The Jesus Saga

An inspiring new translation of the four
gospels, arranged in one seamless,
chronological narrative

by
John Stephen Wright

*"God the Word became a Person, living as the Temple of God among us,
and we gazed with wonder upon the radiance of his revealed glory —
a glory that was utterly unique to the only Son of God, Jesus —
for it was glistening with grace and truth."*

John 1.14

Volume One in the "According to Jesus"
Series by John Stephen

Dedication

To my dad, Morris Wright, a man of rare vision,
wisdom, and creative ability;
devoted husband, father, and friend; career
missionary, church-planter, pastor, engineer,
architect, administrator, and counselor;
an extraordinarily gifted and experienced master
teacher of the life of Jesus;
I salute him for being — more than anything else —
a student of Jesus. Now in his 90s, he continues to study his way through the
life of Jesus many times each year.

It is my prayer that readers of The JESUS SAGA will emulate my Dad, by
becoming passionately and supremely devoted to the life-long pursuit of the
knowledge of Jesus Christ through his precious Word.

This is Jesus' discipleship plan for making us like him,
which is his ultimate purpose for each of us.

Thank you, Dad, for your inspiring, challenging, and enduring life example.

John Stephen Wright
Easter, 2014

"The person who continues to make their home in my word is truly my disciple. And the person who has my commands and makes a practice of obeying them is someone who truly loves me."

Jesus, the Christ

Acknowledgements

To my precious wife Rhonda, for her patience, prayers and
constant support in the time-consuming process of translating, arranging,
and editing the SAGA.

To my family, for their ceaseless encouragement and prayers.

To my daughter Debra, for her assistance in compiling
the Index of Scriptures in Appendix B.

To Denise Long, for her excellent professional editing services.

To Kimberly Brock, for her expertise in copy writing,
and timely advice.

To the late Ernest L Hollaway, for improving the SAGA
with his perceptive suggestions.

To Ed and Sharon Smith, for their eagle eyes in
catching endless errata.

To the apostles who wrote the collection of documents we call the New
Testament, and the myriad scribes and scholars who have worked tire-
lessly and sacrificially to faithfully preserve, translate, and transmit those
Scriptures to us over the last 2000 years.

To the Lord Jesus Christ, who lived, died,
and rose again for the glory of love.
This is HIS Story.

Preface

The JESUS SAGA is a Scriptural biography of the complete life of Jesus. It is composed of the words of Scripture, freshly translated into English from the Greek New Testament, and arranged in chronological order. In addition, the many parallel passages in the gospels have been blended into one composite text including every word in all the passages, while eliminating the repetition among them. The Saga therefore is a "composite style harmony" of the four gospels. This makes it a powerful tool for knowing Jesus.

The JESUS SAGA combines six primary features. These are:

1. a detailed outline structure with clear chronological and geographical development;
2. the blended, composite text of parallel passages in the four gospels;
3. the dynamic translation of the Greek New Testament;
4. the translation of the Greek verbs, especially the present and perfect tenses;
5. the translation of the commands of Jesus; and
6. inclusion of scriptures beyond the four gospels that are related to the life of Christ.

Appendix A at the end of the book explains these six features, preparing the reader to take full advantage of them. Though the JESUS SAGA can be enjoyed without reading Appendix A, becoming familiar with its content will enrich a reader's ability to gain insight into Jesus' life and teachings.

Why Another Translation of the Gospels/Harmony of the Life of Jesus?

The JESUS SAGA is the culmination of my life work and experience as a follower of Jesus, Bible teacher, career missionary, church-planter, pastor, and seminary teacher of the Greek New Testament. I have three motives for preparing this work.

Motivated to Promote Daily Study of the Life and Teachings of Jesus

Soon after I became a follower of Jesus, I was convinced that systematic, repeated, life-long reading of the four gospels is an essential practice in Jesus' discipleship plan. As he said, *"The person who makes their home in my word is truly my disciple."* John 8.31

Jesus repeated this principle many times in his ministry. It was the practice of the earliest Church described in the New Testament. It has made a profound difference in my own life. The need for every believer to build their life on the sure foundation of Jesus' own word has been reinforced throughout my life and ministry experiences.

Jesus stated the goal of discipleship three different times throughout his ministry: *To become like him in every way* (LK 6.39-40; MT 10.24; JN 13.13-15). We do this through the process of learning about him in his Word, and then adjusting ourselves to conform to his examples, commands, values, attitudes, and character. As we come to know Jesus well enough to become like him, we disciples then make him known to others through our words and deeds.

The life and teachings of Jesus recorded in Scripture equip us to know him in our own experience. The writer to the Hebrews reminded us: *"Jesus Christ remains the same – yesterday, today, and forever."* (Heb. 13.8) The Scriptures reveal Jesus truthfully as he was *"yesterday,"* so we can know him *"today."* Life-long, consistent study of the life and teachings of Jesus in the Holy Spirit's power, and in the fellowship of other disciples is our Lord's discipleship curriculum for changing us into his likeness.

Therefore, I have prepared the JESUS SAGA as an aid for in-depth study of the glorious life of the Lord Jesus Christ. It is not intended to replace direct study of the gospels, but the SAGA should supplement reading the gospels by re-packaging their content in a chronological format. To the degree that a disciple comprehensively learns the whole life of Jesus, his or her understanding of the content of each gospel becomes enriched.

Serious followers of Jesus would do well to alternate reading through the Gospels/Acts, and the SAGA several times a year, every year. (I recommend reading the gospels in the order of Mark, Matthew, Luke/Acts, and then John. Repeat this order in every reading cycle. Reading one chapter a day will take you through all the gospels 3 times a year.) Read The JESUS SAGA the follow-ing month, then return to the gospel cycle.

Motivated to Share the Riches of Jesus Found in the Greek New Testament

Secondly, I was deeply blessed to have the opportunity to study the Greek of the New Testament in college and again in my seminary studies. As I was equipped to read the life of Jesus in the Greek New Testament, I discovered depths of meaning and power in the four gospels in the original language that my English and Japanese translations did not convey.

The translations we regularly use are not erroneous; I do not mean to imply that in any way. The many translation available today are a wonderful bless-ing and fully reliable. But they do not include the full meaning of everything that the Greek original communicates. It is similar to the difference between watching a silent, black and white film of the 1920s or a full color, digitally enhanced 21st century version of the same film. The script and story would be the same, but the degree of clarity, insight, and impact would be different. This kind of change occurs, in some degree, when any original document is compared to its translation, and it is also true of the Greek New Testament.

Appendix A describes my translation approach to three crucial Greek verb components: the present tense, perfect tense, and imperatives (or com-mands). Please refer to these explanations. The SAGA translation particularly highlights the commands (imperatives) of Jesus. Thus, the English phrase *"I command you to..."* has been used to translate the Lord's use of imperatives in the SAGA. This translation is intended to encourage loving obedience to the Lord Jesus Christ.

My life-long reading and study of the New Testament in Greek has fueled my desire to share some of the riches of insight not contained in most transla-tions in a fuller, more dynamic rendering of its message. The translations in the SAGA attempt to do this. The Jesus presented in the Greek of the four gospels is loving, decisive, honest, forthright, wise, powerful, captivating, inspiring, and beautiful beyond any earthly comparison. Oh, for readers of the SAGA to see Jesus in all of his glory!

Motivated to Make the Chronology of Jesus' Life Clear

Thirdly, I long for readers of the JESUS SAGA to know and recall the entire life of Jesus with greater clarity. The apostles could reflect on the life of Jesus and know precisely when and where each event or teaching in the gospels actually occurred. They were intimately acquainted with his life as a whole, and this knowledge enriched each individual incident for them. The JESUS SAGA can equip readers to become as familiar with the chronology of Jesus' life as the apostles themselves, through their own eye-witness accounts.

We live in a scientific age that values accurate chronological description of events. However, the gospel writers did not think that chronology was particularly important in their accounts. Thus, the timing of events was not a focus in their writings, except where it was necessary for understanding. (Please see Appendix A for more discussion of this issue.)

Because of this, many believers are not very clear on the chronology of Jesus' life. How much richer would be their understanding if they knew the setting in which the action occurred! Believers should know and value the life of Jesus the way lovers cherish their shared memories. Knowledge of Jesus is the most precious information that serious followers of Jesus can acquire in this world.

The chronology in the SAGA is the fruit of my lifetime of study of Jesus' life. I used the chronological hints and nuances in the gospels to arrange the material into a clear, step-by-step development. Then, I blended the parallel accounts together into one narrative equal to reading all four gospels simultaneously. The result is that the SAGA has all of the impact of the Scriptures that comprise its text, with the added clarity of clear logical and historical arrangement of Jesus' life story.

The chronology and inter-relatedness of the events in Jesus' life are important. It is my hope that the Holy Spirit will use the SAGA text to make Jesus come alive to my readers in the life-changing ways he has graciously done for me in the process of compiling it.

Organizational Structure of the SAGA

The SAGA utilizes three structural tools to organize the events of Jesus' life into a clear chronological and logical development. A reader can more fully understand the timeline and development of Jesus' ministry by noting these tools on every page: the nine major Stages of Jesus life, the 52 Chapter divisions, and the 365 numbered Section Titles.

Jesus concentrated each major stage of his life in a particular geographical area. He intentionally moved from one region of Palestine to another for strategic reasons throughout his ministry. Nothing was by chance. The events that occurred in each region were, therefore, inter-related and fit together as a whole. A brief explanation of the significant characteristics of each of the nine Stages of Jesus' life has been included in the text. These nine introductions have been placed throughout the SAGA, just before the chapters related to each Stage. Refer to the Table of Contents to see the relationship between the nine Stages and the Chapter divisions.

The JESUS SAGA contains 52 chapter divisions, which function differently than the chapter divisions in the Bible. The Scriptures in each SAGA chapter are closely inter-related, grouping together events that occurred in sequence near the same time and location in Jesus' life. The events in each chapter should be viewed as a whole. A new chapter indicates a transition in the time and place when a portion of Jesus' life occurred. Most of the chapters are short, averaging two to four pages. Some are only one page. Others are close to ten.

Within each chapter of the SAGA, material is further grouped into consecutive numbered sections. (The SAGA starts with section #001 and ends with #365.) Each section has a title that summarizes its content. These titles function as an interpretive guide to the life of Jesus. A reader can construct a detailed, comprehensive outline of the complete life of Jesus in chronological order by connecting the section titles. Each section header also lists the Scripture passage(s) from which it was translated.

An important feature of The JESUS SAGA is that over 800 pages of in-depth, free study material on each numbered SAGA section by John Stephen Wright is available in the "Free Saga Commentary" menu at our ATJ Ministries website. Visit www.atjministries.org to access this powerful discipleship teaching. By combining the content of the SAGA with this free teaching material, any reader can enhance the extensive discipleship training that Jesus intended his Word to provide for us.

The nine Stages, 52 Chapters, and 365 numbered Sections organize the life of Jesus into the most clear chronological arrangement the author could conceive. Please see Appendix A for more discussion of the chronological arrangement of the SAGA.

Blended Text Passages and the Superscript ID System

About 1/3 of the content of the gospels is repeated in more than one gospel. We call these "parallel passages." Some stages of Jesus' life abound in parallel texts. The JESUS SAGA blends these parallel passages into one composite text that includes every word in all the parallels, while eliminating the repetition between them. The rationale and process used to compile the blended texts is explained in Appendix A. Please go there for more information.

The SAGA uses a "Superscript ID" system to identify the origin of every word in a "blended text" section. The "base text" is the first Scripture given in the section head. Then the parallel accounts are shown in parentheses. At each place a word, phrase, or sentence from a parallel text has been inserted into the "base text," the appropriate Superscript ID of [MT] (for Matthew), [M] (for Mark), [L] (for Luke), [J] (for John), or [A] (for Acts) is included to indicate the origin of those inserted words.

When the parallel text has ended and the wording returns to the "base text," a Superscript ID also shows this transition back to the base. (If no parentheses with parallel texts are included in the section header, that means that no parallel passages of the base text exist.) Using this system, every word in the SAGA can be traced to its original Scriptural passage.

Writing for Ordinary People

The JESUS SAGA was not compiled as a scholarly tool. New Testament scholars have direct access to the Scriptures in the original languages, and the wealth of research tools that are the fruit of 2000 years of scholarship in the New Testament. True scholars have no need of a work like the SAGA. Therefore it does not contain the footnotes, qualifications, nuanced arguments, and jargon of scholarly writing. The gospels themselves were written in the language of ordinary people. This, too, was the hope in publishing it for the benefit of seekers, and serious followers of Jesus who do not have access to the gospels in their original language.

Supporting Wycliffe Bible Translation Ministries

Wycliffe Bible Translators is a non-profit Christian organization founded in 1942, with the mission of making the Scriptures available in every language spoken in the world through Bible translation. Wycliffe is the world leader in Bible translation work among languages with no current Bible translation. (Visit www.wycliffe.org for more information.)

At the time of publication of The JESUS SAGA, Wycliffe has worked in the translation of the entire Bible in 518 languages, and the New Testament in 1275 more. They are currently in the process of producing the first translation of the Bible in over 1500 languages. Beyond those, about 2000 more language groups do not have any translation of the Bible available to them; most of those groups have never heard the name of Jesus in their history. These 3500 language groups currently without the Scriptures represent over 350 million people.

Fifty percent of the profits from sales of the SAGA are being donated to Wycliffe ministries. By purchasing this book, you are helping to finish the task of spreading God's Word to the hands and hearts of all of the still unreached language/people-groups in the world.

The Blessing of Compiling the SAGA

I cannot conclude this preface without expressing my unceasing gratitude to the Lord Jesus himself; the Father, who gave us his Son; and the Holy Spirit, who reveals Jesus to us through the Scriptures. Although I have been unspeakably blessed to read the life and teachings of Jesus for almost 40 years in Greek, the process of compiling, blending, and translating the SAGA has given me more fresh insight and revelation regarding Jesus than my heart and mind can absorb. It has been the greatest spiritual blessing of my life—bar none.

If readers of the SAGA gain just a fraction of the fresh insight into Jesus that I received in preparing it, then they will be blessed to unimaginable levels. This is my prayer for them.

While the blessings have all come from God, any shortcomings in the work are mine. I stand by the translation. However, the blending and arranging processes were my own work, as are the editorial comments I have placed in the text. Please contact me with any suggestions for improvement you might have.

It is my fervent prayer that the Holy Spirit will thrill your mind and heart with the radiant glory of Jesus in new and transforming ways through this compilation of his precious Word that presents his life, work and teachings. I pray that you will become more like him, more pleasing to him, filled with him, and useful in his unfinished mission of making disciples of all the peoples of the world.

May God the Trinity be praised!

John Stephen Wright
john@atjministries.com
www.atjministries.org

The JESUS SAGA
Table of Contents

STAGE I OF THE LIFE OF JESUS CHRIST:
THE PROLOGUE: THE ETERNAL PREEXISTENCE OF JESUS

STAGE II OF THE LIFE OF JESUS CHRIST: HIS 30 YEARS OF
PREPARATION FOR MINISTRY

STAGE III OF THE LIFE OF JESUS CHRIST: HIS EARLY MINISTRY IN JUDEA

STAGE IV OF THE LIFE OF JESUS CHRIST: HIS GREAT GALILEAN MINISTRY

STAGE V OF THE LIFE OF JESUS CHRIST: HIS WITHDRAWAL TO GENTILE REGIONS

STAGE VI OF THE LIFE OF JESUS CHRIST: HIS LATER MINISTRY IN JUDEA

STAGE VII OF THE LIFE OF JESUS CHRIST: HIS MINISTRY IN PEREA

STAGE VIII OF THE LIFE OF JESUS CHRIST:
JESUS' FINAL WEEK IN THE FLESH—HIS PASSION

STAGE IX OF THE LIFE OF JESUS CHRIST:
HIS RESURRECTION AND ETERNAL MINISTRY

Stage I of the Life of Jesus Christ:

THE PROLOGUE — THE ETERNAL PREEXISTENCE OF JESUS

In order to understand everything else about Jesus' life, we must begin before time and creation itself, with his eternal preexistence as God. Jesus believed that he has always been Divine — the Second Person of the Trinity — living in unbroken fellowship and seamless unity with the Father and the Holy Spirit.

Jesus also considered himself to be the Co-Creator of the universe and everything in it. He revealed himself in his pre-incarnate state to three Old Testament prophets: Isaiah, David, and Daniel. The truths revealed in these three encounters are crucial for understanding Jesus' identity and work in his incarnation because Jesus frequently referred to them.

Because the life of Jesus has no beginning, and he existed before the beginning of everything else he created, it is like no other biography ever written. It is the true story of God.

CHAPTER 1

The Prologue: The Eternal Preexistence of Jesus Christ

#001 Before the Beginning of Time:
Jesus' Eternal Preexistence and Fellowship with the Father
MK 1.1; JN 1.1-2

ᴹThe beginning of the good news about Jesus Christ.

1 ᴶIn the beginning, the Word was already in existence, and the Word was in intimate person fellowship with God (the Father), and the Word was God (fully Divine). 2 He always continued in intimate personal fellowship with God (the Father) in the beginning.

#002 Jesus Creates the Universe out of Nothing
JN 1.3-5; Gen. 1.1-2.4

Genesis 1. 1 In the beginning, God the Word created the heavens and the earth.

ᴶAll things came into existence through him (Jesus), and apart from him nothing came into existence—this is true of everything that was created. (JN 1.3)

2 The earth was without definite shape and not yet complete, and darkness loomed over the surface of the deep, and the Spirit of God continued to hover over the waters.

3 And God the Word said, *"I command that light come into existence,"* and light came to be.

6 And God the Word said, *"I command that a space come into existence between the waters to continue to separate water from water."* 7 So God made the space and separated the water under the space from the water above it. And it became so.

9 And God the Word said, *"I command that the water under the sky be gathered to one place, and I command that dry ground appear."* And it became so.

11 Then, God the Word said, *"I command that the land sprout forth with vegetation: seed-bearing plants and trees on the land that bear fruit with seed in it, according to their various kinds."* And it became so.

14 And God the Word said, *"I command that lights come into existence in the space of the sky to separate the day from the night, and I command that they continue to serve as signs to mark sacred times, and days, and years, 15 and I command that the lights in the space of the sky give light on the earth."* And it became so.

20 And God the Word said, *"I command that the water come forth with living creatures, and that birds fly above the earth across the space of the sky."* 22 God the Word blessed them and said, *"I command that you continue to be fruitful and that you continue to increase in number and I command you to fill the water in the seas, and I command that birds continue to multiply on the earth."*

24 And God the Word said, *"I command that the land produce living creatures according to their kinds, the livestock, the creatures that crawl along the ground, and the wild animals, each according to its kind."* And it became so.

26 Then, God the Word said, *"Let us make mankind in our image, in our likeness, and I command that they continue to rule over the fish in the sea and the birds in the sky, over the livestock and all the wild animals, and over all the creatures that crawl along the ground."*

27 So God the Word created mankind in his own image, in the image of God he created them, male and female he created them.

28 God the Word blessed them and said to them, *"I command that you continue to be fruitful and multiply in number; that you fill the earth and subdue it. I command you all to continue to rule over the fish in the sea and the birds in the sky and over every living creature that crawls on the ground."*

29 Then, God the Word said, *"Look! I have permanently given you every seed-bearing plant on the face of the whole earth and every tree that has fruit with seed in it. They will all be yours for food.* 30 *And to all the beasts of the earth, and all the birds in the sky, and all the creatures that crawl along the ground – everything that has the breath of life in it – I give every green plant for food."* And it became so.

31 God the Word examined all that he had made, and it was very good. 2.1 Thus, the heavens and the earth were completed in all their vast splendor.

4 ᴶIn Him – the Word – God's unique quality of eternal life always existed, and that life has continued to be the light (of revelation) to all people. 5 The light continues to shine in the darkness, and the darkness has never extinguished it.

(Note: The title, "the Word" was added to "God" [thus, "God the Word"] in this section on the basis of the testimony of John 1.3: "All things came into existence through Him [Jesus – The Word], and apart from Him nothing came into existence – this is true of everything that was created." In addition, Jesus was given the eternal Title of "The Word of God" in Revelation 19.13.)

#003 Isaiah Sees a Powerful Vision of the Pre-Incarnate Jesus as God
Isaiah 6.1-13; JN 12.41

1 In the year that King Uzziah died, I saw the Lord, sitting high and permanently exalted on a throne, and his glory filled the temple. 2 Seraphim had taken their place before him, each with six wings. With two wings, they were covering their faces, with two they were covering their feet, and with two they were flying. 3 And they cried out – each to the other, and they were continuing to say:

"Holy, holy, holy is the LORD who rules over his mighty armies;
the whole earth is full of his glory."

4 At the sound of their voices, the doorposts and thresholds shook, and the temple was filled with smoke.

5 And I said, "I myself am wretched, for I have been permanently broken. For I am a man of unclean lips, and I am making my home in the midst of a people of unclean lips, and what's more--my eyes have actually seen the reigning King, the LORD (Jesus) – who rules over his mighty armies ."

6 Then one of the seraphim was sent to me, with a live coal in his hand, which he had grabbed with tongs from the altar. 7 He touched my mouth with it and said, "Look! This has touched your lips; your lawlessness will be taken away and your sin will be atoned for."

8 Then, I heard the voice of the Lord saying, *"Whom will I send? And who will go for us?"*

And I said, "Look! I myself am here. Please send me!"

9 He said, *"I command you to go and tell this people:*
'You will be ever hearing, but never, ever understanding;
you will be ever seeing, but never, ever perceiving.'
10 *For the heart of this people has become calloused;*
and their ears barely hear
and their eyes have shut.
Otherwise, they might possibly see with their eyes,
they might hear with their ears,
they might understand with their hearts,
they might turn back to me and be healed."

ᴶIsaiah said this because he saw Jesus' glory and spoke about him. (JN 12.41)

#004 David and Daniel See Visions of
the Pre-Incarnate Jesus as God's King and Priest
David's Witness: Psalm 110.1-2, 4

The LORD said to my LORD:

"I command you to sit yourself down at my right hand
until I make your enemies
a footstool for your feet."

2 The LORD will extend your powerful scepter out from Zion, saying,
"I command you to continue to rule in the midst of your enemies!"

4 The LORD has sworn an oath
and will never change his mind:
"You are a priest forever,
according to the order of Melchizedek."

The Prophet Daniel's Vision of the
Pre-Incarnate Jesus as the "Son of Man"
Daniel 7.13-14; MK 15.61-62

13 I was looking carefully into a vision in the night, and look!-- there was a person before me like a son of man, coming on the clouds of heaven. He went up to the Ancient of Days and was permanently presented before him.

14 And all authority and all the glory was given to him, and all the nations of the earth and peoples worshiped him. His authoritative dominion is an everlasting authority that will never, ever pass away, and his kingdom is one that will never, ever be destroyed.

At His Trial, Jesus Claims to Be the One Whom David
and Daniel Saw in Their Visions
MK 15.61-62 (Parallel Text: MT 26.63-64)

61 The high priest spoke to him, MT "I charge you under oath by the living God. Tell us, Mare you the Messiah, the Son of MTGod, Mthe Blessed One?"

62 *"I AM,"* said Jesus, MT *"It is as you say. And I say to all of you: in the future* Myou *will see 'the son of Man'* (Dan. 7.13) *'sitting at the right hand of the Mighty One'* (Ps. 110.1) *and 'coming on the clouds of heaven.'"* (Dan. 7.13)

Stage II of the Life of Jesus Christ:

HIS 30 YEARS OF PREPARATION FOR MINISTRY

The Prologue showed us that Jesus has always been God.

In Stage II, we discover the miracle of the ages, that while Jesus will always remain God, he simultaneously became a person in his incarnation — the God-man. It was necessary for Jesus to become a real person to be our perfect Savior. Therefore, before he began his ministry, Jesus' human nature was perfectly prepared through 30 years of sinless growth and development into complete maturity.

In addition, God prepared his covenant people for Jesus' ministry by sending the first prophet in 400 years to Israel: John the Immerser (Baptist). John was to preach a message of repentance, evidenced by immersion in water, so that the people would be ready to believe in Jesus and follow him as their Lord and Savior when he began his ministry.

God does not make mistakes. He prepared the perfect life in the perfect circumstances at the perfect time in history.

Chapters 2 to 5 describe Jesus' 30 years of preparation for ministry.

CHAPTER 2

Preparation: Faith, Prayer, and

Prophecy Prepared for Jesus' Incarnation

#005 The Historical Reliability of the Gospel
LK 1.1-4

1 Because many people have attempted to compile a written declaration of the things that have been permanently fulfilled among us, 2 just as they were handed down to us as authoritative oral traditions by those who were actual eyewitnesses from the beginning of Jesus' ministry and were servants of the Word, 3 it seemed good to me as well to write an orderly account for you, most excellent Theophilus (meaning "friend," or "lover of God").

4 Because I have carefully investigated all of the facts from the very beginning, you can be fully assured of the certainty of the things that you have been taught.

#006 Jesus' Birth was Prepared in Prayer
LK 1.5-10

5 In the days of Herod, king of Judea, there was a certain priest named Zechariah, who belonged to the priestly division of Abijah; his wife was also

a descendant of Aaron, and her name was Elizabeth. 6 They were both righteous in the sight of God, observing all the Lord's commands and ceremonial decrees blamelessly. 7 However, they were childless because Elizabeth was not able to conceive, and they were both advanced in age.

8 It came to pass while Zechariah was serving as a priest before God, as his division was on duty 9 he was chosen by lot, according to the custom of the priesthood, to enter into the temple of the Lord to burn incense. 10 And the crowd of people outside was continuing in prayer when the time for the burning of incense came.

#007 The Promise of a Special Prophet to Prepare the People for Jesus' Ministry
LK 1.11-17

11 Then, an angel of the Lord appeared to him, standing on the right side of the altar of incense. 12 Because Zechariah saw him, he was troubled, and fear gripped him.

13 But the angel said to him, "Stop being afraid, Zechariah, because your prayer has been heard. Your wife Elizabeth will bear you a son, and you are to call him John. 14 He will be a joy and great delight to you, and many will rejoice because of his birth, 15 for he will be great in the sight of the Lord. He must never drink wine or other fermented drink, and he will be filled with the Holy Spirit even before he is born.

16 "He will also turn back many of the people of Israel to the Lord their God. 17 He will go on before the Lord, in the spirit and power of Elijah, to turn the hearts of the parents to their children and the disobedient to the wisdom of the righteous—to make ready a people permanently prepared for the Lord."

#008 God Disciplines Zechariah for His Unbelief
LK 1.18-25

18 Zechariah said to the angel, "How can I know this for sure? I am an old man myself, and my wife has become irreversibly advanced in her years."

19 The angel said to him, "I, myself, am Gabriel. I have taken my stand in the presence of God, and I have been sent to speak to you and to announce

this good news to you. 20 And now you will be silent and not be able to speak until the day this happens because you did not believe my words, which will be fulfilled at the perfect time."

21 Meanwhile, the people were still waiting for Zechariah, and they continued to wonder why he stayed so long in the temple. 22 When he came out, he could not speak to them. They realized he had seen a vision in the temple because he continued making signs to them, but he remained unable to speak.

23 When his time of service was completed, Zechariah returned home. 24 After this, his wife Elizabeth became pregnant and then remained in seclusion for five months. 25 "The Lord has permanently accomplished this for me," she said. "In these days, he has watched over me with favor and taken away my humiliation among the people."

#009 God Prepares For His Son by Providing a Mother of Faith
LK 1.26-38

26 In the sixth month [of Elizabeth's pregnancy] the angel Gabriel was sent from God to a city of Galilee, named Nazareth 27 to a virgin who was engaged to be married to a man named Joseph, a descendant of David. The virgin's name was Mary.

28 And after coming to her, he said, "Greetings, you who are graciously favored! The Lord is with you."

29 But she was greatly troubled by this saying and was carefully considering what kind of greeting this might be.

30 But the angel said to her, "Stop being fearful, Mary, for you have found favor with God. 31 Look, you will conceive in your womb and give birth to a son, and you must give him the name 'Jesus.' 32 He will be great and will be called the 'Son of the Most High.' And the Lord God will give him the throne of his father David. 33 He will reign over the house of Jacob forever; and his kingdom will never end."

34 So, Mary said to the angel, "How will this happen, since I continue to be a virgin?"

35 The angel answered her, "The Holy Spirit will come upon you, and the power of the Most High will overshadow you; so the holy one that will be born will be called 'the Son of God.'

36 "Look, even Elisabeth your relative, has also become pregnant in her old age. This is the sixth month for her who was called barren. 37 For nothing God says will be impossible for him."

38 Mary said, "Yes, I am the bond-slave of the Lord. My wish is for it to happen to me just as you have said."

So, the angel left her.

#010 Mary and Elizabeth Rejoice Together
LK 1.39-45

39 In those days, Mary rose up and went quickly down to a town in the hill country of Judea. 40 She went into Zechariah's home, where she greeted Elizabeth. 41 At the moment Elizabeth heard Mary's greeting, the baby leaped within her, and Elizabeth was filled with the Holy Spirit. 42 She cried out with a booming voice, "You are blessed among women! The child you will have is also blessed! 43 Why is it that the mother of my Lord should come to me?

44 "Look! As soon as the sound of your greeting entered my ears, my baby was overjoyed and leaped within me. 45 And blessed are you who believed that the things that were firmly spoken by the Lord to you will actually be fulfilled."

#011 Mary's Psalm of Praise: The "Magnificat"
LK 1.46-56

46 Mary prayed in praise:

"My soul continues to boast in the Lord, 47
and my spirit has exulted in God my Savior,
48 for he has looked with gracious favor upon
the humiliation of his handmaid.
Look! From now on, all generations will call me profoundly blessed.
49 This is because the Mighty One has done great
things for me—holy is his name!
50 His mercy reaches out to those who fear him,
from generation to generation.

51 He has done powerful deeds with his arm;
He has scattered those who are proud in
the reckoning of their inner thoughts.
52 He has booted princes off their thrones,
but has lifted the humble up in exaltation.
53 He has stuffed the hungry with good things;
but he has sent the rich away empty.
54 He has given help to his servant Israel,
being ever mindful of his mercy,
55 to Abraham and his descendants forever,
just as promised to our fathers."

56 And Mary lived with Elizabeth for about three months and then returned to her house.

#012 The Birth of John; Zechariah's Journey
from Discipline to Praise and Prophecy
LK 1.57-66

57 When the time had come for Elizabeth to have her baby, she bore a son. 58 Her neighbors and relatives heard that the Lord was increasing his mercy to her, and they were rejoicing with her.

59 On the eighth day, they came to circumcise the child, and they were about to name him after his father Zechariah, 60 but his mother spoke up and said, "No! He is to be called John."

61 They said to her, "There is no one among your relatives who has that name."

62 Then, they made signs to his father to find out what he would like to name the child. 63 He asked for a writing tablet and wrote, "His name is John." They all were astonished by this.

64 Immediately, his mouth was opened and his tongue was set free, and he continued speaking and blessing God.

65 All the neighbors were filled with reverent awe, and throughout the hill country of Judea, people continued talking about all these things. 66 All who heard this wondered about it, asking in their hearts, "What is this child going to be?" For the Lord's hand was with him.

#013 Zechariah's Prophecy Prepares for Jesus' Coming
LK 1.67-80

67 His father Zechariah was filled with the Holy Spirit and prophesied,

68 "Blessed be to the Lord, the God of Israel,
because he has come to his people and provided redemption for them.
69 He has raised up a horn of salvation for us in
the house of his servant David
70—just as he spoke through his holy prophets of long ago—
71 salvation from our enemies and from the hand of all who are hating us,
72 to show mercy to our ancestors and to remember his holy covenant,
73 the oath he swore to our father Abraham:
74 to give us deliverance from the hand of our enemies,
and to enable us to serve him without fear,
75 in piety and righteousness before him all our days.

76 "And you, my child, will be called a prophet of the Most High;
for you will go on before the Lord to prepare the way for him,
77 to give his people the knowledge of salvation
through the forgiveness of their sins
78 because of the heartfelt mercy of our God, by which the rising sun will
come to us from heaven
79 to shine on those living in darkness and in the shadow of death,
to guide our feet into the path of peace."

80 And the child grew and became strong in spirit, and he lived in the wilderness until he appeared publicly to Israel.

CHAPTER 3

Preparation: The Birth of Jesus

#014 Jesus' Conception and Nativity from Joseph's Perspective
MT. 1.18-25A

18 The birth of Jesus the Messiah was like this. His mother Mary was engaged for marriage to Joseph, but before they came together as husband and wife, she became pregnant through the Holy Spirit. 19 Joseph, her husband, was a righteous man and yet did not want to expose her to public disgrace, so he wanted to divorce her quietly.

20 But after he had deeply considered this, an angel of the Lord appeared to him in a dream and said,

"Joseph, son of David, do not be afraid to take Mary home as your wife because what is conceived in her is from the Holy Spirit. 21 She will give birth to a son, and you are to give him the name 'Jesus,' because he will save his people from their sins."

22 All this took place to fulfill what the Lord had said through the prophet, 23 "The virgin will conceive and give birth to a son, and they will call him 'Immanuel.'" (Which means "God with us.")

24 When Joseph woke up, he did what the angel of the Lord had commanded him, and he took Mary home as his wife. 25 But he did not have physical relations with her until she had given birth to a son.

#015 The Details of Jesus' Birth in Bethlehem
LK 2.1-7; MT 1.25B

1 In those days, Caesar Augustus issued a decree that the entire Roman world must register for a census. 2 (This was the first census to take place while Quirinius was governor of Syria.) 3 Everyone was traveling for registration, each to his or her own town.

4 Joseph also went up from the town of Nazareth in Galilee to Judea, to Bethlehem the town of David, because he belonged to the house and line of David. 5 He went there to register with Mary, to whom he was engaged to be married, and she was expecting a child.

6 While they were there, the time came for the baby to be born, 7 and she gave birth to her firstborn, a son. She wrapped him in baby cloths and laid him down in a manger because there was no place available for them in the guest room. ^{MT}And Joseph gave him the name Jesus.

#016 Angels Announce Jesus' Birth to the World
LK 2.8-14

8 ^LAnd there were shepherds living out in the fields nearby, staying watchful to guard over their flocks at night. 9 An angel of the Lord suddenly appeared to them, and the glory of the Lord shone radiantly all around them, and they were completely terrified. 10 But the angel said to them,

"Stop being so afraid. Look! I am proclaiming nothing but good news to you that will cause great joy for all the people. 11 Today, in the town of David, a Savior has been born for you; he is Christ (the Messiah) the Lord. 12 This will be a sign to you: you will find a baby wrapped in cloths and lying in a manger."

13 Suddenly a huge gathering of the heavenly army of angels appeared with the angel, praising God and saying, 14 "Glory to God in the highest heaven, and on earth, peace to those on whom his favor rests."

#017 Shepherds Confirm the Good News of Jesus' Birth
LK 2.15-20

15 When the angels had gone away from them into heaven, the shepherds were exclaiming to one another, "Yes, let's go to Bethlehem to see this thing that has happened, which the Lord has made known to us."

16 So they rushed off and found Mary, and Joseph, and the baby, who was lying in the manger. 17 Once they had seen him, they made known the message (2.10-11) that had been spoken to them about this child, 18 and all who heard it marveled at what was spoken by the shepherds to them.

19 Mary was treasuring up all these things and continued to ponder them in her heart.

20 The shepherds returned, as they continued glorifying and praising God for all the things they had heard and seen, which were just as they had been told.

#018 Simeon Confirms that Jesus is the Messiah
LK 2.21-35

21 On the eighth day, when the time had come to circumcise him, Joseph named him Jesus, the name the angel had given him before the baby had been conceived.

22 When the time had been fulfilled for their purification rites required by the Law of Moses, Joseph and Mary took Jesus up to Jerusalem to present him to the Lord 23 just as it stands written in the Law of the Lord, "Every firstborn male must be consecrated to the Lord," (Ex. 13.2, 12, 15) 24 and to offer a sacrifice in accordance with what had been spoken in the Law of the Lord: "A pair of doves or two young pigeons." (Lev. 13.7)

25 Look! There was a man in Jerusalem called Simeon, and this man was righteous and devout. He was waiting for the comfort of Israel (the coming of the Messiah), and the Holy Spirit was resting on him. 26 It had been made fully known to him by the Holy Spirit that he would certainly not die before he had seen the Lord's Messiah.

27 Simeon came into the temple courts under the leadership of the Holy Spirit. When the parents brought in the child Jesus to do for him what the custom of the Law required, 28 Simeon took him in his arms and praised God, saying, 29 "Sovereign Lord, you may now dismiss your servant in peace, according to your promise. 30 For my eyes have seen your salvation, 31 which you have prepared in the sight of all nations, 32 a light of revelation to the Gentiles and the glory of your people Israel."

33 The child's father and mother kept marveling at what was being said about him. 34 Then, Simeon blessed them and said to Mary, his mother: "Look! This child is destined to cause the falling and rising of many in Israel, and to be

a sign that will be spoken against, 35 so that the secret thoughts of many hearts will be revealed. And a sword will pierce your own soul, too."

#019 Anna Confirms that Jesus is the Messiah
LK 2.36-38

36 There was also a prophetess, Anna, the daughter of Penuel, of the tribe of Asher. She had become old, having lived with her husband for seven years after her marriage 37 and then as a widow until she was eighty-four. She never departed from the temple but continued ministering to God night and day, by fasting and praying.

38 Coming up to them at that very moment, she was offering up praise and thanks to God and continued speaking about the child to all who were looking forward to the redemption of Jerusalem.

CHAPTER 4

Preparation: The Infancy and Growth of Jesus

#020 Magi Worship the Infant King
MT 2.1-12

1 After Jesus was born in Bethlehem in Judea, during the days of King Herod, Magi from the east came to Jerusalem 2 and asked, "Where is the one who has been born king of the Jews? For we have seen his star in the east, and we have come to worship him."

3 Because King Herod heard this, he was deeply disturbed, and all Jerusalem with him. 4 Having called together all the chief priests and teachers of the law, he asked them where the Messiah was to be born.

5 "In Bethlehem in Judea," they replied, "for this is what stands written by the prophet. 6 'But you, Bethlehem, in the land of Judah, are by no means least among the leaders of Judah; for out of you will come a ruler who will shepherd my people Israel.'" (Mic.5.2)

7 Then, Herod called the Magi in secret and carefully inquired from them the exact time the star had appeared. 8 Then, he sent them to Bethlehem and said, "Go and make a diligent, careful search for the child. As soon as you find him, report to me, so that I too may go and worship him." 9 After they had heard the king, they went on their way, and amazingly, the star they had seen in the east kept going ahead of them until it stopped over the place where the

child was. 10 Because they saw the star, they rejoiced with a powerful kind of joy.

11 On coming to the house, they saw the child with his mother, Mary, and falling to their knees, they worshiped him. Then, they opened up their treasures and offered him kingly gifts of gold, frankincense, and myrrh.

12 And having been warned in a dream not to go back to Herod, they returned to their country by another route.

#021 God Protects His Son
MT 2.13-18

13 After the Magi had gone, an angel of the Lord appeared to Joseph in a dream. "Get up," he said, "Take the child and his mother and make your escape all the way to Egypt. Continue to stay there until I tell you, for Herod is about to conduct an ongoing search for the child, so he can kill him."

14 So Joseph rose, took the child and his mother, and left for Egypt in the middle of the night, 15 and he stayed there until the death of Herod. And so what the Lord had said through the prophet was fulfilled: "Out of Egypt I have called my son." (Hos. 11.1; Ex. 4.22)

16 When Herod saw that he had been fooled by the Magi, he became extremely enraged; he gave orders to kill all the boys in Bethlehem and the surrounding area who were two years old and younger, in accordance with the time he had learned [of Jesus' birth] from the Magi. 17 Then, what was said through the prophet Jeremiah was fulfilled: 18 "A voice was heard in Ramah, weeping and great mourning; Rachel continually weeping for her children and refusing to be comforted because they are no more." (Jer. 31.15)

#022 God Leads His Son out of Egypt, into Growth
MT 2.19-23 (Parallel Text: LK 2.39-40)

19 After Herod died, [pay careful attention to this...] an angel of the Lord came to Joseph in a dream in Egypt 20 and said, "Get up, for you must take the child and his mother and go all the way to the land of Israel, for those who were trying to take the child's life have all died."

21 So Joseph rose, took the child and his mother, and entered into the land of Israel. 22 But because he heard that Archelaus was reigning in Judea in place of his father Herod, he was afraid to go there.

^LJoseph and Mary had done everything required by the Law of the Lord, ^{MT}so having been warned in a dream, he went back to the district of Galilee, 23 and they went and lived in ^Ltheir own town ^{MT}called Nazareth.

So the word that was spoken through the prophets was fulfilled, that "he will be called 'a Nazarene.'" *(Is. 11.1)

^LAnd the child continued to be filled with wisdom, and kept growing and becoming strong, and the grace of God was always upon him.

+ + + + + + +

*Note: The Hebrew word for "branch" (neser) in Is. 11.1 uses the same consonants as "Nazarene." Multiple prophetic passages relate the Messiah to Galilee, but no single text has the exact phrase that Matthew quoted. Matthew was probably using a Greek translation of the Hebrew. Some reference texts are: Is. 11.1, 49.7, 53.2, 5, 8; Dan. 9.26.

#023 Jesus Communes with His Father in the Temple in Jerusalem
LK 2.41-52

41 Every year, Jesus' parents traveled to Jerusalem for the Festival of the Passover. 42 When Jesus was twelve years old, they went up to the festival, according to their custom.

43 After the festival was over, while his parents were returning home, the boy Jesus stayed behind in Jerusalem, but they were unaware of it. 44 Assuming that he was in their group of travelers, they journeyed on for a day. Then, they began looking for him among their relatives and friends, 45 and because they did not find him, they headed back to Jerusalem to continue searching for him.

46 After three days, they found him in the temple courts, sitting in the midst of the teachers, continuing to listen to them and asking them questions. 47 Everyone who heard him was in a state of amazement at his understanding and his answers.

48 When his parents saw him, they were astonished. His mother said to him, "Son, why have you done this to us? Your father and I have been anxiously searching for you."

49 *"Why were you searching for me?"* he asked. *"Did you not know that I had to be focused on my Father's interests?"*

50 But they did not understand what he was saying to them. 51 Then, he went down to Nazareth with them and was continually obedient to them. But his mother treasured all these things in her heart. 52 And Jesus continued growing in wisdom, in stature, and in favor with God and man.

CHAPTER 5

Preparation: John the Immerser Prepares

the People for Jesus' Ministry

#024 John Begins His Ministry
JN 1.6-9; LK 3.1-6 (Parallel Texts: MT 3.1-3; MK 1.2-4)

JN 1.6-9. 6 A man sent from God appeared; his name was John. 7 This man came in order to witness – to testify concerning the Light, so that everyone might believe (in the Light) through his ministry.

8 John himself was not the Light; he came specifically to bear witness to the Light. 9 The true Light (Jesus), who continually shines upon all people – HE was soon to appear before the world as Messiah.

LK 3.1 In the fifteenth year of the reign of Tiberius Caesar – when Pontius Pilate was governor of Judea, Herod tetrarch of Galilee, his brother Philip tetrarch of Iturea, and Traconitis and Lysanias was tetrarch of Abilene – 2 during the high-priesthood of Annas and Caiaphas, the voice of God came to John, son of Zechariah in the wilderness of Judea.

3 ^{MT}In those days, John the Immerser came. ^LHe went into all of the regions around the Jordan ^{MT}in the Desert of Judea, ^Lpreaching an immersion of repentance based on having received the forgiveness of sins, ^{MT}saying, "I

command you to continue repenting, for the kingdom of heaven has drawn near — permanently!"

4 This is he who was spoken of through the prophet Isaiah, ᴸas it stands written in the book of the words of Isaiah:

"A voice crying out in the wilderness,
'You must all prepare the way for the Lord,
you must all make straight paths for his feet.
5 Every valley will be filled in,
every mountain and hill will be made low.
The crooked roads will become straight,
the rough ways smooth.
6 And all people will see God's salvation for themselves. (Isaiah 40.3-5)

And...

ᴹ "Look! I am sending my messenger just before you, who will prepare your way." (Mal. 3.1)

#025 A Sample of John's Christ-Exalting Preaching
JN 1.15, MT 3.4-10 (Parallel Texts: MK 3.5-6, LK 3.7-10)

ᴶJohn witnessed incessantly about Jesus, crying out with a loud voice, and saying, "This is he of whom I spoke, 'He who comes after me has totally surpassed me, because he existed before me.'"

MT 3.4 John's clothes were made of camel's hair, and he had a leather belt around his waist. His food was locusts and wild honey. 5 Streams of ᴹᴷall different kinds of people from Jerusalem ᴹᵀand all Judea, and the whole region of the Jordan kept going out to him. 6 They were being immersed by him in the Jordan River because they were confessing their sins.

7 But when he saw many of the Pharisees and Sadducees coming to where he was immersing, John said to the crowds coming out to him, "You brood of vipers! Who warned you to flee from the coming wrath? 8 You must produce fruit worthy of your repentance!

9 "And you must not think you can say to yourselves, 'We have Abraham as our father.' I tell you that God has the power to raise up children for Abraham out of these stones. 10 The ax is already laid squarely at the root of

the trees; every tree that is not producing good fruit will certainly be cut down and thrown into the fire."

#026 The People Respond to John
LK 3.10-18 (Parallel Texts: MT 3.11-12, MK 1.7-8)

10 [L]The crowd sought John's counsel, saying, "What should we do [to show our repentance]?"

11 [M]This was his message. [L]John commanded, "Anyone who has two shirts must share with the one who has none, and anyone who has food must continue to share it in the same way."

12 Even tax collectors came to be immersed. "Teacher," they asked his guidance, "what should we do?"

13 "You must continue to refuse to collect any more than you are required to," he told them.

14 Then, some soldiers sought his instruction, saying, "And what should we do?" He replied, "You must be content with your wages, so do not extort money, and do not accuse people falsely for personal gain."

15 The people were waiting expectantly, and they all continued wondering in their hearts if John might possibly be the Messiah. 16 John answered them all, "I immerse you in water for [MT]repentance. But one who is much more powerful than I will come [M]after me, [L]the straps of whose sandals I am not worthy to [M]stoop down and [L]untie, [MT]nor carry. He will immerse you in the Holy Spirit and fire.

17 "His winnowing fork is in his hand to clear his threshing floor and to gather the wheat into his barn, but he will burn up the chaff with unquenchable fire."

18 And with many other words, John exhorted the people as he kept on proclaiming the good news to them.

(Translator's note: John preached for about nine months before Jesus began his ministry.)

Stage III of the Life of Jesus Christ:

HIS EARLY MINISTRY IN JUDEA

Jesus was ready. John had prepared the people. Everything had been set in place at the perfect time and place for Jesus to begin his ministry.

It was finally time.

Jesus concentrated his first period of ministry in Judea. The Immerser was preaching in the Judean wilderness, and sending a stream of repentant, prepared seekers to Jesus. The Lord wisely focused on personal evangelism and individual discipleship training of the people John sent to him. All of the early disciples of Jesus, some of whom were destined to become apostles, came to Jesus from John. In addition, Jesus reached out in personal evangelism on his own initiative to many individuals during his ministry in Judea.

Some scholars call this the "Year of Obscurity" in Jesus' life because we know so little about it compared to the rest of his ministry. John's gospel is our only source of information about most of this stage. Although Jesus did not preach and heal publicly in this period (except at Passover) as he would later on, he did lay a strong foundation for his later ministry by concentrating on key individuals during his six months in Judea.

John includes extensive descriptions of Jesus witnessing to two vastly different people in this period: the respected Pharisee, Nicodemus, and the scandalous Samaritan woman. They represent the wide variety of people to whom Jesus quietly, yet effectively, ministered in these early months of his ministry in Judea. Some of Jesus' most famous promises were spoken in the quietness of those two private conversations.

Chapters 6 to 9 cover Jesus' early ministry in Judea.

CHAPTER 6

Early Judea: The Beginning of Jesus' Ministry

#027 Introduction: The Nature and Results of Jesus' Ministry
LK 3.23A; JN 1.14, 10-13, 16-18

^LNow Jesus Himself was about 30 years old when he began his ministry.

14 ^JGod the Word became a Person, living as the Temple of God among us, and we gazed with wonder upon the radiance of his revealed glory — a glory that was utterly unique to the only Son of God, Jesus — for it was glistening with grace and truth.

10 He, the true light that gives light to everyone, came into the world. He was living in the world, and although the world was made through him, the world did not recognize him. 11 He came to that which was his own, but his very own did not receive him. 12 Yet to all who did receive him — to those who believed in his name — he gave the favored status to become children of God, 13 children born not of natural descent, nor of a mere human decision, or a husband's will, but children born of God Himself.

16 Out of his Divine fullness, we (who have believed in him) have all received grace, constantly being replaced with new flows of grace. 17 For the law was given through Moses, but unbounded grace and the reality of truth came through Jesus Christ.

18 No one has ever fully seen God with their physical eyes before Jesus, but the one and only Son—who is himself God and lives in closest relationship with the Father—has made him fully known.

#028 Jesus' Legal Qualification to be the Messiah: His Genealogy
MT. 1.1-17; LK 3.23B-38

^{MT}This is the genealogy of Jesus the Messiah the son of David, the son of Abraham.

Jesus' Lineage from Abraham to Adam (LK 3.34B-38)

34B ^LAbraham [was] the son of Terah, the son of Nahor, 35 the son of Serug, the son of Reu, the son of Peleg, the son of Eber, the son of Shellac, 36 the son of Cainan, the son of Arphaxad, the son of Shem, the son of Noah, the son of Lamech, 37 the son of Methuselah, the son of Enoch, the son of Jared, the son of Mahalalel, the son of Kenan, 38 the son of Enosh, the son of Seth, the son of Adam, the son of God.

Jesus' Lineage from Joseph to Abraham through David (MT 1.2-17)

2 ^{MT}Abraham was the father of Isaac, Isaac the father of Jacob, Jacob the father of Judah and his brothers, 3 Judah the father of Perez and Zerah, whose mother was Tamar, Perez the father of Hezron, Hezron the father of Ram, 4 Ram the father of Amminadab, Amminadab the father of Nahshon, Nahshon the father of Salmon, 5 Salmon the father of Boaz, whose mother was Rahab, Boaz the father of Obed, whose mother was Ruth, Obed the father of Jesse, 6 and Jesse the father of King David.

David was the father of Solomon, whose mother had been Uriah's wife, 7 Solomon the father of Rehoboam, Rehoboam the father of Abijah, Abijah the father of Asa, 8 Asa the father of Jehoshaphat, Jehoshaphat the father of Jehoram, Jehoram the father of Uzziah, 9 Uzziah the father of Jotham, Jotham the father of Ahaz, Ahaz the father of Hezekiah, 10 Hezekiah the father of Manasseh, Manasseh the father of Amon, Amon the father of Josiah, 11 and Josiah the father of Jeconiah and his brothers at the time of the exile to Babylon.

12 After the exile to Babylon: Jeconiah was the father of Shealtiel, Shealtiel the father of Zerubbabel, 13 Zerubbabel the father of Abihud, Abihud the father of Eliakim, Eliakim the father of Azor, 14 Azor the father of Zadok, Zadok the father of Akim, Akim the father of Elihud, 15 Elihud the father of Eleazar, Eleazar the father of Matthan, Matthan the father of Jacob, 16 and Jacob the father of Joseph, the husband of Mary, and Mary was the mother of Jesus, who is called the Messiah.

17 Thus, there were fourteen generations in all from Abraham to David, fourteen from David to the exile to Babylon, and fourteen from the exile to the Messiah.

Mary's Lineage to King David
(LK 3.23B-31)

23B ᴸIt was commonly thought that Jesus was the son of Joseph [but actually he was the Son of God, as his lineage shows].

24 Mary's father was Heli, the son of Matthat, the son of Levi, the son of Melki, the son of Jannai, the son of Joseph, 25 the son of Mattathias, the son of Amos, the son of Nahum, the son of Esli, the son of Naggai, 26 the son of Maath, the son of Mattathias, the son of Semein, the son of Josek, the son of Joda, 27 the son of Joanan, the son of Rhesa, the son of Zerubbabel, the son of Shealtiel, the son of Neri, 28 the son of Melki, the son of Addi, the son of Cosam, the son of Elmadam, the son of Er, 29 the son of Joshua, the son of Eliezer, the son of Jorim, the son of Matthat, the son of Levi, 30 the son of Simeon, the son of Judah, the son of Joseph, the son of Jonam, the son of Eliakim, 31 the son of Melea, the son of Menna, the son of Mattatha, the son of Nathan, the son of David.

**#029 Jesus is Immersed: The Father and
Holy Spirit Confirm Jesus' Identity and Ministry
MT. 3.13-17 JN 1.32-34 (Parallel Texts: M 1.9-11; L 3.21-22)**

13 ᴸIn those days, when all the people were being immersed, ᴹJesus came from Nazareth of ᴹᵀGalilee to the Jordan to be immersed by John. 14 But John was trying to deter him, saying, "I myself need to be immersed by you, and you come to me?"

15 Jesus replied, *"I command you to permit it now; it is proper for us to do this to fulfill all righteousness."* Then, John consented.

16 As soon as Jesus was immersed, he went up out of the water, ᴸand he was praying. ᴹᵀAt that moment, heaven was ripped open, and he saw the Spirit of God descending ᴸin bodily form ᴹᵀlike a dove and resting on him.

17 And a voice from heaven said, *"ᴹYou are my Son, whom I love; in you I am well pleased."*

32 ᴶJohn gave this testimony: "I have distinctly seen the Spirit come down from heaven as a dove, and abide on him. 33 And I myself did not know him, but the one who sent me to immerse in water told me, 'The man on whom you see the Spirit come down and abide is the one who will immerse in the Holy Spirit.' 34 I have seen this, and I lay down my irrevocable testimony that this is the Son of God."

#030 Jesus Begins His Ministry with Forty Days of Fasting and Prayer
MT. 4.1-11 (Parallel Texts: MK 1.12-13; LK 4.1-13)

1 ᴸJesus, full of the Holy Spirit, returned from the Jordan and was ᴹᵀled forcefully by the Spirit into the wilderness ᴸwhere he was tempted by the devil (ᴹsatan) for forty days, and ᴹhe was with the wild animals. ᴸHe ate nothing during those days, and at the end of them, 2 ᴹᵀafter fasting forty days and forty nights, he was hungry.

3 The tempter came to him and said, "Because you are the Son of God, speak to these stones so they will turn into bread."

4 Jesus answered, *"It stands written: 'I command that man will not live on bread alone, but on every word that comes from the mouth of God.'"* (Duet. 8.3)

5 Then, the devil took him to the holy city ᴸof Jerusalem ᴹᵀand had him stand on the highest point of the temple. 6 "Because you are the Son of God," he said, "throw yourself down. For it stands written, 'He will command his angels concerning you to ᴸguard you, ᴹᵀand they will lift you up in their hands so that you will not strike your foot against a stone.'" (Ps. 91.11-12)

7 Jesus answered him, *"It also stands written: 'I command that you will not put the Lord your God to the test.'"* (Duet 6.16)

8 Again, the devil took him to a very high mountain and showed him all the kingdoms of the world and their splendor ᴸin one moment of time. 9 ᴹᵀ "All of this I will give you, ᴸall their authority and splendor, for it has been

given to me, and I can give it to anyone I want to," he said. ^{MT}"So if you will bow down and worship me, ^Lit will all be yours."

10 ^{MT}Then, Jesus said to him, *"I command you to go way from me, Satan! For it stands written: 'I command you to worship the Lord your God, and serve him only.'"* (Duet. 6.13)

11 ^LWhen the devil had finished all his tempting, ^{MT}he left Jesus ^Luntil a favorable time, ^{MT}and angels came and ministered to him.

CHAPTER 7

Early Judea: The First Glorious Week of Disciple-Making

#031 Day One: John Confesses that He is Not the Messiah
JN 1.19-28

19 Now this was John's testimony when the Jewish leaders in Jerusalem sent priests and Levites to ask him who he was. 20 He confessed and did not deny the truth, but he confessed freely, "I myself am NOT the Messiah."

21 They asked him, "Then, who are you? Are you Elijah? He said, "I am not." "Are you the Prophet?" He answered, "No." 22 Finally they said, "Then who are you? Give us an answer to take back to those who sent us. What do you say about yourself?"

23 John replied, "I myself am a voice crying out in the wilderness, 'Make straight the way for the Lord,' just as Isaiah the prophet said."

24 Now, some who had been sent were of the party of the Pharisees. 25 They questioned him, "Why then are you immersing if you are not the Messiah, nor Elijah, nor the Prophet?"

26 "I myself immerse in water," John replied, "but one has taken his stand in your midst, whom you do not know. 27 HE is the one who comes after me, the straps of whose sandals I am not worthy to untie."

28 This all happened at Bethany on the other side of the Jordan, where John was immersing.

#032 Day Two: John Presents Jesus as "The Lamb of God"
JN 1.29-31

29 The next day John focused his eyes on Jesus as he was coming toward him and said, "Look! The Lamb of God, who truly takes away the sins of the world! 30 This is the one on whose behalf I said, 'A man who comes after me has totally surpassed me because HE existed long before me.' 31 I myself did not know him, but the reason I began immersing in water was so that he might be revealed to Israel."

#033 Day Three: The First Three Disciples Believe in Jesus
JN 1.32, 35-42

32 On the next day, John was once again standing with two of his disciples. … 36 Because he had seen Jesus as he was passing by, he said, "Look, the Lamb of God!" 37 The two disciples of John heard him saying this, and they followed Jesus.

38 Turning around, Jesus looked deep into them as they were following him and said to them, *"What are you really seeking after?"*

They said, "Rabbi" (which means "Teacher"), "where are you making your home?"

39 *"I command you to come,"* he said, *"and you will see."*

So they went and took a good look at where he was staying, and they remained in fellowship with him that day. It was about four in the afternoon.

40 Andrew, Simon Peter's brother, was one of the two who heard what John had said and who had followed Jesus. 41 The first thing Andrew did was to find his brother Simon and tell him, "We have truly found the Messiah!" [That is, the Christ.]

42 And Andrew brought Simon to Jesus. Jesus looked intently at him and said, *"You are presently called Simon son of John. You will be called Cephas."* [Which, when translated, is Peter, or "Rock."]

#034 Day Four: The Fourth and Fifth Disciples Believe in Jesus
JN 1.43-51

43 The next day Jesus decided to leave for Galilee. He found Philip, and said to him, *"I command you to continue following me."*

44 Philip, like Andrew and Peter, was from the town of Bethsaida. 45 Philip found Nathanael and told him, "We have found the one Moses wrote about in the Law, and about whom the prophets also wrote—Jesus of Nazareth, the son of Joseph."

46 "Nazareth! Can anything good come from there?" Nathanael asked. "Come and see," said Philip.

47 When Jesus saw Nathanael approaching, he said of him, *"Look! This is truly an Israelite in whom there is no deceitfulness."*

48 "How do you know me?" Nathanael asked. Jesus answered, *"I saw you while you were still under the fig tree, before Philip called you."*

49 Then, Nathanael declared, "Rabbi, you are the Son of God; you are the king of Israel."

50 Jesus said, *"You believe because I told you I saw you under the fig tree. You will see much greater things than that!"* 51 He then added, *"Very truly I tell you, you all will see 'heaven open, and the angels of God ascending and descending'* (Gen 28.12) *on the Son of Man."*

(Days Five and Six were spent traveling)

#035 Day Seven
Miracle 1: Jesus Turns Ceremonial Cleansing Water into Wine
JN 2.1-11

1 On the third day [from the fourth day of the week, when the journey to Cana began], a wedding took place at Cana in Galilee. Jesus' mother was there, 2 and Jesus and his disciples had also been invited to the wedding. 3 After the wine had run out, Jesus' mother said to him, "They have no more wine."

4 *"Woman, how does that involve you and me?"* Jesus replied. *"My hour has not yet come."*

5 His mother said to the servants, "DO whatever he tells you to do." 6 There were six large stone water pots standing nearby, the kind used by the Jews for ceremonial washing; each held twenty to thirty gallons.

7 Jesus commanded the servants, *"Fill the pots with water."* The servants filled them to the brim.

8 Then, he commanded them, *"Now draw some out, and continue taking it to the master of the banquet."*

9 They did so, and the master of the banquet tasted the water that had been turned into wine. He did not realize where it had come from, although the servants who had drawn the water knew. Then, he called the bridegroom aside 10 and said, "Everyone brings out the choice wine first and then the cheaper wine after the guests have had too much to drink; but you have saved the best till now!"

11 What Jesus did in Cana of Galilee was the first of the signs through which he revealed his glory, and his disciples believed in him.

CHAPTER 8

Early Judea: The First Passover of Jesus' Ministry

#036 Jesus' First Cleansing of the Temple
JN 2.12-22

12 After this [the first miracle at Cana] he went down to Capernaum with his mother, his brothers, and his disciples. They stayed there for a few days.

13 The time for the Jewish Passover was near, so Jesus went up to Jerusalem. 14 In the temple courts, he found people selling cattle, sheep, and doves, and others sitting at tables exchanging money.

15 He made a whip out of cords and drove them all out from the temple courts, both sheep and cattle; he poured out the coins of the moneychangers and flipped their tables upside down. 16 To those who were selling doves he said, *"I command you to get these out of here right now! Stop turning my Father's house into a market!"*

17 His disciples later remembered that it stands written, "Zeal for your house will consume me." (Ps. 69.9)

18 The Jews then responded to him, "What sign can you show us to prove your authority to do all this?"

19 Jesus answered them, *"Destroy this temple, and I will raise it up again in three days."*

20 They replied, "It has taken forty-six years to build this temple, and you are going to raise it in three days?"

21 But the temple he had spoken of was his body. 22 After he was raised from the dead, his disciples recalled what he had said. Then, they believed the scripture and the words that Jesus had spoken.

#037 Jesus' First Major Public Healing Ministry, in the Temple
JN 2.23-25

23 While Jesus was in Jerusalem at the Passover Festival, many people believed in his name as they saw the signs he was continually performing. 24 But Jesus himself would not commit himself to them, for he knew all people. 25 He did not need anyone to testify to him about mankind, for he always knew what was in each person.

#038 Jesus' Conversation with Nicodemus, Part I:
The Holy Spirit's Role in the Work of Salvation
JN 3.1-10

1 Now, there was a Pharisee named Nicodemus, a ruler of the Jewish people. 2 This man came to Jesus under the cover of night and said, "Rabbi, we know that you are a teacher who has come from God. For no one could perform the signs you are doing if God were not with him."

3 Jesus said to Nicodemus, *"Very truly I tell you, no one can see the kingdom of God unless one is born again from above."*

4 "How can they be born when they are old?" Nicodemus asked. "Surely they cannot enter a second time into their mother's womb to be born!"

5 Jesus answered, *"Very truly I tell you, no one can enter the kingdom of God unless one is born of water and the Spirit. 6 That which has been permanently born of the flesh is flesh, but that which has been permanently born of the Spirit is spirit. 7 I command you all to stop being shocked that I said, 'You must all be born again from above.' 8 The wind blows wherever it pleases. You hear its sound, but you cannot tell where it comes from or where it is going. So it is with everyone born of the Spirit."*

9 "How can this be?" Nicodemus asked.

10 Jesus answered: *"You are the teacher of Israel, and yet you do not understand these things?"*

#039 Jesus' Conversation With Nicodemus, Part II:
Jesus' Role in the Work of Salvation
JN 3.11-15

11 *"Very truly I tell you, we speak of what we really know, and we are testifying to what we can never forget having seen, but still you people continue to reject our testimony. 12 Because I have spoken to you of earthly things and you do not believe, how then will you believe if I speak of heavenly things?*

13 *"No one has ever permanently ascended up into heaven, except the one who came down out of heaven — the Son of Man. 14 Just as Moses in the wilderness lifted up the snake, it is necessary for the Son of Man to be lifted up in exaltation, 15 so that everyone who believes in him may continue to have eternal life."*

#040 Jesus' Conversation with Nicodemus, Part III:
The Father's Role in the Work of Salvation
JN 3.16-21

16 *"For God (the Father) loved every sinful person in the world so much that he gave his one and only Son, in order that whoever keeps on believing in him will not perish, but will continue to have God's own kind of eternal life. 17 For God did not send his Son into the world for the purpose of judging the world, but in order that the world might be saved through him.*

18 *"Whoever continues to believe in him is not condemned, but whoever continues to refuse to believe stands condemned already because he made the decision not to believe in the name of God's one and only Son. 19 This is the judgment: Light has come into the world, but people loved the darkness instead of the light, because their deeds were evil.*

20 *"Everyone who is practicing evil continues hating the light and will not come into the light for fear that their deeds will be exposed. 21 But whoever lives by the truth continues to come into the light so that it may be seen plainly that what they have done has been fully accomplished in them by God."*

#041 Jesus' Four Months of Disciple-Making in Judea
JN 3.22-24, 4.1-2

22 After the Passover, Jesus and his disciples went out into the Judean countryside, where he was spending time with them and continuing to immerse.

23 Now, John also was immersing at Aenon near Salim because there was plenty of water, and people were still coming to him and being immersed. 24 [This was before John was put in prison.]

4.1 Now, Jesus learned that the Pharisees had heard that he was gaining and immersing more disciples than John was, 2 although in fact it was not Jesus who immersed, but his disciples who did so.

#042 John the Immerser's Final Witness about Jesus
JN 3.25-36

25 It happened that a dispute developed between some of John's disciples and a certain Jew over the matter of ceremonial washing. 26 They came to John and said to him, "Rabbi, that man who was with you on the other side of the Jordan, the one about whom you gave your conclusive testimony; look, he keeps immersing, and everyone is going to him."

27 To this John replied, "A person can only have as much ministry as God has already decided for him in heaven. 28 You yourselves can testify that I said, 'I am not the Messiah, but I am sent ahead of him.' 29 The bride belongs to the bridegroom. The friend who attends the bridegroom waits and listens for him and is full of joy when he hears the bridegroom's voice. That joy is mine, and it has now been made fully complete. 30 It is necessary that he constantly become greater; I must continue to decrease."

31 The one who comes from above is above all; a person who is from the earth belongs to the earth and speaks as one from the earth. The one who comes from heaven is above all. 32 He testifies to what he has seen and heard, but no one fully accepts his testimony. 33 Whoever has accepted it has certified that God is truthful. 34 For the one whom God has sent speaks the words of God, for the Messiah gives the Spirit without limit.

35 The Father loves the Son and has placed everything in his hands. 36 Whoever believes in the Son has eternal life, but whoever rejects the Son will not receive eternal life, for God's wrath remains on that person.

CHAPTER 9

Jesus Ends His Early Ministry by Making Disciples in Samaria

#043 Jesus Decides to End His Ministry in Judea
by Traveling Through Samaria
JN 4.3-6

3 In order to avoid any appearance of competition with John the Immerser's ministry, Jesus left Judea and returned once more to Galilee.

4 The Lord sensed that it was necessary for him to travel through Samaria. 5 He came to a town in Samaria called Sychar, near the plot of ground Jacob had given to his son Joseph. 6 Jacob's well was there. Jesus, thoroughly exhausted as he was from the journey, sat down by the well. It was about noon.

#044 Jesus Offers the Gift of "Living Water" to a Samaritan Woman
JN 4.7-14

7 Look at this! A Samaritan woman came to draw water. Jesus took the initiative to speak to her, *"Will you give me a drink?"* 8 [His disciples had gone into the town to buy food.]

9 The Samaritan woman said to him, "How is that you, being a Jew, are asking for a drink from me, a Samaritan woman?" [Jews have nothing to do with Samaritans.]

10 Jesus answered her, *"If you knew the gift of God [but you do not], and who it is that is asking you for a drink, you would have asked him, and he would have given you living water."*

11 "Sir," the woman said, "you have nothing to draw with and the well is deep. Where are you going to get this living water? 12 I do not think you are greater than our father Jacob, who gave us the well and drank from it himself, as did also his sons and his livestock, but are you greater?"

13 Jesus answered, *"Everyone who drinks this water is going to be thirsty again, 14 but whoever drinks the water that I give them will never, ever be thirsty again. Indeed, the water I give them will become a spring of water inside them that continues gushing with eternal life."*

#045 The Woman Asks Jesus for "Living Water"
JN 4.15-19

15 The woman said to him, "Master, give me this water so that I can stop being thirsty and no longer have to keep coming here to draw water."

16 He commanded her, *"Go then, call your husband, and come back here."*

17 "I have no husband," she replied. Jesus said to her, *"You are right when you say you have no husband. 18 The fact is, you have had five husbands, and the man you now have is not your husband. What you have just said is quite true."*

19 "Master," the woman said, "I am perceiving that you are a prophet."

#046 Jesus Teaches about True Worship
JN 4.20-26

20 The woman said, "Our ancestors worshiped on this mountain, but you all claim that the place necessary for worship is in Jerusalem."

21 Jesus commanded her, *"You must continue to believe me, woman, a time is coming when you all will worship the Father neither on this mountain nor in Jerusalem. 22 You Samaritans continue worshipping what you do not know; we continue to worship what we do know, for salvation is from the Jews. 23 Yet a time is coming and has now come, when the true worshipers will worship the Father in spirit and in truth, for they are the kind of worshipers that the Father is seeking. 24 God is spirit; it is therefore necessary for his worshipers to worship in Spirit and in truth."*

26 The woman said, "I know that the Messiah [called Christ] is coming. When he comes, he will explain everything to us."

26 Then, Jesus declared, *"I AM the Messiah — the one speaking to you."*

#047 Jesus Trains His Disciples in Evangelism
JN 4.27-38

27 Just then, Jesus' disciples returned and were marveling that he was in an ongoing conversation with a woman. But no one asked, "What are you seeking?" or "Why are you talking with her?"

28 Then, leaving her water jar, the woman went back to the town and said to the people, 29 "Come! You have to see a man who told me everything I ever did. He is the Christ, is he not?" 30 They came out of the town and were coming toward him. 31 Meanwhile his disciples urged him, "Rabbi, eat something."

32 But he said to them, *"I, myself, always have food to eat that you know nothing about."*

33 Then, his disciples said to each other, "Could someone have brought him food?"

34 *"My food,"* said Jesus, *"is to do the will of him who sent me and to finish his work. 35 Do you not have a saying, 'It's still four months until harvest'? I command you, open your eyes up, and look at the fields! They are ripe for harvest. 36 Even now, the one who reaps draws a wage and harvests a crop for eternal life so that the sower and the reaper may rejoice together. 37 Thus, the saying 'One sows and another reaps' is true. 38 I sent you to reap what you have not rigorously labored for. Others have done the really hard work, and you have reaped the benefits of their labor."*

#048 Jesus Evangelizes the Town of Sychar
JN 4.39-42

39 Many of the Samaritans from Sychar believed in Jesus because of the woman's testimony, "He told me everything I ever did."

40 So, when the Samaritans came to him, they asked him to abide with them, and he stayed there two days. 41 And many more people became believers because of his own teaching.

42 They continued saying to the woman, "We no longer believe just because of what you said. Now, we have heard him in a decisive way for ourselves, and we know for sure that this One truly is the Savior of the world."

HIS GREAT GALILEAN MINISTRY

Jesus' outreach in Samaria signaled a crucial transition point in his ministry. Because John the Immerser had been arrested by Herod Antipas, Jesus began to preach publicly to the masses (as he had done in Samaria) with great power. He no longer had to be concerned about the appearance of competition with John.

The world had never seen a communicator as effective as Jesus, for he was anointed by the Holy Spirit immeasurably more so than anyone else; his gifting was greater, and his human speaking skills were nothing less than perfect. Jesus burst onto the scene in Galilee preaching the gospel with a fiery passion that quickly took the region by storm.

The Galilean Ministry was also characterized by almost non-stop miracles of healing, exorcisms, and displays of Jesus' authority over nature. Thirty-five specific miracles of Jesus are recorded in the gospels; nineteen of them occurred during his Galilean campaign. Many more unspecified, mass-healing events also occurred during this roughly twenty month period.

Jesus' strategy in Galilee was to make three systematic, exhaustive tours of the twenty-five towns and villages in the region. Each tour took about six months to complete, and a major transition in Jesus' ministry occurred on each one. This period of Jesus' life is best understood in terms of these tours.

The combination of Jesus' mighty public preaching and teaching, his non-stop miraculous healings, and his tours into every town created huge crowds and great initial popularity for him. This acclaim peaked at the end of his first tour. On the second tour, the Pharisees made the decision to kill him and publicly accused him of being a Satanist. They began to turn the people against Jesus. By the end of the third tour, even his own disciples had abandoned him in droves. Jesus' ministry in Galilee was the best of times, and the beginning of the worst of times for him.

The "Synoptic Gospels" (Matt., Mark, Luke) all describe this period extensively. Chapters 10 to 18 cover Jesus' ministry in Galilee.

CHAPTER 10

Galilee: Jesus Begins His Ministry

#049 Jesus Returns to Galilee in the Power of the Spirit
LK 3.19-20; 4.14-15 (Parallel Texts: MK 1.14-15; MT 4.12; JN 4.43, 45)

19 ᴸWhen John rebuked Herod the tetrarch because of his marriage to Herodias, his brother's wife, and all the other evil things he had done, 20 Herod added this to them all; he locked John up in prison.

ᴹWhen Jesus heard that John had been put in prison, ᴶhe left Sychar after two days to go to Galilee. ᴸSo, Jesus returned in the power of the Holy Spirit to Galilee, and the exciting news about him spread quickly throughout the entire countryside.

ᴶWhen Jesus came into Galilee, they received him gladly, because they had taken careful note of all the things he had done in Jerusalem during the feast [of Passover], because they also had gone to the feast.

ᴹJesus was proclaiming the good news about God:

15 *"The prepared time has fully come, and the heavenly kingdom of God has come close to you-- it's right here! I command you all to continue repenting — permanently changing your mind to agree with me — and continue to believe everything I am proclaiming to you in this good news."*

#050 Miracle 2: Jesus Heals from a Distance, with Just a Word
JN 4.46-54

46 Once again, Jesus visited Cana in Galilee, where he had turned the water into wine. A certain royal official's son was lying sick at Capernaum. 47 Having heard that Jesus had come to Galilee from Judea, this man went to him and continued to plead with him to come and heal his son, who was lingering on the edge of death.

48 Jesus said, *"Unless you all see signs and wonders, you absolutely refuse to believe."*

49 The royal official said, "Sir, please come down now, before my child dies."

50 *"Go,"* Jesus commanded him, *"your son will have an abundant life."* The man believed the words that Jesus had spoken to him and departed on the journey back home.

51 While he was still on the way, his servants met him with the news that his boy was living. 52 When he inquired as to the time when his son became better, they said to him, "Yesterday, at one in the afternoon the fever left him."

53 Then the father realized this was the exact time when Jesus had said to him, *"Your son will have an abundant life."* So, he and his whole household believed.

54 This was the second sign Jesus performed, after coming from Judea to Galilee.

#051 Jesus is Rejected at Nazareth
LK 4.16-30 (Parallel Text: JN 4.44)

ᴶNow Jesus himself had pointed out that a prophet has no honor in his own country.

16 ᴸJesus went on to Nazareth, where he had been brought up, and on the Sabbath day, he went into the synagogue, as was his fixed custom. He stood up to read, 17 and the scroll of the prophet Isaiah was handed to him. Unrolling it, he found the place where it stands written, and read:

18 *"The Spirit of the Lord is on me, because he anointed me*
to proclaim good news to the poor.

He has sent me to proclaim release to the captives and recovery of sight to the blind,
To set people whose lives have been destroyed free —
19 *To proclaim the time of the Lord's favor."* (Isaiah 61.1-2)

20 Then, he rolled up the scroll, gave it back to the attendant, and sat down. Everyone in the synagogue fastened their eyes firmly on him.

21 He began by saying to them, *"Today this scripture has been permanently fulfilled, in your hearing."*

22 All were speaking well of him, and they continued to marvel at the gracious words that came from his lips. "Is this not Joseph's son?" they asked.

23 Jesus said to them, *"Surely you will quote this proverb to me: 'Physician, heal yourself!' And you will say to me, 'Do here in your hometown what we have heard that you did in Capernaum.'* 24 *Truly I tell you, no prophet is accepted in his own hometown.* 25 *I assure you that there were many widows in Israel in Elijah's time, when the sky was shut for three and a half years, and there was a severe famine throughout the land.* 26 *Yet Elijah was not sent to any of them, but to a widow in Zarephath in the region of Sidon.* 27 *And there were many in Israel with leprosy in the time of Elisha the prophet, yet not one of them was cleansed — only Naaman the Syrian."*

28 All the people in the synagogue were furious when they heard this. 29 They got up, drove him out of town, and took him to the brow of the hill on which the town was built in order to throw him off the cliff.

30 But he walked right through the crowd and went his own way. 31 Then, he went down to Capernaum, a town in Galilee.

#052 Jesus Establishes His Headquarters in Capernaum
MT 4.13-16

13 Leaving Nazareth, Jesus went and lived in Capernaum, which was by the lake in the area of Zebulun and Naphtali, 14 to fulfill what was said through the prophet Isaiah:

15 "The land of Zebulun and the land of Naphtali — the way of the Sea,
beyond the Jordan,
'Galilee of the Gentiles' —
The people living in darkness have seen a great light;
16 On those living in the shadow of death, a light has dawned." (Isaiah 9.1-2)

**#053 After Miracle 3, Jesus Calls Four Key Disciples to
Follow Him on a Full-time Basis
LK 5.1-11 (Parallel texts: MT 4.18-22; MK 1.16-20)**

1 [L]One day as Jesus was standing by the Lake of Gennesaret—[MT]the sea of Galilee—[L]the people were crowding around him and listening to the word of God. 2 He saw two boats at the shore, left there by the fishermen, [MT]two brothers—Simon, who was called Peter, and his brother Andrew—[L]who were washing their nets.

3 He got into one of the boats—the one belonging to Simon—and asked him to put out a little way from the shore. Then, he sat down and taught the people from the boat.

4. When he had finished speaking, he said to Simon, *"I command you to go out again into the deep water, and let down the nets for a catch."*

5 Simon answered, "Master, we've labored hard all night long and have not caught anything. But because you say so, I will let down the nets."

6 When they had done so, they caught such a large number of fish that their nets were tearing. 7 So, they signaled their partners in the other boat to come and help them, and they came and filled both boats so full that they were beginning to sink!

8 When Simon Peter saw all of this, he fell down at Jesus' knees and said, "Get away from me, Lord; I am a thoroughly sinful man!"

9 For he and all his companions were shocked at the catch of fish they had taken, 10 as were James and John, the sons of Zebedee, Simon's partners. Then Jesus said to Simon, *"I command you to stop being afraid;* [MT]*you must come and follow after me.* [L]*From now on* [MT]*I will make both of you* [L]*fishers of people."*

11 So, when they pulled their boats up on shore, they left everything behind and followed him.

[M]And going on a little farther, he saw [MT]two other brothers—[M]James the son of Zebedee and John his brother—sitting in the boat [MT]with Zebedee, their father, [M]mending their nets. Immediately he called them. [MT]Right away [M]they left [MT]the boat [M]and their father Zebedee in it with the hired workers, and they followed him.

#054 Miracles 4 and 5: Jesus Shakes Capernaum
with a Powerful Day of Ministry
MK 1.21-34 (Parallel texts: MT 8.14-16; LK 4.31B-42)

Miracle 4: In the morning...

21 They went into Capernaum. When the Sabbath came, Jesus went straight into the synagogue and began to teach. 22 The people were in a state of continual amazement at his teaching; he was teaching them as one who possessed authority, unlike the manner of the teachers of the law.

23 Just then, a man in their synagogue who was possessed by an impure spirit cried out, 24 "What is there between us and you, Jesus of Nazareth? Have you come to destroy us? I know who you are—the Holy One of God!"

25 Jesus rebuked the spirit, saying, *"I command you to be silenced! You come out of him!"*

26 The impure spirit shook the man violently, ᴸand when he had thrown him down in the midst of everybody, ᴹcame out of him with a massive scream, ᴸhaving done him no harm.

27 ᴹThe people were all so amazed that they continued asking each other, "What is this? A new teaching, and with authority! He even gives orders to impure spirits and they obey him." 28 The news about Jesus spread quickly over the whole region of Galilee.

Miracle 5: That afternoon...

29 As soon as they left the synagogue, they went with James and John to the home of Simon and Andrew. 30 Simon's mother-in-law had been laid out in bed with a raging fever, so they immediately told Jesus about her. 31 Having come near to the bed, He took hold of her hand firmly and raised her up. The fever left her instantly, and she began waiting on them.

That night... many healing miracles

32 That evening after the sun had set, the people started bringing all the sick and demon-possessed people to Jesus. 33 The whole town gathered outside the door, 34 and Jesus healed many people who had various diseases. He also drove out many demons, ᴹᵀso that what was spoken through Isaiah

the prophet might be fulfilled, "He himself took our infirmities and bore our diseases." (Isaiah 53.4)

^MBut Jesus would not let the demons speak because they knew who he was.

CHAPTER 11

Galilee: Jesus' First Tour

#055 Jesus' First Tour of Galilee is Birthed in Prayer
MK 1.35-39 (Parallel Texts: MT 4.23-35; LK 4.42-44)

35 Very early in the morning, while it was still pitch dark, Jesus got up, left the house, and went out to a desolate, solitary place, where he continued to pray ᴸat daybreak. ᴹSimon and his companions scoured the countryside looking for him. 37 When they finally found him, they exclaimed, "Everyone is looking for you!" ᴸThe people would have tried to prevent him from leaving them, but he said:

38 ᴹ "Let us go elsewhere – to the nearby villages ᴸand other towns – for I must ᴹpreach ᴸthe good news of the kingdom of God there also. This is why I was sent, ᴹwhy I have come."

39 So, he traveled throughout ᴹᵀall ᴹGalilee, constantly preaching ᴹᵀand teaching in the synagogues, ᴹdriving out demons, ᴹᵀproclaiming the good news of the kingdom, and healing every disease and sickness among the people.

The news about him spread out all over Syria, and people brought to him all who were ill with various diseases — those suffering severe pain, the demon-possessed, those having seizures, and the paralyzed — and he healed them. Large crowds from Galilee, the Decapolis, Jerusalem, Judea, and the [Perean] region across the Jordan followed him.

#056 Miracle 6: Jesus Compassionately Heals a Man of Leprosy
MK 1.40-45 (Parallel Texts: MT 8.2-4; LK 5.12-16)

40 ^LWhile Jesus was in one of the towns, ^Ma man ^Lcovered ^Mwith leprosy came to him. ^LSeeing Jesus, the man fell on his face ^Mand begged him on his knees, ^L"Lord, ^Mif you are willing, you have the power to make me clean."

41 Jesus was filled with compassion and reached out his hand and touched the man. *"I am willing,"* he said, *"I command you to be made clean!"*

42 Immediately, the leprosy left him and he was cleansed. 43 Jesus sent him away at once with a stern warning, 44 *"I command you: see that you do not tell this to anyone. But you must go, show yourself to the priest, and you must offer the sacrifices (^{MT}gift) that Moses commanded for your cleansing as a testimony to them."*

45 Instead, the man went out and began to proclaim what had happened to many people, and he continued to spread the news. As a result, Jesus could no longer enter a town openly, but he was forced to stay outside in lonely places.

^LThe reports about Jesus continued to go out into the surrounding regions, so that crowds of ^Mpeople came to him from everywhere ^Lto hear him and to be healed of all their sicknesses.

And Jesus continued to go out regularly to desolate places so that he could pray.

#057 Miracle 7: Jesus Forgives and Heals a Paralyzed Man
MK 2.1-12 (Parallel Texts: MT 9.1-8; LK 5.17-26)

1 A few days later, ^{MT}Jesus stepped into a boat, crossed over, and came into his own town, ^MCapernaum, and the people heard that he had come home. ^LOn one of those days that he was teaching, Pharisees and teachers of the law were there, having come from every village of Galilee and from Judea and Jerusalem. The power of the Lord was present with him to heal the sick. 2 ^MThey gathered in such large numbers that no room was left, not even outside the door, and Jesus was speaking the word to them.

3 Some men came, bringing to him a paralyzed man, ^{MT}who was permanently immobilized on a mat ^Mcarried by four men. ^LThey were trying to take

him into the house to lay him before Jesus. 4 ᴹBecause they could not reach Jesus because of the crowd, ᴸthey went up onto the roof ᴹand chopped an opening in the roof above Jesus by digging through it, and then they lowered the mat the man was lying on ᴸthrough the tiles into the middle of the room, right in front of Jesus.

5 ᴹBecause Jesus saw their faith, he said to the paralyzed man, ᴹᵀ *"Son, I command you to be courageous!* ᴸFriend, ᴹyour sins are forgiven."*

6 Now some teachers of the law ᴸand Pharisees ᴹwere sitting there, thinking to themselves, 7 "Why is this fellow talking like that? ᴸWho is this who ᴹis blaspheming? Who has the power to forgive sins but God alone?"

8 Immediately, Jesus knew in his spirit that this was what they were reasoning in their hearts, and he said to them, *"Why are you thinking these ᴹᵀevil ᴹthings ᴹᵀin your hearts? 9 Which is easier: to say to this paralyzed man, 'Your sins are forgiven,' or to say, 'Get up for good, pick up your mat, and continue walking'? 10 "But I want you to be fully convinced that the Son of Man has authority on earth to forgive sins."* So, he said to the man, 11 *"I command you, get up for good, pick up your mat, and go home."*

12 ᴸImmediately, the man stood up in front of them, ᴹtook up his mat, walked out in full view of them all, ᴸand headed home praising God.

ᴹᵀWhen the crowd saw this, they were in a state of continual amazement, and they ᴸwere filled with a sense of awe ᴹᵀand they kept on praising God who had given this display of authority to the people. ᴹThey said, "We have never seen anything like this before; ᴸwe have truly seen remarkable things today!"

#058 Jesus Calls Matthew to Follow Him
MT 9.9-13 (Parallel Texts: MK 2.13-17; LK 5.27-32)

ᴹOnce again, Jesus went out beside the lake. A large crowd came to him, and he was teaching them.

9 ᴹᵀAs Jesus went on from there, he saw a man named Matthew, ᴸa tax collector also called Levi, ᴹthe son of Alphaeus, sitting at ᴹᵀthe tax collector's booth. *"I command you to continue following me,"* he said. So, Matthew ᴸleft everything, ᴹᵀand having risen up, he followed him.

10 ᴸLevi made Jesus a great feast ᴹᵀat his house; while Jesus was having dinner, ᴸa large crowd ᴹᵀof many tax collectors and 'sinners' came and sat

down ᴸat the table, and they ate with him and his disciples, ᴹfor there were many who followed him.

11 ᴹᵀWhen the Pharisees ᴹand their scribes ᴹᵀsaw this — ᴹthat he was eating with tax collectors and 'sinners,' — ᴸthey murmured against his disciples ᴹᵀand asked: "Why does your teacher eat with tax collectors and sinners?"

12 On hearing this, Jesus said, *"It is not the healthy who need a doctor, but the sick. 13 But I command you all to go and really learn what this means: 'I desire mercy, not sacrifice.' (Hos. 6.6). For I have not come to call the righteous, but sinners* ᴸ*to repentance."*

#059 The First Tour Ends with a Question about Fasting
MK 2.18-22 (Parallel Texts: MT 9.14-17; LK 5.33-39)

18 Now John's disciples and the Pharisees were making a practice of fasting. Some of ᴹᵀJohn's disciples ᴹcame and asked Jesus, "How is it that John's disciples ᴸoften fast and pray, ᴹand the disciples of the Pharisees are fasting, but yours are not? ᴸThey go on eating and drinking."

19 ᴹJesus answered, *"How can* ᴸ*you make* ᴹ*the guests of the bridegroom fast* ᴹᵀ*and mourn* ᴹ*while he is with them? They cannot, so long as they have him with them. 20 But the time will come when the bridegroom will be taken from them, and* ᴸ*in those days,* ᴹ*they will fast.*

21 *"No one* ᴸ*tears a patch from a new garment* ᴹ*and sews the patch of unshrunk cloth on an old garment. Otherwise, the new piece will pull away from the old, making the tear worse,* ᴸ*and he will have torn the new garment, and the patch from the new will not match the old.*

22 ᴹ*"And no one pours new wine into old wineskins. Otherwise, the* ᴸ*new* ᴹ*wine will burst the skins,* ᴹᵀ*the wine will run out,* ᴹ*and both the wine and the wineskins will be ruined. No, they* ᴸ*must* ᴹ*pour new wine into new wineskins,* ᴹᵀ*and both are preserved.* ᴸ*Furthermore, after drinking the old wine, no one wants the new, for he says, 'the old is better.'"*

CHAPTER 12

Jesus Ministers in Jerusalem at His Second Passover

#060 Miracle 8: Jesus Heals a Paralyzed Man on a Sabbath
JN 5.1-14

1 Some time later, Jesus went up to Jerusalem for one of the Jewish (Passover) festivals.

2 Now there is in Jerusalem near the Sheep Gate a pool, which in Aramaic is called Bethesda, and which is surrounded by five covered courts. 3 A great number of disabled people used to lie there—the blind, the lame, and the paralyzed.

[Note: Less reliable manuscripts include the following here: "And they waited for the waters to move. 4 The people thought that from time to time an angel of the Lord would come down and stir up the waters. The first one into the pool after that would be cured of whatever disease they had."]

5 A certain man was there who had been an invalid for 38 continuous years. 6 When Jesus saw him lying there and became aware that he had been in this condition for such a long time, he asked him, *"Do you really want to become well?"*

7 "Sir," the invalid replied, "I have no man to help me into the pool when the water is stirred. While I am still crawling along, trying to get in, someone else always goes down ahead of me."

8 Then, Jesus commanded him, *"Get up for good! Pick up your mat, and continue to walk."* 9 Instantly, the man was made whole; he picked up his mat and began walking. The day on which this took place was a Sabbath, 10 and so the Jewish leaders said to the man who had been permanently healed of his paralysis, "It is the Sabbath; the law forbids you to carry your mat."

11 But he replied, "The man who made me well said to me, 'Pick up your mat and continue walking.'"

12 So, they asked him, "Who is this fellow who told you to pick it up and walk?"

13 The man who was healed had no idea who it was, for Jesus had slipped away into the crowd that was there. 14 Later on, Jesus found him at the temple and said to him, *"Look, you have become permanently whole. I command you to stop sinning, or something far worse may happen to you."*

#061 Jesus Claims to be Equal with God the Father
JN 5.15-20

15 The man went away and announced to the Jewish leaders that Jesus had made him whole. 16 So, because Jesus was doing these things on the Sabbath, the Jewish leaders were persecuting him.

17 In his defense, Jesus said to them, *"My Father is always at his work to this very moment, so I too, am always working."*

18 For this reason, they were seeking to kill him even more; for not only was he continually breaking the Sabbath, but he continued calling God his own Father, making himself equal with God.

19 Jesus answered by saying to them, *"Very truly I tell you, the Son can do nothing by himself, except for what he is seeing that his Father is in the process of doing -- because whatever the Father is doing, that is what the Son does in the same way. 20 For the Father is always loving the Son and showing him all he does. Yes, and he will show him even greater works than these, so that you will be in a constant state of amazement."*

#062 Jesus is Both Judge and Giver of Eternal Life
JN 5.21-30

21 *"Just as the Father raises the dead and gives them eternal life, in the same way, the Son gives eternal life to whom he is pleased to give it. 22 Moreover, the Father*

judges no one, but has permanently entrusted all judgment to the Son, 23 so that all people may continue to honor the Son, just as they honor the Father. Whoever is not honoring the Son is not honoring the Father who sent him.

24 *"Very truly I tell you, whoever hears my word and continues to believe in him who sent me has eternal life and will not ever be judged, but has crossed over permanently from death to life. 25 Very truly I tell you, a time is coming and has now come, when the dead will hear the voice of the Son of God, and those who hear will live. 26 For just as the Father has eternal life in himself, he has granted the Son eternal life in himself. 27 And he has given him authority to judge because he is the Son of Man.*

28 *"I command you to stop being amazed at this -- for a time is coming when all who are in their graves will hear his voice 29 and come out; those who have done what is good will rise to live eternally, and those who have done what is evil will rise to be condemned. 30 By myself I can do nothing; I judge only as I hear, and my judgment is just, for I always seek not to please myself, but to please him who sent me."*

#063 Five Key Witnesses Certify Jesus as the Son of God
JN 5.31-47

Jesus testified, 31 *"If I alone testify about myself, my testimony is not valid."*

John the Immerser testified, 32 *"There is another like me, who testifies in my favor, and I know that his testimony about me--which he continues to declare-- is true. 33 You have sent to John and he has set forth his decisive witness to the truth. 34 Not that I accept human testimony, but I mention it that you may be saved. 35 John was a lamp that burned and gave light, and you chose for a time to bask in his light.*

The Miracles of Jesus testified, 36 *"I have a witness far greater than that of John. For the works that the Father has given over to me to finish – the very works that I am continuing to do – these continue bearing witness that the Father has sent me.*

The Father testified, 37 *"And the Father who sent me has himself testified conclusively concerning me. You have never heard his voice nor seen his form, 38 nor does his word dwell in you at all, for you are refusing to believe in the one he sent."*

The Scripture (Moses) testified, 39 *"You continue to study the Scriptures diligently because you think that in them you have eternal life. These very Scriptures are bearing witness about me, 40 yet you continue to refuse to come to me so that you could actually have eternal life!*

41 *"I do not accept praise or glory from human beings, 42 but I have come to fully know you. I know for sure that you do not have the love of God making its home in your hearts. 43 I have come in my Father's name, and you do not accept me; but if*

someone else comes in his own name, you will accept him. **44** *How can you possibly believe, given that you accept glory from one another, but you do not seek the glory that comes from the only God?*

45 *"I command you to stop thinking I will accuse you before the Father. Your accuser is Moses, on whom you have set all your hope.* **46** *If you really believed in Moses — and you do not — you would have believed me, for he wrote about me.* **47** *But because you do not believe what he wrote, how are you going to believe what I say?"*

CHAPTER 13

Galilee: Crucial Sabbath Controversies Continue as

Jesus Returns to the Region

#064 A Controversy over Picking Grain on the Sabbath
MT 12.1-8 (Parallel Texts: MK 2.32-28; LK 6.1-5)

1 At an opportune time, Jesus went through the grain fields on the Sabbath. His disciples were hungry and began picking some heads of grain, ᴸrubbing them in their hands ᴹᵀand eating them. 2 Having seen this, the Pharisees said to him, "Look! Your disciples are doing what is unlawful on the Sabbath."

3 He answered, *"Have you never read what David did when he and his companions were hungry* ᴹ*and in need? In the days of Abiathar the high priest,* 4 ᴹᵀ*he entered the house of God, and he and his companions ate the consecrated bread, which was not lawful for them to do, but only for the priests?*

5 *"Or have you not read in the Law that the priests on Sabbath duty in the temple continue desecrating the Sabbath, and yet are innocent?* 6 *I tell you that something greater than the temple is here.* 7 *If you had only understood what these words mean, 'I desire mercy and not sacrifice,'* (Hos. 6.6; Mic. 6.6-8) *you would not have condemned the innocent.* 8 *For the Son of Man is Lord of the Sabbath.* ᴹ*The Sabbath was made for man, but man was not made for the Sabbath."*

#065 Miracle 9: The Sabbath Day Healing of A Man with a Shriveled Hand
MK 3.1-6 (Parallel Texts: MT 12.9-14; LK 6.6-11)

1 ^{MT}Going on from that place, ^Lon another Sabbath ^MJesus went into their synagogue ^Land was teaching, ^Mand a man with a shriveled right hand was there. 2 ^LThe scribes and the Pharisees ^Mwere watching him like hawks, to see if Jesus would heal him on the Sabbath. Looking for a reason ^{MT}to bring charges against Jesus, they asked him, "Is it lawful to heal on the Sabbath?"

Jesus answered, *"If any of you has a sheep and it falls into a pit on the Sabbath, will you not take hold of it and lift it out? Any person is so much more valuable than a sheep!"*

^LBut he knew their thoughts perfectly. 3 ^MSo, he commanded the man with the shriveled hand, ^L*"Rise up for good and* ^M*take your stand in the midst of everybody."*

The man rose up and stood there. 4 Then, Jesus said to them all, ^L*"I ask you,* ^M*which is lawful on the Sabbath, to do good or to do evil? To save life or to destroy it?"*

5 But they continued to maintain their silence. And having looked around at all of them with anger, because he was deeply grieved by the stubbornness of their hearts, Jesus commanded the man, *"Stretch out your hand."* So he stretched it out and it was completely restored ^{MT}just as whole as the other. Jesus said, *"Therefore, doing good on the Sabbath is always lawful."*

6 ^LBut the Pharisees were filled with anger, ^Mand they went out and were plotting together with the Herodians on how they might utterly destroy Jesus.

#066 Jesus Withdraws to the Sea of Galilee and Ministers There
MK 3.7-12 (Parallel Text: MT 12.15-21)

7 ^{MT}Because he was aware of the intention to kill him, ^MJesus withdrew with his disciples to the lake, and a large crowd from Galilee followed them. 8 When they heard about all that he was continuing to do, many people also came to him from Judea, Jerusalem, Idumea, and the regions across the Jordan and around Tyre and Sidon, ^{MT}and he healed all their sick.

9 ^MOn account of the crowd, Jesus told his disciples to have a small boat prepared and ready for him to keep the people from crowding him. 10 He had healed many, and those with diseases continued pushing forward to touch him.

11 As the impure spirits saw him, they were falling down before him and crying out, "You are the Son of God." 12 But he gave them strict commands not to make his identity known to the people.

^{MT}This all happened to fulfill what was spoken through the prophet Isaiah:

> "This is my servant whom I have chosen,
> the one I love, in whom I take my delight;
> I will place my spirit on him,
> and he will proclaim justice to the nations,
> he will not quarrel or cry out;
> no one will hear his voice in the streets.
> He will not break even a bruised reed,
> and he will not put out a smoldering wick
> until he has brought justice all the way through to victory.
> And the nations will put their hope in his name." (Is. 42.1-4)

CHAPTER 14

Galilee: The Appointment of the Twelve Apostles and the

"Teaching on the Mount"

#067 Jesus Appoints the Twelve Apostles
MK 3.13-19 (Parallel Text: LK 6.12-16)

13 ᴸOne of those days Jesus went out to the mountain to pray, and he continued in prayer for the entire night. And when it became day, ᴹhe went up on the mountainside and called ᴸhis disciples — ᴹthose he wanted — and they came to him. 14 And he chose twelve from among them and appointed his twelve that they might be with him and that he might send them out to preach, 15 and to have the authority to drive out demons.

16 The names of the twelve he appointed are Simon, whom he named Peter; 17 James, son of Zebedee; James' brother John (to them he gave the name Boanerges, which means "sons of thunder"); 18 Andrew; Philip; Bartholomew; Matthew; Thomas; James, son of Alphaeus; Thaddaeus; Simon who was called "the Zealot"; 19 and Judas Iscariot, who betrayed him, ᴸa traitor.

#068 The Core Attitudes of a Jesus Follower
MT 5.1-12 (Parallel Text: LK 6.17-26)

ᴸJesus went down with the apostles and stood on a level place on the mountain.

1 ᴹᵀNow, when Jesus saw the crowd ᴸof his disciples and the great multitudes of people, ᴹᵀhe sat down. ᴸThey came from all over Judea, from Jerusalem, and from the coast of Tyre and Sidon. They had come to hear him and to be healed of their diseases. Those troubled by evil spirits were cured, and the people were all trying to touch him because power was coming from him and healing them all.

ᴹᵀHis disciples came to him, 2 and ᴸlooking at his disciples, ᴹᵀhe was teaching them, saying, 3 *"Blessed are the poor in spirit, for theirs is the kingdom of heaven. ᴸBut woe to you who are rich, for you have already received your comfort.*

4 ᴹᵀ*Blessed are those who mourn ᴸand weep now, ᴹᵀfor they will be comforted, and ᴸlaugh. Woe to you who laugh now, for you will mourn and weep.*

5 ᴹᵀ*"Blessed are the meek, for they will inherit the earth.*

6 *Blessed are those who hunger ᴸnow ᴹᵀand thirst for righteousness, for they will be filled. ᴸWoe to you who are full now, for you will hunger.*

7 ᴹᵀ*Blessed are the merciful, for they will be shown mercy.*

8 *"Blessed are the pure in heart, for they will see God.*

9 *Blessed are the peacemakers, for they will be called 'children of God.'*

10 *Blessed are those who are persecuted because of righteousness, for theirs is the kingdom of heaven. ᴸWoe to you when all men speak well of you, for that is what their fathers did to the false prophets.*

11 ᴹᵀ*"Blessed are you when people ᴸhate you, and when they exclude, and ᴹᵀinsult you, and persecute you, ᴸtrash your name as evil, ᴹᵀand falsely say all kinds of evil against you because of me, ᴸthe son of man. 12 ᴹᵀI command you all to continually rejoice in that day and you all must make yourselves glad – ᴸleap for joy – ᴹᵀbecause great is your reward in heaven, for they persecuted the prophets before you in the same way."*

#069 Disciples Live in Jesus' Righteousness
MT 5.13-20

13 *"You are the salt of the earth. But if the salt loses its saltiness, how can it be made salty again? It is no longer good for anything, except to be thrown out and constantly trampled underfoot.*

14 *"You are the light of the world. A town built on a hill cannot be hidden.* 15 *Nor do people keep a lamp burning and then set it under a bowl. Instead, they put it on its stand, and it keeps shining light upon everyone in the house.* 16 *In the same way, I command you to let your light shine before others, in such a way that they see your good deeds, and glorify your Father in heaven.*

17 *"Do not think that I have come to abolish the Law or the Prophets; I have not come to abolish them but to fulfill them.* 18 *"For truly I tell you, until heaven and earth disappear, the smallest letter or the least stroke of a pen will never, ever disappear from the Law, until everything has been fulfilled.*

19 *"Therefore anyone who sets aside one of the least of these commands and teaches others accordingly will be called least in the kingdom of heaven, but whoever practices and teaches these commands will be called great in the kingdom of heaven.*

20 *"For I tell you that unless your righteousness surpasses that of the Pharisees and the teachers of the law, you will certainly not enter the kingdom of heaven."*

Six Examples: The Way Love More than Fulfills the Old Covenant Commands

#070 Love Deals Righteously with Anger and Broken Relationships MT 5. 21-48 (Parallel Text: LK 6.27-30, 32-36)

21 (Example One) *"You have heard that it was said to the people long ago, 'You shall not murder,'* (Exodus 20.13) *and 'anyone who murders will be subject to judgment.'*

22 *"But I tell you that anyone who is angry with a brother or sister will be subject to judgment. Again, anyone who says to a brother or sister, 'You idiot!' is answerable to the court. And anyone who says, 'You fool!' will be in danger of the fires of hell.*

23 *"Therefore, if you are in the process of offering your gift at the altar and remember that your brother or sister is holding something against you,* 24 *I command you to leave your gift right there in front of the altar. I command that you make the effort to go and try to be reconciled to them and then come and finish offering your gift.*

25 *"I command you to think about it like this: You must settle matters quickly with your adversary who is taking you to court. Do it while you are still together on the way, or your adversary may hand you over to the judge, and the judge may hand you over to the officer, and you may be thrown into prison.* 26 *I tell you truthfully that you will not get out until you have paid the last penny."*

#071 Love Deals Righteously with
Sexuality, Marriage, and Promise Keeping
MT 5.27-37

27 (Example Two) *"You have heard that it was said, 'You shall not commit adultery.'* (Ex. 20.14)

28 *"But I myself tell you that anyone who continues to look at a woman lustfully has already committed adultery with her in his heart.*

29 *"If your right eye is causing you to stumble, I command you to gouge it out and throw it away. It is better for you to lose one part of your body than for your whole body to be thrown into hell. 30 And if your right hand causes you to stumble, I command you to cut it off and throw it away. It is better for you to lose one part of your body than for your whole body to go into hell.*

31 (Example Three) *"You have heard, 'Anyone who divorces his wife must give her a certificate of divorce.'* (Duet. 24.1) 32 *But I myself tell you that anyone who divorces his wife, except for sexual immorality, makes her the victim of adultery, and anyone who marries a divorced woman is committing adultery.*

33 (Example Four) *"Again, you have heard that it was said to the people long ago, 'Do not break your oath, but fulfill the oaths you have made to the Lord.'* (Duet. 23.21) 34 *But I myself command you not to swear an oath at all: either by heaven, for it is God's throne; 35 or by the earth, for it is his footstool; or by Jerusalem, for it is the city of the Great King. 36 And do not swear by your head, for you cannot make even one hair white or black.*

37 *"All you need to say is simply 'Yes' or 'No'; anything beyond this comes from the evil one."*

#072 Unconditional Love is the Basis of True Righteousness
MT 5.38-48 (Parallel Texts: LK 6.27-30, 32-36)

38 (Example Five) *"You have heard that it was said, 'Eye for eye, and tooth for tooth.'* (Ex. 21.24) 39 *But I myself command you -- do not resist an evil person. If anyone is slapping you on the right cheek, I command you to turn the other cheek to him also. 40 And if anyone wants to sue you and take your shirt, I command you to give up your coat as well. 41 If anyone forces you to go one mile, I command you to continue going with him for two miles.*

42 *"I command you to give to the one who asks you, and do not turn away from the one who wants to borrow from you.* ᴸ*If anyone takes what belongs to you, I command*

you not to take it back from him. I command you to lend to them without expecting anything back. Even sinners lend to sinners, expecting to be repaid in full.

43 (Example Six) ᴹᵀ "*You have heard that it was said, 'Love your neighbor' (Lev. 19.18) and 'Hate your enemy.' (Duet. 23.6) 44 But I myself command you to continue loving your enemies;* ᴸ*continue doing good to those who hate you; I command you to continue blessing those who curse you,* ᴹᵀ *continue praying for those who persecute you* ᴸ*and mistreat you 45* ᴹᵀ*so that you may be children of your Father in heaven. He causes his sun to rise on the evil and the good and sends rain on the righteous and the unrighteous.*

ᴸ "*I command you to be merciful, just as your heavenly Father is merciful. Then, your reward will be great, and you will be children of the Most High because he is kind to the ungrateful and wicked.*

46 ᴹᵀ "*If you love those who love you,* ᴸ*what credit is that to you?* ᴹᵀ*What reward will you get?* ᴸ*Even sinners love those who love them. And if you do good to those who are good to you, what credit is that to you?* ᴹᵀ*Are not even the* ᴸ*sinners and* ᴹᵀ*tax collectors doing that? 47 And if you greet only your own people, what are you doing more than others? Do not even pagans do that? 48 Therefore, I command you to be complete in love* ᴸ*and mercy,* ᴹᵀ*just as your heavenly Father is complete in love* ᴸ*and mercy.*"

#073 Love For God Motivates Giving and Fasting in Secret
MT 6.1-4, 16-18

The Principle: 1 "*I command you to continue to pay careful attention that you do not practice your righteousness in front of others in order to be seen by them. If you do, you will have no reward from your Father in heaven.*

The Principle Applied to Giving: 2 "*So when you are giving to the needy, I command you not to announce it with trumpets, as the hypocrites are doing in the synagogues and on the streets, to be honored by others. Truly I tell you, they have received their reward in full.*

3 *But when you give to the needy, I command you not to let your left hand know what your right hand is doing, 4 so that your giving may be in secret. Then your Father, who is seeing what is done in secret, will reward you.*

The Principle Applied to Fasting: 16 "*When you are fasting, I command you not to look gloomy as the hypocrites do, for they deliberately put their misery on their faces to show others they are fasting. Truly I tell you, they have received their reward in full.*

17 *"But when you fast, I command you to keep oil on your head and wash your face* 18 *so that it will not be obvious to others that you are fasting, but only to your Father, who is unseen; and your Father, who is seeing what is done in secret, will reward you."*

#074 Love for God Motivates Private Prayer
MT 6.1-4, 16-18 (Repeated Text: LK 11.2-4)

5 *"And when you pray, I command you not to be like the hypocrites, for they love to pray standing in the synagogues and on the street corners to be seen by others. Truly I tell you, they have received their reward in full.*

6 *"But when you pray, I command you to go into your room, close the door, and pray to your Father, who is unseen. Then, your Father, who sees what is done in secret, will reward you.* 7 *And when you pray, I command you not to continue babbling like pagans, for they think they will be heard because of their many words.* 8 *I command you not to be like them, for your Father knows what you need before you ask him.*

9 *"When you pray, I command you to continue to make these requests:*

'Our Father in heaven,
cause your name to be honored as holy,
10 *cause your sovereign reign to be fully acknowledged by all people,*
cause your will to be done on earth with the same attitude that characterizes heaven.
11 *Give us this day our daily allotment of bread.*
12 *And forgive us our debts, as we also have forgiven our debtors.*
13 *And do not lead into temptation, but deliver us from the evil one.'*

14 *"For if you forgive other people when they sin against you, your heavenly Father will also forgive you.* 15 *But if you do not forgive others their sins, your Father will not forgive your sins."*

#075 Love for God Requires Unrivaled Loyalty to Him Alone
MT 6.19-24

19 *"I command you not to store up for yourselves treasures on earth, where moths and vermin destroy and where thieves break in and steal.* 20 *But store up for your-selves treasures in heaven, where moths and vermin do not destroy and where thieves do not break in and steal.* 21 *For where your treasure is, there your heart will be also.*

22 *"The eye is the lamp of the body. If your eyes are healthy, your whole body will be full of light. 23 But if your eyes are unhealthy, your whole body will be full of darkness. If then the light within you is darkness, how great is that darkness?*

24 *"It's impossible to serve two masters. Either you will hate the one and love the other, or you will be devoted to the one and will despise the other. You cannot serve both God and money."*

#076 Love for God Means Living under His Control Alone
MT 6.25-34

25 *"Therefore, I tell you, do not worry about your life, what you will eat or drink, or about your body, what you will wear. Is not life more than food and the body more than clothes? 26 Look at the birds of the air; they do not sow or reap or store away in barns, and yet your heavenly Father feeds them. Are you not much more valuable than they are? 27 Can any one of you add a single hour to your life by worrying about it?*

28 *"And why do you worry about clothes? See how the flowers of the field grow. They do not labor or spin. 29 Yet I tell you that not even Solomon in all his splendor was dressed like one of these. 30 If that is how God clothes the grass of the field, which is here today and tomorrow is thrown into the fire, will he not also clothe you? Oh you of little faith!*

31 *"So I command you to stop worrying, saying, 'What shall we eat?' or 'What shall we drink?' or 'What shall we wear?' 32 For the pagans run after all these things, and your heavenly Father knows that you need them. 33 But I command you to constantly seek first to surrender yourselves to his reign in you, and his righteousness, and all these other things will be given to you as well. 34 Therefore, do not worry about tomorrow, for tomorrow will worry about itself. Each day has enough trouble of its own."*

#077 Love for God Means Judging Ourselves, Not Others
MT 7.1-6 (Parallel Text: LK 6.37-42)

1 *"I command you to stop judging, so that you ⌐will be never, ever, be judged. I command you likewise to stop condemning, so that you will never, ever, be condemned. I command you to continue forgiving, and you will be forgiven. I command you to continue giving, and it will be given to you, in full measure, pressed down to the rim, with all the excess shaken off together and overflowing into your own lap. 2*

^MT*For in the same way you judge others, you too will be judged, and with the same standard of measure that you are measuring, it will be measured back to you."*

^L Then he told them this illustration. *"Can a blind man lead a blind man? Will both of them not fall down into a pit? A disciple is not above his teacher, but everyone who has been completely, permanently trained will be like his teacher.*

3 ^MT *"Why, then, are you looking at the speck of sawdust in your brother's eye and paying no attention to the plank in your own eye? 4 How can you say to your brother, 'Let me take the speck out of your eye,' when* ^L all the time you are failing to see ^MT the *plank in your own eye? 5 You hypocrite, I command you to first take the plank out of your own eye, and then you will see clearly to remove the speck from your brother's eye.*

6 *"I command you not to give what is sacred to dogs; do not throw your pearls to pigs. If you do, they may trample them under their feet and turn and tear you to pieces."*

#078 Love for God Means Persisting in Prayer
MT 7.7-12 (Parallel Text: LK 6.31; 11.5-13))

7 *"I command you to continue asking, and it will be given to you; likewise, continue seeking and you will find; continue knocking and the door will be opened to you. 8 For everyone who continues to ask, receives; the one who continues to seek, finds; and to the one who continues to knock, the door will be opened.*

9 *"Which of you will give your son a stone if he asks you for bread? 10 Or if he asks for a fish, will you give him a snake?*

11 *"Since you, then, though you are evil, know how to give good gifts to your children, how much more will your Father in heaven give good gifts to those who continue asking him?*

12 *"So, in everything, I command you to continue behaving toward others in the same way you are wanting them to do for you, for this sums up the Law and the Prophets."*

#079 Jesus Warns about Two Different Paths, with Different Outcomes
MT 7.13-23 (Parallel Text: LK 6.43-46)

13 *"I command you to enter through the narrow gate. For wide is the gate and broad is the road that is leading to destruction, and many enter through it. 14 But small is the gate and narrow is the road that is leading to life and only a few find it.*

15 *"I command you to watch continually for false prophets. They come to you in sheep's clothing, but inwardly they are ferocious wolves. 16 You will recognize them by their fruit.*

[L]*"Each tree is known by its own fruit.* [MT]*Do people pick grapes from thorn bushes or figs from thistles? 17 Likewise, every good tree bears good fruit, but a bad tree bears bad fruit. 18 A good tree cannot bear bad fruit, and a bad tree cannot bear good fruit. 19 Every tree that does not bear good fruit is cut down and thrown into the fire. 20 Thus, by their fruit you will recognize them.*

[L]*"The good man brings good things out of the good stored in his heart, and the evil man brings forth evil things out of the evil stored in his heart. For the mouth speaks out of the overflow of what is in the heart.*

"Why do you call me 'Lord, Lord,' and do not obey what I say? 21 [MT]*Not everyone who says to me, 'Lord, Lord,' will enter the kingdom of heaven, but only the one who is doing the will of my Father who is in heaven.*

22 *"Many will say to me on that day, 'Lord, Lord, did we not prophesy in your name, and in your name drive out demons, and in your name perform many miracles?' 23 Then, I will speak out to them, 'I never knew you. Stay away from me, you evildoers!'"*

#080 The Sure Foundation of Jesus' Authoritative Word
MT 7.24-29 (Parallel Text: LK 6.47-49)

24 *"Therefore* [L]*I will show you what the person is like who comes to me,* [MT]*continues hearing these words of mine, and actually makes a practice of doing them. He is like a wise man who* [L]*dug down deep and* [MT]*built his house on the rock. 25 The rain came down, the rivers rose, the winds blew and beat against that house,* [L]*and when the flood came, the torrent struck the house but could not shake it,* [MT]*and it did not fall because its foundation had been firmly set on the rock.*

26 *"But everyone who is hearing these words of mine and does not continue to put them into practice is like a foolish man who built his house on sand,* [L]*on the bare ground without a foundation. 27* [MT]*The rain came down, the rivers rose, the winds blew and beat against that house, and* [L]*when the torrent struck, that house* [MT]*collapsed with a great crash,* [L]*and its destruction was complete."*

28 When Jesus had finished saying these things, the crowds were in continual amazement at his teaching 29 because he was teaching with authority, and not as their teachers of the law had taught.

CHAPTER 15

Galilee: Crucial Events Preceding the Second Tour

#081 Miracle 10: The Greatest Faith Jesus Ever Saw
LK 7.1-10 (Parallel Text: MT 8.1, 5-13)

1 [L]When Jesus had finished speaking his message to the people who were listening, [MT]he came down from the mountain. Large crowds were following him, [L]and he entered Capernaum. 2 There was a centurion's servant, whom his master valued highly, who was lying sick and about to die, paralyzed at home, in terrible distress. 3 Having heard about Jesus, the centurion sent some elders of the Jews to him, asking him to come and heal his servant.

4 When they came to Jesus, they were pleading earnestly with him, "Lord, This man deserves to have you do this 5 because he truly loves our nation and has built our synagogue. [MT]He said to tell you: 'Help, Lord. My servant lies at home paralyzed and in terrible suffering.'"

Jesus said, *"I will go myself, and heal him."*

6 [L]So, Jesus was going along with them. He was not far from the house when the centurion sent friends to say to him, "Lord, do not trouble yourself, for I am not worthy to have you come under my roof. 7 That is why I did not even consider myself worthy to come to you. But only say the word, and my servant will be healed. 8 For I myself am a man under authority with sol-

diers under me. I tell this one, 'Go,' and he goes, and that one, 'Come,' and he comes. I say to my servant, 'Do this,' and he does it."

9 When Jesus heard this, he was ᴹᵀastonished and ᴸamazed at him, and turning to the crowd following him, he said, *"Truly I tell you, I have not found* ᴹᵀ*anyone with* ᴸ*such great faith, even in Israel.* ᴹᵀ*"I say to you that many will come from the east and the west and will take their places at the feast with Abraham, Isaac, and Jacob in the kingdom of heaven. But the subjects of the kingdom will be thrown outside into the darkness, where there will be weeping and gnashing of teeth."*

Then, Jesus said to the centurion (through his friends), *"Go! I command that it will be done for you, just as you believed it would."*

And his servant was healed at that moment. 10 ᴸThen, the men who had been sent returned to the house and found the servant had been made fully whole.

#082 Miracle 11: Jesus Raises a Man from the Dead with Just a Word
LK 7.11-17

11 Next, Jesus went to a town called Nain, and his disciples and a large crowd was going along with him. 12 As he approached the town gate, a dead person—the only son of his mother—was being carried out, and the woman was a widow. And a large crowd from the town was with her.

13 Because the Lord saw her, he was filled with compassion for her, and he said, *"I command you not to continue to cry."*

14 Then, he went up and touched the bier they were carrying the son on, and the bearers stood still. He said, *"Young man, I command you to get up!"* 15 The dead man sat up and began to speak, and Jesus gave him back to his mother.

16 They were all filled with awe and were giving glory to God. "A great prophet has appeared among us," they said. "God has come to help his people!"

17 This news about Jesus spread throughout Judea and all the surrounding regions.

#083 John the Immerser Seeks Reassurance from Jesus, who Gives it
LK 7.18-23 (Parallel Text: MT 11.2-6)

18 ᴸJohn's disciples told him about all these things. So, ᴹᵀwhen John had heard in prison about the works of Christ, ᴸhe called two of his disciples 19

and sent them to the Lord to ask, "Are you the one who is to come, or should we be expecting someone else?"

20 When the men came to Jesus, they said, "John the Immerser sent us to you to ask, 'Are you the one who is to come, or should we be expecting someone else?'"

21 At that very time, Jesus cured many who had diseases, sicknesses, and evil spirits, and he gave sight to many who were blind. 22 So, he replied to the messengers, *"Go back and report to John what you have seen and heard. The blind are receiving sight, the lame are walking, those who have leprosy [skin diseases] are being cleansed, the deaf are hearing, the dead are being raised, and the good news is being proclaimed to the poor.* (Is. 35.5-6; 61.1)

23 *"Anyone who does not stumble on account of me is truly blessed."*

#084 Jesus Praises John the Immerser
MT 11.7-19 (Parallel Text: LK 7.24-35)

7 ᴹᵀAs John's disciples were leaving, Jesus began to speak to the crowd about John, *"What did you go out into the wilderness to see? A reed swayed by the wind? If not, what did you go out to see? A man dressed in fine clothes? No, you will find those who wear fine, expensive clothes and indulge in luxury in kings' palaces.*

9 *"Then what did you go out to see? A prophet? Yes, I tell you and more than a prophet. 10 This is the one about whom it stands written, 'I will send my messenger ahead of you, who will prepare the way before you.' (Mal. 3.1) 11 Truly I tell you, among those born of women there has not risen anyone greater than John the Immerser; yet whoever is least in the kingdom of heaven is greater than he is. 12 From the days of John the Immerser until now, the kingdom of heaven has been subjected to violence, and violent people have been raiding it. 13 For all the Prophets and the Law prophesied until John. 14 And if you are willing to accept it, he is the Elijah who was to come. 15 Whoever has ears, I command him take care to continue listening carefully.*

16 *"To what can I compare this generation? They are like children sitting in the marketplaces and calling out to others, 17 'We played the pipe for you, and you did not dance; we sang a dirge, and you did not mourn.' 18 For John came neither eating nor drinking, and they say, 'He has a demon.' 19 The Son of Man came eating and drinking, and they say, 'Here is a glutton and a drunkard, a friend of tax collectors and sinners.' But wisdom is proved right by her deeds."*

ᴸWhen they heard Jesus' words, all the people, even the tax collectors, acknowledged that God's way was right because they had been immersed by

John. But the Pharisees and the experts in the law rejected God's purpose for themselves because they had not been immersed by John.

#085 Jesus Rebukes Unrepentant Towns and Welcomes the Repentant
MT 11.20-30

20 Then, Jesus began to speak against the towns in which most of his miracles had been performed because they did not repent.

21 *"Woe to you, Chorazin! Woe to you, Bethsaida! For if the miracles that were performed in you had been performed in Tyre and Sidon, they would have repented long ago in sackcloth and ashes. 22 But I tell you, it will be more bearable for Tyre and Sidon on the day of judgment than for you. 23 And you, Capernaum, will you be lifted up to the skies? No, you will go down into the depths. For if the miracles that were performed in you had been performed in Sodom, it would have remained to this day. 24 But I tell you that it will be more bearable for Sodom on the day of judgment than for you."*

25 At that time Jesus said, *"I voice my agreement with you, Father, Lord of heaven and earth, because you have hidden these things from the wise and intelligent and revealed them to little children. 26 Yes, Father, for this is your good pleasure.*

27 *"All things have been handed over to me by my Father. No one has experienced true knowledge of the Son except the Father, and no one has experienced true knowledge of the Father except the Son, and those to whom the Son chooses to reveal him.*

28 *"Oh, I command you all to come to me -- all you who are weary and have become heavily burdened down -- and I will give you rest. 29 I command you all to take my yoke upon you and to learn from me, for I am gentle and humble in heart, and you will all find rest for your souls. 30 For my yoke is easy on you, and my burden is light."*

#086 A Woman Who Was Forgiven Much, Loved Much
LK 7.36-50

36 One of the Pharisees invited Jesus to have dinner with him, so he went into the Pharisee's house and reclined at the table.

37 Look! A woman in that town who lived a sinful life learned that Jesus was eating at the Pharisee's house, so she came there with an alabaster jar of perfume. 38 As she stood behind him at his feet and continued to weep, she

began drenching his feet with her tears. Then, she was wiping them with her hair, while kissing them and pouring her perfume on them.

39 When the Pharisee, who had invited him, saw this, he said to himself, "If this man were a real prophet—and surely he is not—he would know who is touching him and what kind of woman she is, that she is a sinner."

40 Jesus answered him, *"Simon, I have something to tell you."*

"Tell me, teacher," he said.

41 *"Two people owed money to a certain moneylender. One owed him five hundred days of wages, and the other fifty days of wages. 42 Neither of them had the money to pay him back, so he graciously forgave the debts of both. Now which of them will love him more?"*

43 Simon replied, "I suppose the one who had the bigger debt forgiven."

"You have judged correctly," Jesus said.

44 Then, he turned toward the woman and said to Simon, *"Do you see this woman? I came into your house. You did not give me any water for my feet, but she drenched my feet with her tears and wiped them with her hair. 45 You did not give me a kiss, but this woman, from the time I entered, has not stopped kissing my feet. 46 You did not put oil on my head, but she has poured perfume on my feet. 47 Therefore, I tell you, her many sins have been permanently forgiven, as her great love has shown. But whoever has been forgiven little, loves just a little."*

48 Then Jesus said to her, *"Your sins are permanently forgiven."*

49 The other guests began to say among themselves, "Who is this who even forgives sins?"

50 Jesus said to the woman, *"Your faith has permanently saved you; I command you to go and continue to live in peace."*

CHAPTER 16

Galilee: Jesus' Second Tour

#087 Jesus Begins His Second Tour of Galilee
LK 8.1-3

1 After this, Jesus was traveling through all of the towns and villages, teaching in their synagogues and proclaiming the good news of the kingdom of God. The Twelve were with him, 2 and also some women who had been cured of evil spirits and diseases; Mary (called Magdalene) from whom seven demons had gone out; 3 Joanna the wife of Chuza, the manager of Herod's household; Susanna; and many others. These women were helping to support them out of their own means.

#088 Miracle 12: Jesus is Publicly Rejected by
the Jewish Leadership for the First Time
MT 12.22-37 (Parallel Text: MK 3.22-30)

ᴹAnd the multitude gathered together again to such an extent that they could not even eat a meal.

22 ᴹᵀThen, they brought him a demon-possessed man who was blind and mute, and Jesus healed him so that he could both talk and see. 23 All the people were amazed and kept saying, "Could this be the Son of David?"

24 But when the Pharisees ᴹand the scribes who came down from Jerusalem ᴹᵀheard this, they said, "It is only by Beelzebul, the prince of demons, that this fellow is driving out demons."

25 Jesus knew their thoughts and said to them, ᴹ*"How can Satan cast out Satan?* ᴹᵀ*Every kingdom divided against itself will be ruined, and every city or household divided against itself will not stand.* 26 *If Satan drives out Satan, he is divided against himself. How then can his kingdom stand?* 27 *And if I myself am driving out demons by Beelzebul, by whom are your people driving them out? So then, they will be your judges.* 28 *But since it is by the Spirit of God that I am driving out demons, then the kingdom of God has come upon you.* 29 *Or again, how can anyone enter a strong man's house and carry off his possessions unless he first ties up the strong man? Then, he can plunder his house.*

30 *"Whoever is not with me is against me, and whoever is not gathering with me scatters.* 31 *And so I tell you, every kind of sin and slander can be forgiven, but blasphemy against the* ᴹ*Holy* ᴹᵀ*Spirit will not be forgiven.* 32 *Anyone who speaks a word against the Son of Man will be forgiven, but anyone who speaks against the Holy Spirit will not be forgiven – either in this age or in the age to come –* ᴹ*but is guilty of an eternal sin."*

He said this because they were saying, "He has an unclean spirit."

33 Jesus replied, ᴹᵀ*"Make a tree good and its fruit will be good, or make a tree bad and its fruit will be bad; a tree is recognized by its fruit.* 34 *You brood of vipers, how can you who are evil say anything good? For the mouth speaks out of what fills the heart.* 35 *A good man brings good things out of the good stored up in him, and an evil man brings evil things out of the evil stored up in him.* 36 *But I tell you that everyone will have to give account on the day of judgment for every empty word they have spoken.* 37 *For by your words, you will be acquitted, and by your words, you will be condemned."*

#089 Jesus Rejects a Request for an Immediate Sign, yet Promises the "Sign of Jonah" MT 12.38-45

38 Then, some of the Pharisees and teachers of the law said to him, "Teacher, we want to see a sign from you."

39 He answered, *"A wicked and adulterous generation constantly seeks for a sign! But none will be given it except the sign of the prophet Jonah.*

40 *"For just as Jonah was three days and three nights in the belly of a huge fish, so the Son of Man will be three days and three nights in the heart of the earth.* 41 *The*

men of Nineveh will stand up at the judgment with this generation and condemn it; for they repented at the preaching of Jonah, and now something greater than Jonah is here. 42 The Queen of the South will rise at the judgment with this generation and condemn it; for she came from the ends of the earth to listen to Solomon's wisdom, and now something greater than Solomon is here.

43 *"When an impure spirit comes out of a person, it goes through arid places seeking rest and does not find it. 44 Then, it says, 'I will return to the house I left.' When it arrives, it finds the house in an unoccupied state, having been swept clean and put in full order. 45 Then, it goes and takes with it seven other spirits more wicked than itself, and they go in and live there. And the final condition of that person becomes much worse than the first. That is how it will be with this wicked generation."*

#090 Jesus Affirms the Priority of Kingdom Relationships
MK 3.20-21, 31-35 (Parallel Texts: MT 12.46-50; LK 8.19-21)

20 Then, Jesus entered a house, and again, a crowd gathered so much so that he and his disciples were not even able to eat. 21 When his family heard about this, they went to take charge of him, for they said, "He is out of his mind."

31 ^LSo Jesus' mother and brothers came to see him. ^{MT}While Jesus was still speaking to the crowd, ^Mhis mother and brothers arrived, ^{MT}wanting to speak to him. ^MStanding outside, they sent someone in to call him. 32 A crowd was sitting around him, and they told him, "Your mother and brothers are outside looking for you and ^{MT}wanting to speak to you."

33 ^M*"Who are my mother and my brothers?"* he asked.

34 Then, he looked at those seated in a circle around him ^{MT}and pointing to his disciples ^Mhe said, *"Here are my mother and my brothers! 35 Whoever does ^{MT}the will of my Father in heaven — ^Lwho continually hears and puts God's Word into practice — ^Mthat person is my brother and my sister and my mother."*

#091 The Parable of the Seed and Four Kinds of Soil
MT 13.1-9, 18-23 (Parallel Texts: MK 4.1-9, 13-20; LK 8.4-8, 11-15)

1 ^{MT}That same day, Jesus went out of the house and sat by the lake. 2 ^LPeople were coming to him from town after town, ^{MT}and such large crowds gathered around him that he climbed into a boat and sat in it, while all the people stood on the shore.

3 Then, he told them many things in parables, saying, ^M *"Listen up!* ^{MT}*A farmer went out to sow his seed. 4 As he was scattering the seed, some fell along the path* ^L*where it was trampled underfoot,* ^{MT}*and the birds came and ate it. 5 Some fell on rocky places, where there was not much soil. It sprang up quickly because the soil was shallow. 6 But when the sun came up, the plants were scorched, and they withered away because they had no root* ^L*and so they had no moisture. 7* ^{MT}*Other seeds fell among thorns, which grew up and choked the plants* ^M*so they bore no fruit. 8* ^{MT}*Still other seeds fell on good soil,* ^M*where they came up and grew and* ^{MT}*kept producing fruit,* ^M*multiplying a hundred, sixty, or thirty times what was sown."*

9 ^LWhen he had said this, he cried out, ^{MT} *"Whoever has ears, I command them to continue to pay full attention to this!"*

18 ^MThen, Jesus said to his disciples: ^M *"Do you not understand this parable? How then will you understand any parable? Listen then to what the parable of the sower means:* ^L*the seed is the word of God and* ^M*the farmer sows the word. 19* ^{MT}*When people hear the message about the kingdom and do not understand it, the evil one,* ^M*Satan,* ^{MT}*comes and snatches away what was sown in their hearts* ^L*so that they may not be saved by believing it.* ^{MT}*This is the seed sown along the path.*

20 *"The seed falling on rocky ground refers to someone who hears the word and at once receives it with joy. 21 But because they have no root, they last only a short time.* ^L*They believe for a while, but in the time of testing –* ^{MT}*when trouble or persecution comes because of the word -- they quickly fall away.*

22 *"The seed falling among the thorns refers to someone who hears the word, but the worries of this life, the deceitfulness of wealth,* ^L*the pleasure of this life,* ^M*and strong desires for other things* ^{MT}*keep choking out the word, making it unfruitful,* ^L*so it does not mature.*

23 *"But the seed falling on good soil refers to someone* ^L*with an honest and good heart* ^{MT}*who hears the word and understands it,* ^M*fully accepts it,* ^L*and retains it.* ^{MT}*This is the one who constantly produces fruit, yielding a hundred, sixty, or thirty times what was sown."*

#092 The Reason Jesus Began to Use Parables
MT 13.10-17 (Parallel Texts: MK 4.10-12; LK 8.9-10)

10 ^MWhen he was alone, ^{MT}the disciples ^Mwho were traveling with Jesus, along with the twelve ^{MT}came to him and asked, "Why do you speak to the people in parables?"

11 He replied, *"Because the experiential knowledge of the secrets of the kingdom of heaven has been given permanently to you, but not to them.* ᴹFor those on the outside, everything is now expressed in parables.*

12 ᴹᵀ *"Whoever is in possession of knowledge will be given more, and they will have an abundance. Whoever does not have experiential knowledge, even the information they have will be taken from them.* ᴹOtherwise, they would turn to me, and they would be forgiven.* 13 ᴹᵀThis is why I speak to them in parables: 'Although seeing, they do not see; although hearing, they do not listen or understand.'* (Jer. 5.21)

14 *"The prophecy of Isaiah is being actively fulfilled in them:*

'You will be ever hearing but never understanding;
you will be ever seeing but never perceiving.
15 For the people's heart has become calloused;
they hardly hear with their ears, and they have closed their eyes.
Otherwise, they might see with their eyes, hear with their ears,
understand with their hearts, and in turn, I would heal them.' (Isaiah 6.9-10)

16 *"But blessed are your eyes because they are seeing and your ears because they are hearing. 17 For truly, I tell you, many prophets and righteous people have longed to see what you are seeing, but they do not see it, and they have longed to hear what you are hearing but do not hear it."*

#093 The Kingdom Parable of the Weeds
MT 13.24-30, 36-43

24 Jesus told them [the Weeds in the Field] parable: *"The kingdom of heaven is like a man who sowed good seed in his field. 25 But while everyone was asleep, his enemy came, sowed weeds among the wheat, and went away. 26 When the wheat sprouted and formed heads, then the weeds also appeared. 27 The owner's servants came to him and said, 'Sir, did you not sow good seed in your field? So where did the weeds come from?'*

28 *"'An enemy did this,' he replied.*

"The servants asked him, 'Do you want us to go and pull them up?'

29 *"'No,' he answered, 'because while you are pulling up the weeds, you may uproot the wheat with them too. 30 Let both grow together until the harvest. At that time I will tell the harvesters to first collect the weeds and tie them in bundles to be burned and then to gather all the wheat and bring it into my barn.'"*

36 Then, Jesus left the crowd and went into the house. His disciples came to him and said, "Please explain the parable of the weeds in the field to us."

37 Jesus answered them, *"The one who sowed the good seed is the Son of Man. 38 The field is the world, and the good seed stands for the people of the kingdom. The weeds are the people of the evil one, 39 and the enemy who sows them is the devil. The harvest is the end of the age, and the harvesters are angels.*

40 *"As the weeds are pulled up and burned in the fire, so it will be at the end of the age. 41 The Son of Man will send out his angels, and they will weed out of his kingdom everything that causes sin and all who do evil. 42 They will throw them into the blazing furnace where there will be weeping and gnashing of teeth. 43 Then, the righteous will shine like the sun in the kingdom of their Father. Whoever has ears, I command to continue hearing."*

#094 Five More Kingdom Parables
MT 13.31-33, 44-50 (Parallel Text: MK 4.30-32)

31 He told them [the Mustard Seed] parable: ᴹ *"What can we say the kingdom of God is like, or what parable shall we use to describe it?* ᴹᵀ*The kingdom of heaven is like a mustard seed, which a man took and sowed in his field. 32 Although it is the smallest of all seeds* ᴹ*you plant in the ground,* ᴹᵀ*as it continues growing, it becomes the largest of garden plants and turns into a tree* ᴹ*with such big branches* ᴹᵀ*that the birds come and make their perch in its branches."* (Ps. 104.12; Ez. 17.23, 31.6; Dan. 4.12)

33 He told them still another parable [of the Yeast]: *"The kingdom of heaven is like yeast that a woman took and mixed into about thirty kilograms of flour, until it worked its way all through the dough."*

[The Parable of the Treasure Hidden in a Field:] 44 *"The kingdom of heaven is like treasure that had been well hidden in a field. When a man found it, he hid it again, and then in his great joy, he went and sold all he had and bought that field."*

[The Parable of the Pearl of Great Price:] 45 *"Again, the kingdom of heaven is like a merchant who was ever searching for fine pearls. Because he found one of great value, he went away and sold everything he possessed and then bought it."*

[The Parable of the Net:] 47 *"Once again, the kingdom of heaven is like a dragnet that was let down into the lake and caught all kinds of fish. 48 When it was full, the fishermen pulled it up on the shore. Then, they sat down and collected the good fish in baskets but threw the bad fish away. 49 This is how it will be at the end of the age. The angels will come and separate the wicked from the righteous 50 and will surely throw them into the blazing furnace, where there will be weeping and gnashing of teeth."*

#095 Jesus Concludes the Teaching Session Using Three More Parables
MK 4.21-29; MT 13.34-35, 51-53 (Parallel Texts: MK 4.33-34; LK 8.16-18)

ᴹ21 [In the Parable of the Lamp on its Stand] he said to them, *"Do you bring in a lamp to put it under a bowl,* ᴸ*or hide it in a jar,* ᴹ*or under a bed? Instead, do you not put it on its stand* ᴸ*so that those who come in can see the light? 22* ᴹ*Whatever is hidden is meant to be disclosed, and whatever is concealed is meant to be brought out into the open.*

23 *"Anyone who has ears to hear, I command to continue listening. 24* ᴸ*Therefore,* ᴹ*I command you to make a practice of carefully considering what you hear. With the measure you are using, it will be measured to you, and even more. 25 Whoever has will be given more; whoever does not have, even what he has will be taken from him."*

26 [In the Parable of the Growing Seed] he also said, *"This is what the kingdom of God is like. A man scatters seeds on the ground. 27 Night and day, whether he sleeps or gets up, the seeds continue sprouting and growing, though he does not know how. 28 All by itself the soil continually produces fruit – first the stalk, then the head, and then the full kernel in the head. 29 As soon as the grain is ripe, he puts the sickle to it because the harvest has come and remains."*

34 ᴹᵀJesus spoke all of these things to the crowd, ᴹwith many similar parables he spoke the word to them as much as they could understand; ᴹᵀHe did not say anything to them without using a parable. ᴹBut when he was alone with his disciples, he would explain everything. 35 ᴹᵀThus, what was spoken through the prophet was fulfilled, "I will open my mouth in parables; I will utter things hidden since the creation of the world." (Ps. 78.2)

51 At the end, Jesus asked: *"Have you understood all these things?"*

"Yes," they replied.

52 He said to them, [using the Parable of the Owner of the House with New and Old Treasures], *"Therefore every teacher of the law who has become a disciple in the kingdom of heaven is like the owner of a house who brings out of his storeroom new treasures as well as old."*

53 When Jesus had finished these parables, he moved on from there.

#096 Miracle 13: Stormy Wind and Waves Obey Jesus
MK 4.35-41 (Parallel Texts: MT 8.23-27; LK 8.22-25)

35 ^MThat day when evening came, Jesus said to his disciples, *"Let us go over to the other side* ^L*of the lake."* 36 Leaving the crowd behind, they took him along, just as he was, in the boat. There were also other boats with him, ^{MT}and his disciples followed him.

37 ^MA furious squall came up, and the waves kept crashing over the boat, so that it was nearly swamped by the waves, ^Land they were in grave danger. 38 Jesus was in the stern and fell asleep on a cushion. The disciples woke him and said to him, ^M "Teacher! ^LMaster! ^{MT}Lord! ^MDo you not care that we are perishing?"

39 He got up, rebuked the wind, and commanded ^Lthe raging waves, *"Be quiet! I command you to become completely still!"*

Then, the wind died down and a deep calm settled over the lake. 40 He said to his disciples, *"Why are you so afraid,* ^{MT}*men of little faith?* ^L*Where is your faith?* ^M*Do you still have no faith?"*

41 ^MThey were terrified ^Land marveled, ^Masking each other, "Who is this? ^LHe commands, and ^Meven the wind and the waves obey him!"

#097 Miracle 14: A Legion of Demons Obey Jesus
MK 5.1-20 (Parallel Texts: MT 8.28-34; LK 8.26-40)

1 ^MThey went across the lake to the region of the Gerasenes. 2 When Jesus got out of the boat, a man with an impure spirit came from the tombs to meet him; ^{MT}he was possessed by many demons ^Land had not worn any clothes for a long time and did not live in his own house.

3 ^MThis man was living in the tombs ^{MT}and was extremely fierce, so much so that no one could approach him, ^Mand no one was able to bind him anymore, not even with a chain. 4 He had often been firmly chained hand and foot, but he tore the chains apart and permanently destroyed the irons on his feet. No one was strong enough to subdue him. 5 Night and day among the tombs and in the hills, he would continue crying out and cutting himself with stones.

6 Because he saw Jesus from a distance, the man ran up and fell on his knees in front of him. 7 He shouted out at the top of his voice, "What do you want with me, Jesus, Son of the Most High God? ^{MT}Have you come to torment us before the appointed time? ^LI beseech ^Mand implore you in God's name, do not torture me!"

8 For Jesus had been saying to him, *"I command you to come out of this man, you impure spirit!"* 9 Then, Jesus asked him, *"What is your name?"*

"My name is Legion," he replied, "for we are many." 10 And he pleaded with Jesus again and again not to send them out of the area, ᴸnor to command them to depart into the abyss.

11 ᴹA large herd of pigs was feeding on the nearby hillside. 12 The demons begged Jesus, ᴹᵀ "Because you will cast us out, ᴹsend us among the pigs; permit us to go into them." 13 He gave them permission, and the impure spirits came out and went into the pigs. The herd, about two thousand in number, rushed down the steep bank into the lake, and they were drowned.

14 Those tending the pigs took off and reported this in the town and countryside, and the people went out to see what had happened. 15 When ᴹᵀthe whole city ᴹcame to Jesus, they took a long look at the man who had been possessed by the legion of demons, sitting, dressed, and functioning in his right mind; and they were afraid. 16 Those who had seen it told the people what had happened to the demon-possessed man, and they told about the pigs as well.

17 Then, the people began to plead with Jesus to leave their region, ᴸfor their hearts were gripped with overpowering fear. So Jesus climbed into the boat and returned.

18 ᴹAs Jesus was stepping into the boat, the man who had been demon-possessed begged to go with him. 19 Jesus did not permit him, but said, *"I command you to go home to your own people and tell them what the Lord has done for you, and how he has had mercy on you."*

20 So the man went away and began to tell in the Decapolis how much Jesus had done for him. And all the people continued to be amazed.

#098 Miracle 15: Jesus Raises a Young Woman from the Dead
MK 5.21-24, 35-43 (Parallel Texts: MT 9.18-19, 23-26; LK 8.40-42, 49-56)

21 ᴹWhen Jesus had again crossed by boat to the other side of the lake, a huge crowd gathered around him while he was by the lake. 22 Then, one of the synagogue leaders, named Jairus, came, and when he saw Jesus, he fell at his feet. ᴸFor he had an only daughter, about twelve years of age, and she was dying. 23 ᴹHe pleaded earnestly with him, "My little daughter is dying. Please come and put your hands on her so that she can be made whole and really live." 24 So Jesus went with him ᴹᵀand so did his disciples.

35 ᴹWhile Jesus was still speaking, some people came from the house of Jairus, the synagogue leader. "Your daughter is dead," they said. "Why make any further trouble for the teacher?"

36 Having heard what they said, Jesus refused to acknowledge it and told him, *"Stop being afraid; I command you to just continue believing, ᴸand she will be made whole."*

37 ᴹHe did not let anyone follow him except Peter, James, and John, the brother of James. 38 When they came to the home of the synagogue leader, Jesus saw a commotion, ᴹᵀand flute players, ᴹand people crying and wailing loudly. 39 He went in and said to them, *"Why all this commotion and wailing? The child is not dead, but she is sleeping."*

40 But they were laughing at him. After he put them all out, he took the child's father and mother and the disciples who were with him and went in where the child was. 41 And having taken her by the hand, he said to her, *"Talitha koum!"* [*"Little girl...ᴸChild, ᴹI command you, rise up!"*]

42 ᴸHer spirit returned ᴹand immediately the [twelve-year-old] girl stood up and began to walk around the house. At this, they were completely astonished. 43 Jesus gave strict orders not to let anyone know about this, and he told them to give her something to eat. ᴹᵀAnd the report about this went out into all the region.

#099 Miracle 16: Jesus Heals a Woman's 12-Year Hemorrhage
MK 5.25-34 (Parallel Texts: MT 9.20-22; LK 8.43-48)

24B ᴹ[As Jesus was on the way to Jairus' house] a large crowd was following him and kept pressing up against him, ᴸalmost crushing him. 25 ᴹA woman was there who had been subject to bleeding for twelve years, ᴸbut no one could heal her. 26 ᴹShe had suffered a great deal under the care of many doctors and had spent everything she had, yet instead of becoming better, she only grew worse.

27 Having heard about Jesus, she came up from behind him in the crowd and touched ᴸthe bottom hem ᴹof his cloak 28 because she was saying ᴹᵀwithin herself, ᴹ "If I just touch his clothes, I will be healed." 29 Immediately, her bleeding stopped, and she felt sure in her body that she had been permanently healed of her suffering.

30 Because Jesus immediately realized that power had gone out from him, he turned around in the crowd and asked, *"Who touched my clothes?"*

31 [L]When all the people denied it, Peter and [M]his disciples were saying to him, "You see the people crowding against you, and yet you can ask, 'Who touched me?'"

[L]But Jesus said, *"Someone touched me, for I know that power has gone out from me."* 32 [M]Jesus kept looking around him to see who had done it.

33 Then, the woman, knowing what had happened to her [L]and seeing that she was not hidden from Jesus, [M]came out of the crowd and fell at his feet. Trembling with fear, she told him the whole truth [L]and spoke plainly in the presence of all the people about why she had touched him, and how she had been instantly healed.

34 [M]He said to her, *"Daughter,* [MT]*take courage.* [M]*Your faith has made you permanently whole. I command you to go on and continue to live in peace. I command that you continue to be set free from your suffering."*

[MT]And the woman was healed from that very hour.

#100 Miracles 17 and 18: Jesus Heals the Blind and Mute
MT 9.27-34

27 As Jesus went on from there, two blind men were following him, crying out, "Please have mercy on us, Son of David!" 28 When he had gone indoors, the blind men came to him, and he asked them, *"Do you really believe that I am able to do this?"*

"Yes, Lord," they replied.

29 Then, he touched their eyes and said, *"I command that it be done to you as you have believed,"* 30 and their sight was restored. Jesus commanded them sternly, *"Make sure that no one knows about this."*

31 But they went out and spread the news about him all over that region. 32 While they were going out, a man who was demon-possessed and could not talk was brought to Jesus. 33 After the demon was driven out, the man who had been mute spoke. The crowd was amazed and said, "Nothing like this has ever been seen in Israel."

34 But the Pharisees said, "It is by the prince of demons that he drives out demons."

#101 Jesus' Second Rejection in Nazareth
MK 6.1-6A (Parallel Text: MT 13.54-58)

1 ᴹJesus left there and went to his hometown, and his disciples continued to follow him. 2 When the Sabbath came, he began to teach in the synagogue, and many who heard him were amazed. "Where did this man get these things?" they asked. "What's this wisdom that has been given him? What are these incredible miracles he is performing? 3 Is this not the ᴹᵀcarpenter's son, ᴹthe carpenter? Is this not Mary's son and the brother of James, Joseph, Judas, and Simon? Are his sisters not all here with us?" And they were being offended by him.

4 Jesus said to them, *"A prophet is not without honor except in his own town, among his relatives, and in his own home."*

5 He could not perform many miracles there ᴹᵀbecause of their unbelief, ᴹexcept to lay his hands on a few sick people and heal them. 6 He could not stop being amazed at their unbelief.

#102 Jesus Issues a Call to Prayer in the Latter Part of the Second Tour
MT 9.35-38 (Parallel Text: MK 6.6B)

35 ᴹᵀJesus continued to go through all the towns and villages, teaching in their synagogues, preaching the good news of the kingdom, and healing every disease and sickness.

36 As he saw the crowds, he had compassion on them because they were in a beaten down state and had become helpless, like sheep that do not have a shepherd. 37 Then, he said to his disciples, *"The harvest is plentiful but the workers are few. 38 Therefore, I command you to pray and ask the Lord of the harvest to send out workers into his harvest field."*

CHAPTER 17

Galilee: Jesus Trains the Twelve Prior to the Third Tour

#103 The Locale, Message, Gifting, and Grace for Their Ministries
MT 10.1-8 (Parallel Texts: MK 6.7; LK 9.1-2)

1 ᴹᵀJesus called his twelve disciples to him and gave them the ᴸpower and ᴹᵀauthority to drive out impure spirits and to heal every disease and sickness. ᴸHe sent them out to continue proclaiming the kingdom of God and to continue healing the sick.

2 ᴹᵀThese are the names of the twelve apostles. First, Simon (who is called Peter) and his brother Andrew; James, son of Zebedee, and his brother John; 3 Philip and Bartholomew; Thomas and Matthew, the tax collector; James, son of Alphaeus, and Thaddaeus; 4 Simon the Zealot; and Judas Iscariot, who betrayed him.

5 Jesus sent out the twelve, ᴹtwo by two, ᴹᵀwith the following instructions: *"I command you not to go among the Gentiles or enter any town of the Samaritans. 6 Rather, I command you to continue going to the lost sheep of Israel. 7 As you go, continue to proclaim this message: 'The kingdom of heaven has come near.' 8 I command that you continue healing the sick, raising the dead, cleansing those who have leprosy, and driving out demons. Freely you have received; freely give."*

#104 The Principles of Support and the People's Response
MT 10.9-15 (Parallel Texts: MK 6.8-11; LK 9.3-5)

9 *"I command you all not to take* ^M*anything for your journey except for a staff—
no bread, no* ^MT*gold or silver or copper to take with you in your belts,* 10 *no bag for
the journey or extra shirt or sandals or extra staff—for the worker is worthy of his
support."*

11 *"Whatever town or village you enter, I command you all to search there for
some worthy person and to stay at their house until you leave.* 12 *As you enter the
home, I command you all to give it your greeting.* 13 *If the home is deserving, let your
peace rest on it; if it is not, let your peace return to you."*

14 *"If anyone will not welcome you or listen to your words, when you leave that home
or town, I command you all to shake the dust off your feet.* 15 *Truly I tell you, it will be
more bearable for Sodom and Gomorrah on the day of judgment than for that town."*

#105 How to Handle Opposition and Persecution as Jesus Did
MT 10.16-23

16 *"Pay attention: I am sending you out like sheep surrounded by wolves.
Therefore, become as shrewd as snakes and as innocent as doves.* 17 *I command you
all to be on your guard constantly; you will be handed over to the local councils and
be flogged in the synagogues.* 18 *You will be brought on my account before governors
and kings as witnesses to them and to the Gentiles.* 19 *But when they arrest you, I
command you all not to worry for a minute about what to say or how to say it. At that
time, you will be given what to say,* 20 *for it will not be you speaking, but it will be the
Spirit of your Father who is speaking through you.*

21 *"Brother will betray brother to death, and a father his child; children will rebel
against their parents and have them put to death.* 22 *You will be hated by everyone
because of me, but the one who stands firm to the end will be saved.* 23 *When you are
persecuted in one place, I command you all to flee to another. Truly I tell you, you will
not finish going through the towns of Israel before the Son of Man comes."*

#106 Jesus' Goal for Discipleship and its Impact on Ministry
MT 10.24-31

24 *"The student is not greater than the teacher, nor is the servant greater than his
master.* 25 *It is sufficient for students to become like their teachers, and servants like
their masters. Because the head of the house has been called Beelzebul, how much more*

the members of his household! 26 I command you all not to be afraid of them, for noth-ing has been safely hidden away that will not be disclosed, or concealed that will not be made known. 27 What I am telling you in the dark, I command you all to speak in the daylight; what is being whispered in your ear, you must all proclaim from the roofs.

28 "I command you all not to continue to fear those who kill the body but do not have the power to destroy the soul. Rather, I command you to hold in the utmost reverence the One who can destroy both soul and body in hell. 29 Are not two spar-rows being sold for a penny? Yet not one of them will fall to the ground apart from your Father's care. 30 And even the very hairs of your head have all been counted up and known. 31 So I command you not to stay afraid; you are always worth more than many sparrows."

#107 Jesus' Absolute Authority over His Disciples
and His Oneness with Them
MT 10.32-42

32 "Whoever acknowledges me before others, I will also acknowledge before my Father in heaven. 33 But whoever disowns me before others, I will disown before my Father in heaven. 34 Do not think that I have come to bring peace upon the earth. I did not come to bring peace, but a sword. 35 For I have come to turn

'A man against his father,
a daughter against her mother,
and a daughter-in-law against her mother-in-law.
36 A man's enemies will be the members of his own household...' (Mic. 7.6)

37 "Anyone who loves their father or mother more than they love me is not wor-thy of me; anyone who loves their son or daughter more than they love me is not worthy of me. 38 Whoever does not wholeheartedly take up their cross and continue following after me is not worthy of me. 39 Whoever finds their life apart from me will lose it, and whoever loses their life for my sake will actually find it.

40 "Anyone who welcomes you is actually welcoming me, and anyone who wel-comes me is welcoming the one who sent me. 41 Whoever welcomes a prophet as a prophet will receive a prophet's reward, and whoever welcomes a righteous person as a righteous person will receive a righteous person's reward. 42 And if anyone gives even a cup of cold water to one of these little ones who is my disciple, truly I tell you for sure, that person will absolutely not lose their reward."

CHAPTER 18

Galilee: Jesus' Third Tour and its Aftermath

**#108 Jesus and the Apostles Depart for His Third and Final Tour of Galilee
MT 11.1 (Parallel Texts: MK 6.12-13; LK 9.1, 6)**

^{MT}After Jesus had finished giving commands to his twelve disciples, ^Lthey went out among the villages, preaching the gospel ^Mthat people must repent. And they were casting out many demons and anointing many sick people with oil and healing them ^Leverywhere.

^{MT}Jesus went out from there to continue teaching and preaching in their towns.

**#109 The Death of John the Immerser
MK 6.14-29 (Parallel Texts: MT 14.1-12; LK 9.7-9)**

14 ^MKing Herod heard about what was happening on Jesus' third tour, for Jesus' name had become well known. ^LAnd he was very perplexed, ^Mfor some were saying, "John the Baptist is alive, having been raised from the dead, and that is why miraculous powers are at work in him."

15 Others said, "He is Elijah." And still others claimed, "He is a prophet, like one of the prophets of long ago."

16 But when Herod heard this, he said, "John, whom I beheaded has been raised from the dead?!" 17 For Herod himself had given orders to have John arrested, and he had him bound and put in prison. He did this because of Herodias, his brother Philip's wife, whom he had married. 18 For John kept saying to Herod, "It is not lawful for you to have your brother's wife."

19 So, Herodias nursed a grudge against John and persisted in wanting to kill him. But she was not able to do so 20 because Herod feared John and protected him, knowing him to be a righteous and holy man. ^{MT}When he would have otherwise killed John, he was scared to do so because of the multitudes because they believed that John was a Prophet. ^MEvery time Herod heard John, he was greatly puzzled; yet he loved to listen to him.

21 Finally the perfect opportunity came. On his birthday, Herod gave a banquet for his high officials, military commanders, and the leading men of Galilee. 22 When the daughter of Herodias came in and danced, she greatly pleased Herod and his dinner guests. The king said to the girl, "Ask me for anything you want, and I will give it to you." 23 And he promised her with an oath, "Whatever you ask for, I will give you, up to half my kingdom."

24 She went out and said to her mother, "What shall I ask for?"

"The head of John the Baptist," she answered.

25 At once, the girl hurried in to the king with the request: "I want you to give me the head of John the Baptist on a platter—right now!"

26 The king was greatly distressed, but because of his oaths and his dinner guests, he did not want to refuse her. 27 So, he immediately sent an executioner with orders to bring John's head. The man went, beheaded John in the prison, 28 and brought back his head on a platter. He presented it to the girl, and she gave it to her mother. 29 On hearing of this, John's disciples came and took his body and laid it in a tomb, ^{MT}and they went and told Jesus.

#110 Jesus Withdraws to Bethsaida with the Twelve
MK 6.30-34 (Parallel Texts: MT 14.13-14; LK 9.10-11; JN 6.1-3)

^{MT}Now when Jesus heard about John's death, he withdrew from there. 30 ^MThe apostles, ^Lwhen they had returned from their mission work, ^Mgathered around Jesus and reported to him all they had done and taught. 31 Then, because so many people were coming and going that they did not even have

a chance to eat, Jesus said to them, *"I command you all to come with me by your-selves to a quiet place and get some rest."*

32 So they went away by themselves in a boat to a solitary place, ᴸto a city called Bethsaida, ᴶon the other side of the sea of Galilee, which is also called Tiberias. 33 ᴹᵀBut when the multitudes heard this, ᴹand many who saw them leaving recognized them, they ran on foot from all the towns and arrived there ahead of them. And a great multitude followed him because they had seen the signs that he had performed on those who were sick.

34 When Jesus landed and saw a large crowd, he had compassion on them, ᴸwelcomed them, ᴹᵀand healed their sick ᴹbecause they were like sheep without a shepherd. So, he began teaching them many things.

#111 Miracle 19: Jesus Feeds the 5000
MK 6.35-44 (Parallel Texts: MT 14.15-21; LK 9.12-17; JN 6.3-15)

JN 6.3 ᴶThen, Jesus went up on a mountainside and sat down with his disciples. 4 The Jewish Passover Festival was near. 5 When Jesus looked up and saw a great crowd coming toward him, he said to Philip, *"Where shall we buy bread for these people to eat?"* 6 He asked this just to test him, for he had already decided what he was going to do.

7 Philip answered him, "It would take more than half a year's pay to buy enough bread for each one to have even a little!"

MK 6.35 ᴹBy this time, it was late in the day, so his disciples came to him. "This is a remote place," they said, "and it's already very late. 36 Send the people away so that they can go to the surrounding countryside and villages and buy themselves something to eat."

37 But Jesus answered, ᴹᵀ *"They do not need to go away. ᴹI command you to give them something to eat."*

They said to him, "That would take more than half a year's wages! Are we to go and spend that much on bread and give it to them to eat?"

38 *"How many loaves do you have?"* he asked. Then, he commanded them, *"Go and see."*

ᴶAnother of his disciples, Andrew, Simon Peter's brother, spoke up, "Here is a boy with five small barley loaves and two small fish, but how far will they go among so many?"

MTJesus commanded, *"Bring them here to me."* 39 MThen, Jesus directed them to have all the people sit down in groups Lof fifty Mon the green grass. 40 So they sat down in groups of hundreds and fifties.

41 Taking the five loaves and the two fish and looking up to heaven, he gave thanks and broke the loaves. Then, he gave them to his disciples to distribute to the people. He also divided the two fish among them all. 42 They all ate and were satisfied.

JWhen they had all had enough to eat, he commanded his disciples, *"Gather the pieces that are left over. Let nothing be wasted."*

43 MThe disciples picked up twelve basketfuls of broken pieces of bread and fish. 44 The number of the men, MTbesides women and children, Mwho had eaten was five thousand. JAfter the people saw the miraculous sign that Jesus had performed, they began to say, "Surely this is the prophet who is to come into the world."

#112 Miracle 20: Jesus (and Peter) Walk on Water in a Storm
MT 14.22-33 (Parallel Texts: MK 6.45-52; JN 6.16-21)

22 MTImmediately, Jesus made the disciples climb into the boat and go on ahead of him to the other side-- Mto Bethsaida to--MTwhile he dismissed the crowd. JWhen evening came, his disciples went down to the lake, where they climbed into a boat and set off across the lake for the area near Capernaum. By now it was dark, and Jesus had not yet joined them.

23 MTAfter he had dismissed them, Jknowing that they intended to come and make him King by force, MThe went up on a mountainside by himself to pray. Later that night, he was there alone, 24 and the boat was already a considerable distance from land, being buffeted by the waves because a Jstrong wind was blowing against it and the waters were rough.

25 MTShortly before dawn, Jwhen they had rowed about three miles (or five kilometers), MJesus saw them straining mightily at the oars, MTand he went out to them, walking on the lake. MHe intended to pass them by. 26 MTWhen the disciples saw him walking on the lake, they were terrified. "It's a ghost," they said and cried out in fear.

27 But Jesus immediately commanded them, *"Take courage! It is 'I AM.' I command you to stop being afraid."*

28 Peter replied, "Lord, because it's you, command me to come to you on the water."

29 *"Come,"* Jesus commanded him.

Then, Peter climbed down from the boat, walked on the water, and came toward Jesus. 30 But because he kept looking at the wind, he became afraid and, beginning to sink, cried out, "Lord, save me!"

31 Immediately, Jesus reached out his hand and caught him. *"You of little faith,"* he said, *"why did you doubt?"*

32 And when they climbed into the boat, the wind died down, ᴹand they were totally astonished. They had learned nothing from the miracle of the loaves; their hearts were hardened.

33 Then those who were in the boat worshiped him, saying, "Truly you are the Son of God."

ᴶAnd immediately they arrived at the shore where they were going.

#113 Jesus Ministers in Gennesaret
MK 6.53-56 (Parallel Text: MT 14.34-35)

53 ᴹWhen they had crossed over, they landed at Gennesaret and anchored there. 54 As soon as they climbed out of the boat, the people ᴹᵀof that area ᴹrecognized Jesus. 55 The people came running from throughout the whole region, and they carried the sick on mats to where they heard Jesus was.

56 For wherever he went — into villages, towns, or the countryside — they placed the sick in the marketplace. They begged him to let them touch even the edge of his cloak, and all who touched it were healed.

#114 Jesus Begins the "Bread of Life" Discourse in Capernaum
JN 6.22-29

22 ᴶOn the next day [after the 5000 had been fed], the crowd that had stayed on the opposite shore of the lake [at Bethsaida] realized that only one boat had been there, and that Jesus had not entered it with his disciples, but that they had gone away alone. 23 Then, some boats from Tiberias landed near the place where the people had eaten the bread after the Lord had given thanks. 24 Once the crowd saw that neither Jesus nor his disciples were there, they got into the boats and went to Capernaum in search of Jesus. 25 When they found him on the other side of the lake, they asked him, "Rabbi, when did you get here?"

26 Jesus answered, *"Very truly I tell you, you are looking for me, not because you saw the signs I performed, but because you ate the loaves and had your fill. 27 I*

command you to stop working for the kind of food that spoils, but work for food that endures forever – that is eternal life--which the Son of Man will give you. For God the Father has stamped his seal of approval on him."

28 Then, they asked him, "What must we do to continually engage in the works that God requires?"

29 Jesus answered, *"This is the work of God: to continue believing in the one he has sent."*

#115 Jesus Declares, "I AM the Bread that Gives Eternal Life"
JN 6.30-40

30 So, they asked him, "What sign then will you give that we may see it and believe you? What will you do? 31 Our ancestors ate the manna in the wilderness; as it stands written, 'He gave them bread from heaven to eat.'" (Ex. 16.4; Neh. 9.15; Ps. 78.24-25)

32 Jesus said to them, *"Very truly I tell you, it is not Moses who has given you the kind of bread from heaven that remains, but it is my Father who is giving you that true bread from heaven. 33 For the bread of God is the bread that comes down from heaven and imparts eternal life to the world."*

34 "Please, sir," they said, "always give us this bread."

35 Then, Jesus declared, *"I AM the bread that gives eternal life. Whoever comes to me is certain never to go hungry, and whoever keeps believing in me is certain never to be thirsty. 36 But as I told you, you have really seen me, and still you do not believe. 37 All those the Father gives me will come to me, and whoever comes to me I will never, ever push away.*

38 *"For I have come down from heaven not to do my will, but to do the will of him who sent me. 39 And this is the will of him who sent me, that I shall lose none of all those he has permanently given me, but raise them up at the last day. 40 For my Father's will is for everyone who sees the Son and continually believes in him to have eternal life, and I myself will raise them up at the last day."*

#116 Jesus Assures Believers of Eternal Life
JN 6.41-51

41 At this, the Jews there were grumbling about him because he said, *"I am the bread that came down from heaven."* 42 They were saying, "Is this not Jesus,

the son of Joseph, whose father and mother we know? How can he now say, '*I have come down permanently from heaven?*'"

43 "*Stop grumbling among yourselves,*" Jesus commanded them. 44 "*No one has the ability to come to me unless the Father who sent me draws them, and I myself will raise them up at the last day. 45 It stands written in the Prophets: 'They will all be taught by God.' (Is. 54.13) Everyone who makes a practice of hearing the Father and learning from him, comes to me.*

46 "*No one has fully seen the Father except the one who is from God; only he has fully seen and comprehended the Father. 47 Very truly I tell you, the person who keeps believing (in me) really has eternal life. 48 I AM the bread that gives eternal life.*

49 "*Your ancestors ate the manna in the wilderness, yet they died. 50 But here is the bread that comes down from heaven, which anyone may eat and not die. 51 I am the living bread that came down from heaven. Whoever eats this bread will live forever. This bread is my flesh, which I myself will give for the eternal life of the world.*"

#117 Believers are United with Jesus Through Faith in Him
JN 6.52-59

52 ᴶThen, the Jews were quarreling among themselves, saying, "How can this man give us his flesh to eat?"

53 Jesus said to them, "*Very truly I tell you, unless you eat the flesh of the Son of Man and drink his blood, you have no life in you. 54 Whoever continually eats my flesh and keeps drinking my blood has eternal life, and I will raise them up at the last day. 55 For my flesh is real food and my blood is real drink.*

56 "*Whoever eats my flesh and drinks my blood continues to make their home in me, and I in them. 57 Just as the living Father sent me and I am living through the Father, so the one who is feeding on me will live through me. 58 This is the bread that came down from heaven. Your ancestors ate manna and died, but whoever is feeding on this bread will live forever.*"

59 He said this while teaching in the synagogue in Capernaum.

#118 Many of Jesus' Disciples Reject Him
JN 6.52-59

60 ᴶOn hearing this, many of his disciples said, "This is a hard teaching. Who is able to fully accept it?"

61 Aware that his disciples were grumbling about this, Jesus said to them, *"Does this offend you? 62 Then what would you do if you were to see the Son of Man ascending to where he was before! 63 It is the Spirit that imparts eternal life; the flesh is useless. The words I myself have spoken to you stand firm – they are full of the Spirit and give eternal life. 64 Yet there are some of you who do not believe."*

For Jesus had known from the beginning which of them did not believe and who would betray him. 65 He went on to say, *"This is why I told you that no one is able to come to me unless the Father has permanently enabled them."*

66 From this time, many of his disciples turned back and no longer followed him.

67 *"You do not want to leave too, do you?"* Jesus asked the Twelve.

68 Simon Peter answered him, "Lord, to whom shall we go? You have the words of eternal life. 69 We have come to irrevocably believe in you, and we really know that you are the Holy One of God."

70 Then, Jesus replied, *"Have I myself not chosen you, the Twelve? Yet one of you is devilish – like the devil."*

71 He meant Judas, the son of Simon Iscariot, who, although one of the Twelve, would later betray Jesus.

#119 The Hypocrisy of Disobeying God's Word to Observe Mere Human Traditions
JN 7.1; MK 7.1-13 (Parallel Text: MT 15.1-9)

^JAfter [the feeding of the 5000], Jesus was in Galilee. He did not want to go about in Judea because the Jewish leaders there were looking for a way to kill him.

1 ^MThe Pharisees and some of the scholars of the law who had come to Jesus from Jerusalem gathered around him 2 and saw some of his disciples eating food with hands that were defiled—that is, unwashed. 3 The Pharisees and all the Jews will not eat unless they give their hands a ceremonial washing, holding to the tradition of the elders. 4 When they come from the marketplace they will not eat unless they wash. And they observe many other traditions, such as the washing of cups, pitchers, and kettles. 5 So, the Pharisees and teachers of the law asked Jesus, "Why do your disciples not live according to the tradition of the elders; by eating their food with defiled hands?"

6 He replied, *"You hypocrites! Isaiah was right when he prophesied about you hypocrites; as it is written:*

> *"'These people honor me with their lips,*
> *but their hearts are far from me.*
> *7 they worship in vain;*
> *their teachings are merely human rules.' (Is. 29.13)*

8 *"You have let go of the commands of God and are holding fast to human traditions."* 9 And he continued, *"You excel at despising the commands of God in order to observe your own traditions! 10 For Moses* ᴹᵀ*commanded you,* ᴹ*saying:*

> *"'Honor your father and your mother' (Ex. 20.12),*
> *and, 'anyone who curses their father or mother is to be put to death.' (Ex. 21.17)*

11 *"But you say that if anyone declares that what might have been used to help their father or mother is 'Corban' (that is, 'devoted to God') – 12 then you no longer let them do anything for their father or mother. 13 Thus, you nullify the word of God for* ᴹᵀ*the sake of* ᴹ*your tradition that you have handed down. And you do many things like that."*

#120 Jesus Identifies the Source of Sinfulness
MK 7.14-23 (Parallel Text: MT 15.10-20)

14 ᴹJesus, having called the crowd to him again was saying, *"I command you all to keep taking to heart what I am saying and truly understand this: 15 "Nothing outside a person can defile them by going into* ᴹᵀ*their mouth.* ᴹ*Rather, it is what comes out of* ᴹᵀ*the mouth of* ᴹ*a person that truly defiles them."*

ᴹᵀThen, the disciples came to him and asked, "Do you know that the Pharisees were offended when they heard this?"

16 He replied, *"Every plant that my heavenly Father has not planted will be pulled up by the roots. I command all of you to leave them alone; they are blind guides. If the blind continue to lead the blind, both will certainly fall into a pit."*

17 ᴹAfter he had left the crowd and entered the house, his disciples asked him about this parable.

18 *"Are you so dull?"* he asked. *"Can you not comprehend that nothing that enters a person from the outside can defile them? 19 For it does not go into a person's*

heart but into the stomach, and then out of the body." [In saying this, Jesus declared all foods clean.]

20 He continued to explain to them: *"What comes out of a person is what defiles them.*21 *For it is from within, out of a person's heart, that evil thoughts come – sexual immorality, theft, murder,* 22 *adultery, greed, malice, deceit, lewdness, envy, slander, arrogance, and folly.* 23 *All these evils come from inside and defile a person.* MT*But to eat with unclean hands does not defile a person."*

Stage V of the Life of Jesus Christ:

HIS WITHDRAWAL TO GENTILE REGIONS

After the intensity of twenty months of non-stop travel and ministry in Galilee, Jesus and his disciples needed a change of pace. In addition, over those months Jesus' popularity had crescendoed to a peak, and then, as the Pharisees began to accuse him of being a Satanist, his public acceptance declined to the point that many of his own disciples abandoned him. It was time for Jesus to end his ministry in Galilee.

This posed a logistical problem for Jesus. Where could he go? It was too early to return to Judea. The Divine plan for his death was still a year away. Going straight to Judea for the Passover festivities would incite an unnecessary and ill-timed uproar among the Jewish leadership and the people. So from April through August, Jesus withdrew from his Jewish homeland and sojourned in the Gentile areas to the North, East, and Southeast of Galilee instead.

The Scriptures report just thirteen events that occurred during this season of withdrawal. Like the early Judean ministry, the lack of quantity of information about these five months is balanced by its quality. Some of the most important and dramatic scenes in Jesus' life took place during this period. The Synoptic gospels continue to narrate these months of withdrawal.

The withdrawal gave Jesus and his disciples time to refresh and prepare for the explosion of ministry that would characterize the last eight months of his life. They spent more than one thousand hours walking and talking together, praying, and conducting discipleship training that would have been impossible in Galilee because of the huge crowds.

The season of withdrawal was the necessary prelude to Jesus' last great journey to Jerusalem and the cross. Chapters 19 to 21 cover Jesus' season of withdrawal to the surrounding Gentile regions.

CHAPTER 19

Withdrawal: Jesus' First Trip North to Tyre and Sidon, and His Return Southeast to the Decapolis

---

**#121 Miracle 21: Jesus Responds to the "Great Faith"
of a Gentile Woman in Tyre
MK 7.24-30 (Parallel Text: MT 15.21-28)**

24 ^MJesus left that place and went to the vicinity of Tyre. He entered a house and did not want anyone to know it, yet he could not keep his presence secret. In fact, as soon as ^{MT}a Canaanite woman of that region, ^Mwhose little daughter was possessed by an impure spirit heard about him, she came and fell at his feet. ^{MT}She cried out to Jesus, saying, "Have mercy upon me, Lord, Son of David. My daughter is horribly troubled by a demon."

25 ^MThe woman was a Greek, born in Syrian Phoenicia. She kept begging Jesus to drive the demon out of her daughter. ^{MT}But Jesus did not answer her with a single word; and his disciples came and entreated him, saying, "Please dismiss her, for she is crying out after us."

26 Jesus answered, *"I was sent to the lost sheep of the house of Israel."*

Kneeling down before him, the woman said, "Lord, please help me."

27 Jesus answered her, ^M *"First let the children eat all they want, for it is not right to take the children's bread and toss it to the dogs."*

28 "Lord," she replied, "even the dogs under the table eat the children's crumbs ᴹᵀthat fall down."

29 ᴹThen, Jesus answered her, ᴹᵀ *"O woman, your faith is great! I command that it be done for you as you will.* ᴹ*Because of this reply, you may go; the demon has left your daughter."*

30 ᴹᵀSo her daughter was healed from that hour. ᴹThe woman went home and found her child lying on the bed, and the demon was gone.

#122 Miracle 22: Jesus Heals a Deaf Man and Many Others
MK 7.31-37; MT 15.29-31

31 ᴹThen, Jesus left the vicinity of Tyre and went up through Sidon, then down ᴹᵀalong ᴹthe Sea of Galilee and into the middle of the region of the Decapolis. ᴹᵀHe went up on a mountainside and sat down. Great crowds came to him, bringing the lame, the blind, the crippled, the mute, and many others. They laid them at his feet, and he healed them. The people were amazed when they saw the mute speaking, the crippled made well, the lame walking, and the blind seeing.

32 ᴹThen, some people brought to Jesus a man who was deaf and could hardly talk, and they begged him to place his hand on him.

33 After he took him aside by himself, away from the crowd, Jesus put his fingers into the man's ears. Then, he spit and touched the man's tongue. 34 He looked up to heaven and with a deep sigh said to him, *"Ephratha!"* (a command that meant: *"Be opened!"*). 35 At this, the man's ears were opened, his tongue was set free, and he began to speak normally.

36 Jesus commanded them not to tell anyone. But the more he did so, the more they continued talking about it. 37 People were completely overwhelmed; they were in a state of amazement. "He has made everything well," they said. "He even makes the deaf to hear and the mute to speak."

ᴹᵀAnd they gave glory to the God of Israel.

#123 Miracle 23: Jesus Feeds 4000 Gentiles
MK 8.1-10 (Parallel Text: MT 15.32-39)

1 ᴹDuring those days, another large crowd gathered. Because they had nothing to eat, Jesus called his disciples to him and said, 2 *"I am feeling compassion for these people; they have already remained together with me for three days*

and now they have nothing to eat. 3 ^{MT}*I am unwilling to* ^M*send them home hungry, for some of them have come a great distance, and they will faint with hunger on their way."*

4 His disciples answered, "But where in this remote place can anyone get enough bread to feed ^{MT}such a great crowd?"

5 ^M*"How many loaves do you have?"* Jesus asked.

"Seven," they replied.

6 He told the crowd to sit down on the ground. When he had taken the seven loaves and given thanks, he broke them and gave them to his disciples to distribute to the people, and ^{MT}the disciples ^Mgave them to the crowd. 7 They had a few small fish as well; he blessed them also and told the disciples to distribute them. 8 The people ate until they were full. Afterward, the disciples picked up seven basketfuls of broken pieces that were left over. 9 About four thousand ^{MT}men ^Mwere present, ^{MT}besides the women and children.

^MAfter he had sent them away, 10 Jesus climbed into the boat with his disciples and crossed over ^{MT}to Magadan ^Min the region of Dalmanutha.

#124 A Second Sinful Request for Jesus to Perform Signs on Demand
MT 16.1-4 (Parallel Text: MK 8.11-13)

1 ^{MT}The Pharisees and Sadducees came to Jesus ^Mand began to argue with him, ^{MT}and they tested him by asking him to show them a sign from heaven. 2 ^MHe sighed deeply in his spirit and ^{MT}replied, *"When evening comes, you say, 'It will be fair weather, for the sky is red,' 3 and in the morning, 'Today it will be stormy, for the sky is red and overcast.' You know how to interpret the appearance of the sky, but you cannot interpret the signs of the times.*

4 *"A wicked and adulterous generation looks for a sign, but* ^M*truly I say to you,* ^{MT}*none will be given it except the sign of Jonah."*

Jesus then left them and ^Mclimbed into the boat again, ^{MT}going away to the other side of the Lake.

#125 Jesus Warns the Disciples about Hypocrisy
MT 16.5-12 (Parallel Text: MK 8.14-21)

5 ^{MT}When they went across the lake, the disciples forgot to take bread, ^Mexcept for the single loaf they had with them in the boat. 6 ^{MT}Jesus said to

them, *"I command you all to stay vigilant. You must all remain on careful guard against the yeast of the Pharisees and Sadducees* ^MT^*and Herod."*

7 ^MT^They were talking about this among themselves and said, "It is because we did not bring any bread."

8 Jesus knew what they were talking about, so he asked, *"You people of little faith, why are you talking among yourselves about having no bread? 9 Do you still not* ^M^*see or* ^MT^*understand?* ^M^*Are your hearts hardened? Do you have eyes but fail to see, and ears but fail to hear?*

^MT^ *"Do you not remember* ^M^*when I broke* ^MT^*the five loaves for the five thousand, and how many full baskets* ^M^*of broken pieces* ^MT^*you gathered?"*

^M^They said to him, "Twelve."

10 ^MT^ *"Or the seven loaves for the four thousand and how many full baskets* ^M^*of broken pieces* ^MT^*you gathered?"*

^M^They said to him, "Seven."

11 ^MT^ *"How is it that you do not understand I was not talking to you about bread? But I command you all to remain on careful guard against the yeast of the Pharisees and Sadducees."*

12 Then, they understood that he was not telling them to guard against the yeast used in bread but against the teaching of the Pharisees and Sadducees.

#126 Miracle 24: Jesus Heals Another Blind Man
MK 8.22-26

22 ^M^They came to Bethsaida, and some people brought a blind man and pleaded with Jesus to touch him. 23 Having taken the blind man by the hand, Jesus led him outside the village. When he had spit on the man's eyes and put his hands on him, Jesus asked, *"Are you seeing anything?"*

24 The man looked up and said, "I see people; they look like trees walking around."

25 Once more, Jesus placed his hands on the man's eyes. Then, his eyes were opened, his sight was restored, and he was looking at everything clearly.

26 Jesus sent him home, after commanding him, *"Do not even go into the village."*

CHAPTER 20

Withdrawal: Jesus' Second Trip Northward to Caesarea Philippi

---

#127 Peter's Great Confession
MT 16.13-16 (Parallel Texts: MK 8.27-29; LK 9.18-20)

13 ^{MT}Jesus went on ^Mwith his disciples to the villages in the region of Caesarea Philippi. On the way, ^Lwhile he was praying alone, his disciples were with him. He asked them, ^{MT}*Who do people say the Son of Man is?"*

14 They replied, "Some say John the Baptist; others say Elijah; and still others, Jeremiah, or one of the ancient prophets ^Lwho has risen from the dead."

15 ^{MT} *"But what about you?"* he asked. *"Who do you say I am?"*

16 Simon Peter answered, "You are the Christ, the Son of the living God."

#128 Jesus Teaches about His Church for the First Time in His Ministry
MT 16.17-20 (Parallel Texts: MK 8.30; LK 9.21)

18 ^{MT}Jesus replied, *"Blessed are you, Simon son of Jonah, for this was not revealed to you by flesh and blood, but by my Father in heaven. And I tell you that you are 'Petros', a piece of rock, and on this 'petra,' a massive bedrock, I will build my church, and the gates of hades will not overcome it.*

19 *"I will give you the keys of the kingdom of heaven; whatever you may bind on earth must be something that already stands bound in heaven, and whatever you may unbind on earth must be something that already stands unbound in heaven."*

20 Then he ᴸstrictly ᴹᵀordered his disciples not to tell anyone that he was the Messiah.

#129 Jesus Teaches about His Cross for the First Time
MT 16.21-28 (Parallel Texts: MK 8.31-9.1; LK 9.22-27)

21 ᴹᵀFrom that time on, Jesus began to reveal to his disciples that he must go to Jerusalem and suffer many things at the hands of the elders, the chief priests, and the teachers of the law, and that he must be killed and on the third day be raised to life.

22 Peter took him aside and began to rebuke him. "Have mercy, Lord!" he said. "There is no way that will ever happen to you!"

23 Jesus turned and said to Peter, *"I command you to remain behind me, Adversary! You are being a stumbling block to me because you do not have in mind the concerns of God, but merely human interests."*

24 Then, Jesus said to his disciples, *"Because you are willing to come after me, I command that you must deny yourself, take up your cross ᴸdaily, ᴹᵀand continue following me. 25 For whoever wants to save his own life will lose it, but whoever loses his life for my sake ᴹand the sake of the gospel ᴹᵀwill find it.*

26 *"Will it do any good for someone to gain the whole world, yet forfeit his own soul? What can anyone give in exchange for his soul? 27 For the Son of Man is going to come in his Father's glory with his angels, and then he will reward each person according to what that person has done.*

ᴹ *"If anyone is ashamed of me and my words in this adulterous and sinful generation, the Son of Man will also be ashamed of him when he comes in ᴸhis own glory and* ᴹ*the glory of his Father with his holy angels. 28* ᴹᵀ *"Truly I tell you, some who stand here will most certainly not taste death before they see the Son of Man coming in his kingdom ᴹwith great power."*

#130 Jesus' Transfiguration
MT 17.1-8 (Parallel Texts: MK 9.2-8; LK 9.28-36A)

1 ᴹᵀAfter six days, Jesus took with him Peter, James, and John, the brother of James, and he led them up a high mountain by themselves ᴸto pray. 2 As he

continued in prayer, ᴹᵀhe was transfigured before them. His face shone like the sun—like a bolt of lightning—and his clothes were ᴹglistening ᴹᵀwhite as light, ᴹas no launderer on earth could bleach them.

3 Just then, Moses and Elijah emerged before them, ᴸappearing in glory, and they were ᴹᵀtalking with Jesus ᴸabout his death and resurrection that he would accomplish at Jerusalem. Now Peter and the men with him were sound asleep, but when they awoke, they saw Jesus in his glory and the two men standing with him.

As Moses and Elijah were starting to leave, 4 ᴹᵀPeter said to Jesus, "Lord, it is good for us to be here. If you wish, I will put up three shelters—one for you, one for Moses, and one for Elijah."

ᴹHe was so scared that he did not really know what he was saying. 5 ᴹᵀWhile he was still speaking, a bright cloud covered them, and a voice from the cloud said, *"This is my Son, whom I love; with him I am well pleased,* ᴸ*my Chosen One.* ᴹᵀ*I command you all to listen to him continually!"*

6 When the disciples heard this, they fell face down on the ground, scared out of their wits.

7 But Jesus came and touched them as he commanded: *"Get up. Stop being afraid."*

8 When they looked up, they saw no one any more, except Jesus himself, alone.

#131 Jesus Reinforces the Lesson of His Transfiguration
MT 17.9-13 (Parallel Texts: MK 9.9-13; LK 9.36B)

9 ᴹᵀAs they were coming down the mountain, Jesus commanded them, *"Do not tell anyone what you have seen, until the Son of Man has been raised from the dead."*

ᴹAnd they kept his saying to themselves as they discussed with each other what *"raised from the dead"* might mean.

10 ᴹᵀThe disciples asked him, "Why then do the teachers of the law say that Elijah must come first?"

11 Jesus replied, *"To be sure, Elijah comes and will restore all things.* ᴹ*And how is it written that the Son of Man should suffer many things and be treated with contempt?* 12 ᴹᵀ*But I tell you, Elijah has already come, and they did not recognize him, but they have done to him everything they wished,* ᴹ*just as it was written of him.* ᴹᵀ*In the same way the Son of Man is going to suffer at their hands."*

13 Then, the disciples understood that he was talking to them about John the Immerser. ^LAnd they kept their silence and told no one during those days about any of the things that they had seen.

#132 Miracle 25: Jesus Heals a Demonized Boy
MK 9.14-27 (Parallel Texts: MT 17.14-18; LK 9.37-43)

14 ^LThe next day, when they came down from the mountain ^Mand rejoined the other disciples, they saw a large crowd around them and the teachers of the law arguing with them. 15 As soon as all the people saw Jesus, they were overwhelmed with wonder and ran to greet him.

16 *"What are you arguing with them about?"* he asked.

17 ^{MT}A man approached Jesus and knelt before him. He said, "Lord, have mercy on my son. He has seizures and is suffering greatly."

^MHe went on, "Teacher, I brought you my son, ^Lmy only child, ^Mwho is possessed by a spirit that has robbed him of speech. 18 Whenever it seizes him, it throws him to the ground. He foams at the mouth, ^Lcries out, ^Mgnashes his teeth, and becomes rigid. ^LThe spirit hardly ever departs from him and injures him severely. ^MI asked your disciples to drive out the spirit, but they could not."

19 *"You unbelieving* ^{MT}*and perverse* ^M*generation,"* Jesus replied, *"How long shall I stay with you? How long shall I put up with you? Bring the boy to me."*

20 So they brought him. When the spirit saw Jesus, it immediately threw the boy into a convulsion, and he fell to the ground and rolled around, foaming at the mouth.

21 Jesus asked the boy's father, *"How long has he been like this?"*

"From childhood," he answered. 22 "It has often thrown him into fire or water to kill him. But if you can do anything, take pity on us and help us."

23 *"'If you can'?"* said Jesus. *"Everything is possible for one who believes."*

24 Immediately, the boy's father exclaimed, "I do believe; help me overcome my unbelief!"

25 When Jesus saw that a crowd was running to the scene, he rebuked the impure spirit. *"You deaf and mute spirit,"* he said, *"I command you, come out of him and never enter him again."*

26 The spirit shrieked, convulsed the boy violently, and came out. The boy looked so much like a corpse that many said, "He's dead." 27 But Jesus took

him by the hand and lifted him to his feet, and he stood up. ᴸJesus gave him back to his father. And they were all astonished by the greatness of God.

#133 Jesus Teaches about Mountain-Moving Faith
MT 17.19-20 (Parallel Text: MK 9.28-29)

19 ᴹAfter Jesus had gone indoors, ᴹᵀhis disciples came to him in private and asked, "Why could we not drive the demon out?"

20 He replied, *"Because you have so little faith.* ᴹ*This kind of demon can only come out by prayer.* ᴹᵀ*Truly I tell you, if you have faith as small as a mustard seed, you can say to this mountain, 'Move from here to there,' and it will move. Nothing will be impossible for you."*

CHAPTER 21

Withdrawal: Jesus Trains His Disciples on

His Final Trip Back to Capernaum

#134 Jesus Teaches His Disciples about His Death the Second Time
MK 9.30-32 (Parallel Texts: MT 17.22-23; LK 9.43B-45)

30 ^MThey left that place and travelled to Galilee. Jesus did not want anyone to know where they were, 31 because he was teaching his disciples. ^{MT}When they came together in Galilee, ^Mhe said to them, ^L *"I command you all to listen carefully to what I am about to tell you. ^MThe Son of Man is going to be delivered into the hands of men. They will kill him, and after three days, he will be raised ^{MT}to life."*

32 ^MBut they did not understand what he meant and were afraid to ask him about it. ^LIt was hidden from them, so that they did not grasp it. ^{MT}And the disciples were filled with grief.

#135 Jesus Pays the Temple Tax with an Unusual Catch of Fish
MT 17.24-27

24 After Jesus and his disciples arrived in Capernaum, the collectors of the two-drachma temple tax came to Peter and asked, "Does your teacher not make a practice of paying the temple tax?"

25 "Yes, he does," he replied.

When Peter came into the house, Jesus was the first to speak. *"What do you think, Simon?"* he asked. *"From whom do the kings of the earth receive duty and taxes – from their own sons or from others?"*

26 "From others," Peter answered.

"Then the sons are exempt," Jesus said to him. 27 *"But so that we may not cause any offense, I command you to go to the lake and throw out your line. Take the first fish you catch; open its mouth, and you will find a four-drachma coin. Take it and give it to them for my tax, and in your behalf."*

#136 Jesus Teaches on True Kingdom Greatness: A Servant Attitude
MT 18.1-6 (Parallel Text: MK 9.33-37; LK 9.46-48)

1 ᴹᵀAt that time, the disciples came to Jesus in the house and asked, *"Who, then, is the greatest in the kingdom of heaven?"* ᴸBut Jesus, perceiving what they were thinking in their hearts, asked them. ᴹ *"What were you arguing about on the road?"*

But they kept quiet because they had argued about who was the greatest on the way.

Sitting down, Jesus called all the Twelve to him and said, *"Anyone who wants to be first must be the very last and the servant of all."*

2 ᴹᵀHe called a little child to him and placed the child among them. 3 And he said, *"Truly I tell you, unless you change and become like little children, you will never enter the kingdom of heaven. ᴹWhoever does not receive the kingdom of God like a child will not enter it.*

4 ᴹᵀ *"Therefore, whoever humbles himself by taking the lowly position of this child is the greatest in the kingdom of heaven. 5 And whoever welcomes one such child in my name welcomes me."*

#137 True Kingdom Greatness: A Good Example
MT 18.7-9 (Parallel Text: MK 9.43-50)

6 *"If anyone causes one of these little ones – those who believe in me – to stumble, it would be better for them to have a large millstone hung around their neck and to be drowned in the depths of the sea. 7 Woe to the world because of the things that cause people to stumble! Such things must come, but woe to the person through whom they come! 8 If your hand or your foot is causing you to stumble, I command you to cut it*

off and throw it away. It is better for you to enter life maimed or crippled than to have two hands or two feet and be thrown into eternal fire.

9 *"And if your eye is causing you to stumble, I command you to gouge it out and throw it away. It is better for you to enter eternal life with one eye than to have two eyes and be thrown into the fire of hell, where 'the worms that eat them do not die, and the fire is not quenched.' (Isa. 66.24)*

"Everyone will be salted with fire. Salt is good, but if it loses its saltiness, how can you make it salty again? Have salt among yourselves, and be at peace with each other."

#138 True Kingdom Greatness: Care-Giving
MT 18.10-14; MK 9.38-41

MT 18.10 ^{MT} *"See that you do not despise one of these little ones. For I tell you that their angels in heaven always see the face of my Father in heaven.*

[Note: The most reliable ancient manuscripts do not contain MT 18.11, as found in the KJV. Thus, we do not include verse 11 in this publication.]

12 *"What do you think? If a man owns a hundred sheep, and one of them wanders away, will he not leave the ninety-nine on the hills and go to look for the one that wandered off? 13 And if he finds it, truly I tell you, he is happier about that one sheep than about the ninety-nine that did not wander off. 14 In the same way, your Father in heaven is not willing that any of these little ones should perish."*

MK 9.38 ^M "Teacher," said John, "we saw someone driving out demons in your name, and we told him to stop because he was not one of us."

39 *"Do not stop him,"* Jesus said. *"For no one who does a miracle in my name can in the next moment say anything bad about me, 40 for whoever is not against us is for us. 41 Truly I tell you, anyone who gives you a cup of water in my name because you belong to the Messiah will certainly not lose their reward."*

#139 True Kingdom Greatness: Practicing Restoration
MT 18.15-20

15 ^{MT} *"If your brother or sister sins [against you], I command you to go and point out their fault, just between the two of you. If they listen to you, you have regained your brother or sister. 16 But if they will not listen, I command you to take one or two others along, so that 'every matter may be established by the testimony of two or three witnesses.' (Duet. 19.15)*

17 *"If they still refuse to listen, I command you to tell it to the church; and if they refuse to listen even to the church, I command you to treat them as you would a pagan or a tax collector. 18 Truly I tell you, whatever you bind on earth must be something already bound in heaven, and whatever you unbind on earth must be something already unbound in heaven.*

19 *"Again, truly I tell you that if two of you on earth agree about anything they ask for, it will be done for them by my Father in heaven. 20 For where two or three have been permanently gathered together in my name, there am I in the midst of them."*

#140 True Kingdom Greatness: Limitless Forgiveness
MT 18.21-35

21 ^{MT}Then, Peter came to Jesus and asked, "Lord, how many times shall I forgive my brother or sister who have sinned against me? Up to seven times?"

22 Jesus answered, *"I tell you, not seven times, but seventy times seven. 23 Therefore, the kingdom of heaven is like a king who wanted to settle accounts with his servants. 24 As he began the settlement, a man who owed him ten thousand bags of gold was brought to him. 25 Because he was not able to pay, the master ordered that he and his wife and his children and all that he had should be sold to repay the debt.*

26 *"At this the servant fell on his knees before him. 'Have mercy upon me,' he begged, 'and I will pay back everything.' 27 The servant's master had compassion for him, canceled the debt, and let him go. 28 But when that servant went out, he found one of his fellow servants who owed him a hundred silver coins. He grabbed him and began to choke him. 'Pay back what you owe me!' he demanded.*

29 *"His fellow servant fell to his knees and begged him, 'Have mercy upon me, and I will pay it back.' 30 But he refused. Instead, he went off and had the man thrown into prison until he could pay the debt. 31 When the other servants saw what had happened, they were outraged and told their master everything that had happened.*

32 *"Then, the master called the servant in. 'You wicked servant,' he said, 'I canceled all that debt of yours because you begged me to. 33 Should you not have had mercy on your fellow servant just as I had on you?' 34 In anger his master handed him over to the jailers to be tortured, until he should pay back all he owed.*

35 *"This is how my heavenly Father will treat each of you unless you forgive your brother or sister from your heart."*

Stage VI of the Life of Jesus Christ:

HIS LATER MINISTRY IN JUDEA

In the beginning of September, Jesus intended to attend the Feast of Tabernacles in Jerusalem and then remain in Judea until the Feast of Dedication in December. After beginning his ministry in this region almost three years earlier, he would return for four months of intense ministry. There would be little similarity between his early and later ministries in Judea.

Just as Jesus had prepared the twelve apostles to go out—two by two—to heal and preach the gospel in all of the towns and villages of Galilee on his third tour there, he had prepared another 70 disciples—35 teams of two—to preach and heal throughout Judea during his later ministry. The effect of these roving 35 teams was profound. Jesus himself joined in the tour of Judea with his twelve apostles. No one had ever seen anything like this before. Unlike the obscurity of his earlier ministry in Judea when he focused on personal evangelism, this time Jesus came with great power to saturate the entire region with his public preaching and teaching, and teams of two.

Along with the tour of Judea, Jesus also continued to concentrate on discipleship training with the larger group of about 120 disciples that traveled with him from Galilee. Luke, who organized his narrative around Jesus' two journeys to Jerusalem during this period, recorded many of the key lessons in discipleship training that Jesus delivered in this four-month period.

John's narrative focused exclusively on what happened in Jerusalem during Jesus' two visits for the Feast of Tabernacles in September, and Dedication in December. Therefore, Luke and John's content complement each other perfectly. Matthew and Mark had little to say about these months.

Chapters 22 to 30 cover Jesus' later ministry in Judea.

CHAPTER 22

Judea: Jesus Travels to Jerusalem for the Feast of Tabernacles

---

#141 Jesus Departs for Jerusalem after His Brothers Mock Him
JN 7.2-10; MT 19.1A; LK 9.51 (MK 10.1)

^LAs the time was approaching for him to be lifted up to heaven, Jesus decided to make his way to Jerusalem. 2 ^JSo, when the Jewish Festival of Tabernacles was near, 3 Jesus' brothers said to him, "Leave Galilee and go to Judea so that your disciples there may see the works you do. 4 No one who wants to become a public figure acts in secret. Because you are doing these things, show yourself to the world."

5 For even his own brothers did not believe in him.

6 Therefore, Jesus told them, *"My time is not yet here; any time will do for you. 7 The world cannot hate you, but it hates me because I testify that its works are evil. 8 You go to the feast. I am not going up to this feast now because my time has not yet fully come."*

9 After he had said this, he stayed in Galilee. 10 However, after his brothers had left for the festival, he went also, not publicly, but in secret. ^{MT}So, when Jesus had finished saying these things, he left ^Mthat place in ^{MT}Galilee and went into the region of Judea.

#142 Jesus Travels Through Samaria to Jerusalem
LK 9.52-56

52 Jesus sent messengers on ahead of him, who went into a Samaritan village to prepare for him, 53 but the people there did not welcome him because they knew he was heading for Jerusalem. 54 When the disciples James and John saw this, they asked, "Lord, do you want us to call fire down from heaven to utterly destroy them?" 55 But Jesus turned and rebuked them. 56 Then, he and his disciples went to another village.

#143 Jesus Copes with Inadequate Discipleship on the Journey
LK 9.57-62 (Parallel Text: MT 8.19-22)

57 As they were walking along the road, a man said to Jesus, "I will follow you wherever you go."

58 Jesus replied, *"Foxes have dens and birds have nests, but the Son of Man has no place to lay his head."*

59 He said to another man, *"I command you to follow me continually."* But he replied, "Lord, first let me go and bury my father." 60 Jesus said to him, *"I command you to let the dead bury their own dead, but you must go and keep proclaiming the kingdom of God."*

61 Still another said, "I will follow you, Lord; but first let me go and say goodbye to my family." 62 Jesus replied, *"No one who puts a hand to the plow and looks back is fit for service in the kingdom of God."*

CHAPTER 23

Judea: Jesus' First Teaching at Tabernacles—

"Rivers of Living Water"

#144 Jesus Claims His Teaching is Divine
JN 7.11-19

11 Now at the festival, the Jewish leaders were searching for Jesus and asking, "Where is that man?" 12 Among the crowds, there was widespread grumbling about him. Some said, "He is a good man." Others replied, "No, he deceives the people." 13 But no one was saying anything publicly about him for fear of the leaders.

14 In the middle days of the festival, Jesus went to the temple courts and began to teach. 15 The Jews there were in a state of amazement and asked, "How did this man become so learned without having been taught as a rabbi?"

16 Jesus answered, *"My teaching is not my own. It comes from the one who sent me. 17 Anyone who is willing to DO the will of God will find out whether my teaching comes from God, or whether I speak on my own initiative. 18 Whoever speaks on their own initiative does so to gain personal glory, but the person who continually seeks the glory of the one who sent him is a person of truth; there is nothing false about him. 19 Has not Moses permanently delivered the law to you? Yet not one of you is keeping the law. Why are you seeking to kill me?"*

#145 Various Responses to Jesus
JN 7.20-27

20 "You are demon-possessed," the crowd answered Jesus. "Who is trying to kill you?"

21 Jesus said to them, *"I performed one miracle, and you all continue to be amazed. 22 Yet, because Moses gave you circumcision as a firm command [although actually it did not come from Moses, but from the patriarchs], you circumcise a boy on the Sabbath as a regular practice. 23 Now, given that a boy can be circumcised on the Sabbath so that the law of Moses may not be broken, why are you angry with me for healing a man's whole body on the Sabbath? 24 Stop judging by mere appearances, but instead judge correctly."*

25 At that point, some of the people of Jerusalem began to ask, "Is this not the man they are trying to kill? 26 Here he is, speaking publicly, and they are not saying a word to him. Have the authorities really concluded that he is the Messiah? 27 But we know where this man is from; when the Messiah comes, no one will know where he is from."

#146 Two Failed Attempts to Arrest Jesus
JN 7.28-36

28 Then, Jesus, still teaching in the temple courts, cried out, *"Yes, you know me, and you know where I am from. I did not come here — permanently — on my own authority, but he who sent me is true. You do not know him, 29 but I myself know him, because I am from him and he sent me."*

30 At this, they began trying to seize him, but no one laid a hand on him because his hour had not yet come. 31 Still, many in the crowd believed in him. They said, "When the Messiah comes, surely he will not perform more signs than this man, will he?"

32 The Pharisees heard the crowd whispering such things about him. Then, the chief priests and the Pharisees sent temple guards to arrest him.

33 Jesus said, *"I am with you for only a short time, and then I am going to the one who sent me. 34 You will look for me, but you will not find me; and where I AM, you are unable to come."*

35 The Jews said to one another, "Where does this man intend to go that we cannot find him? Will he go where our people live scattered among the Greeks and teach them? 36 What did he mean when he says, 'You will look for me, but you will not find me,' and 'Where I am, you cannot come'?"

#147 Jesus Promises the Holy Spirit
JN 7.37-39

37 On the last and greatest day of the festival, Jesus stood and said in a loud voice, *"If anyone is thirsty, I command that person to come to me and continually drink. 38 Whoever believes in me, as Scripture has said, rivers of living water will flow out from within them."*

39 By this, he meant the Spirit, whom those who believed in him were later to receive. Up to that time, the Spirit had not been given because Jesus had not yet been glorified.

#148 The Crowd Divides Because of Jesus
JN 7.40-52

40 On hearing his words, some of the people said, "Surely this man is the Prophet."

41 Others said, "He is the Messiah."

Still others asked, "How can the Messiah come from Galilee? 42 Does not Scripture say that the Messiah will come from David's descendants and from Bethlehem, the town where David lived?"

43 Thus, the people were divided because of Jesus. 44 Some wanted to seize him, but no one laid a hand on him. 45 Finally, the temple guards went back to the chief priests and the Pharisees, who asked them, "Why did you not bring him in?"

46 "No one ever spoke the way that this man does," the guards replied.

47 "You mean he has deceived you also?" the Pharisees retorted.

48 "Have any of the rulers or of the Pharisees believed in him? 49 No! But this mob that knows nothing of the law — there is a curse on them."

50 Nicodemus, who had gone to Jesus earlier and who was one of the Pharisees, asked 51 "Does our law condemn a man without first hearing him to find out what he has been doing?"

52 They replied, "Are you from Galilee, too? Look into it, and you will find that a prophet does not come out of Galilee."

CHAPTER 24

Judea: Jesus' Second Teaching at Tabernacles--

"'I AM' the Light of the World"

Jesus Forgives a Woman Caught in Adultery

#149 Who is Worthy to Judge Others?
JN 8.1-8

1 Jesus went to the Mount of Olives. 2 At dawn, he appeared again in the temple courts, where all the people gathered around him, and he sat down to teach them. 3 The teachers of the law and the Pharisees brought in a woman caught in adultery. 4 They made her stand before the group and said to Jesus, "Teacher, this woman was caught in the act of adultery. 5 In the Law Moses commanded us to stone such women. Now what do you say?"

6 They were using this question as a trap, in order to have a basis for accusing him. But Jesus bent down and started to write on the ground with his finger. 7 When they kept on questioning him, he straightened up and said to them, *"I command that any one of you who is totally innocent – without any sin – be the first to hurl a stone at her."*

8 Again, he stooped down and wrote on the ground.

#150 Jesus Forgives and Transforms the Woman
JN 8.9-11

9 At this, those who heard began to go away one at a time, the older ones first, until only Jesus was left, with the woman still standing there.

10 Jesus straightened up and asked her, *"Woman, where are they? Has no one condemned you?"*

11 "No one, sir," she said.

"Then neither do I condemn you," Jesus declared. *"I command you to go now and permanently leave your life of sin."*

[Note: The text of John 8.1-11 does not appear in the earliest manuscripts of the Gospel of John. In addition, this text is found in some less reliable manuscripts of the Gospel of Luke, rather than John. These facts show us that the pericope was not part of the original manuscript of John's gospel. It was added later by editors and manuscript copiers who felt it was more appropriate to John Chapter Eight. Because the fragment is part of the ancient manuscript tradition of the early church and is consistent with the words and actions of Jesus in the gospels, we have included it in The Jesus Saga.]

Jesus' Second Teaching in the Temple:
#151 "I AM the Light of the World"
JN 8.12-20

12 When Jesus spoke again to the people, he said, *"I AM the light of the world. Whoever follows me will never walk in darkness but will have the light of eternal life."*

13 The Pharisees challenged him, "Here you are, functioning as your own witness; your testimony is not valid."

14 Jesus answered, *"Even if I testify on my own behalf, my testimony is valid, for I know where I came from and where I am going. But you have no idea where I come from or where I am going. 15 You judge by human standards; I pass judgment on no one. 16 But if I do judge, my decisions are true because I am not alone in making them. I stand with the Father, who sent me. 17 In your own Law, it is written that the testimony of two witnesses is true. 18 I am one who testifies for myself; my other witness is the Father, who sent me."*

19 Then, they asked him, "Where is your father?"

"You do not know me or my Father," Jesus replied. *"If you knew me, you would know my Father also."*

20 He spoke these words while teaching in the temple courts near the place where the offering boxes were placed. Yet no one seized him because his hour had not yet come.

#152 Jesus Warns about Dying in Sin
JN 8.21-24

21 Once more, Jesus said to them, *"I am going away, and you will look for me, and you will die in your sin. Where I go, you cannot come."*

22 This made the Jews ask, "Will he kill himself? Is that why he says, 'Where I go, you cannot come'?"

23 But he continued, *"You are from below; I am from above. You are of this world; I am not of this world. 24 Therefore, I told you that you would die in your sins; if you do not believe that I AM he, you will certainly die in your sins."*

#153 Who is Jesus? He is the Crucified Lord!
JN 8.25-30

25 "Who are you?" they asked.

"Just what I have been telling you from the beginning," Jesus replied. 26 *"I have much to say in judgment of you. But he who sent me is trustworthy, and what I have heard from him I tell the world."*

27 They did not understand that he was telling them about his Father. 28 So Jesus said, *"When you have lifted up the Son of Man in exaltation [on the cross], then you will know that 'I AM' and that I do nothing on my own initiative; but rather, I speak just what the Father has taught me. 29 The one who sent me is with me; he has not left me alone, for I always do what pleases him."*

30 Even as he spoke, many believed in him.

#154 True Believers Abide in Jesus' Word
JN 8.31-36

31 To the Jews who had committed themselves to him, Jesus said, *"If you make your home in my teaching, you are really my disciples. 32 Then you will know the truth, and the truth will make you free."*

33 They answered him, "We are Abraham's descendants and have never been slaves of anyone. How can you say that we shall be set free?"

34 Jesus replied, *"Very truly I tell you, everyone who continues to sin is a slave to sin. 35 Now a slave does not abide permanently in the family, but a son abides in it forever.36 Therefore, if the Son sets you free, you will be free indeed."*

#155 Who is a True Descendant of Abraham?
JN 8.37-40

37 *"I know that you are physically Abraham's descendants. Yet, even now you are looking for a way to kill me because you do not hold to my word. 38 I myself am telling you what I have truly seen in the Father's presence, and you are doing what you have heard from your father."*

39 "Abraham is our father," they answered.

"If you were Abraham's children," said Jesus, *"then you would be doing what Abraham did. 40 As it is, you are looking for a way to kill me, a man who has told you decisively about the truth that I heard from God. Abraham did not do such things."*

#156 Children of God or the Devil
JN 8.41-47

41 Jesus said: *"You are doing the works of your own father."*

"We are not illegitimate children," they retorted. "We have one Father, who is God himself."

42 Jesus said to them, *"If God were your Father--and he is not--you would love me, for I have come from God. I have not come on my own; God sent me. 43 Why do you not understand what I am saying to you? Because you are unable to really hear what I say. 44 You belong to your father, the devil, and you always want to carry out your father's desires. He was a murderer from the beginning, not holding to the truth, for there is no truth in him. When he lies, he is speaking his own language, for he is a liar and the father of lies. 45 Yet because I tell the truth, you do not believe me!*

46 *"Can any of you prove me guilty of sin? Because I am speaking the truth, why do you not believe me? 47 Whoever belongs to God hears what God says. The reason you do not hear is that you do not belong to God."*

#157 Jesus is Accused of Demon Possession the Third Time
JN 8.48-53

48 The Jews answered him, "Are we not right in declaring that you are a Samaritan and demon-possessed?"

49 *"I myself am not possessed by a demon,"* said Jesus, *"but I am giving honor to my Father, and you are dishonoring me. 50 I, myself, am not seeking glory for myself; but there is One who is seeking it, and he is the judge. 51 Very truly I tell you, whoever obeys my word will never, ever experience death."*

52 At this, they exclaimed, "Now we really know for sure that you are demon-possessed! Abraham died and so did the prophets, yet you say that whoever obeys your word will never taste death! 53 Are you greater than our father Abraham? He died, and so did the prophets. Who do you think you are?"

#158 Who Is Jesus? He is "I AM"
JN 8.54-58

The Pharisees said, "Who are you making yourself out to be?"

54 Jesus replied, *"If I glorify myself, my glory means nothing. My Father, whom you claim as your God, is the one who is glorifying me. 55 Although you have not come to know him, I really do know him. If I said I do not, I would be a liar like you, but I do know him and obey his word. 56 Your father Abraham rejoiced at the thought of seeing my day; he saw it and was glad."*

57 "You are not yet fifty years old," they said to him, "and you have really seen Abraham?"

58 Jesus answered, *"Very truly I tell you, before Abraham was born, I AM."*

59 At this, they picked up stones to stone him, but Jesus hid himself, slipping away from the temple grounds.

Jesus is the Light of the Blind

#159 Miracle 26: Jesus Lights a Blind Man's Eyes
JN 9.1-7

1 As he went along, Jesus saw a man blind from birth. 2 His disciples asked him, "Rabbi, who sinned, this man or his parents, that he was born blind?"

3 *"Neither this man nor his parents sinned,"* said Jesus, *"but this happened so that the works of God might be displayed in him. 4 As long as it is day, we must continue doing the works of him who sent me. Night is coming when no one can work. 5 While I am in the world, I AM the light of the world."*

6 After saying this, he spit on the ground, made some mud with the saliva, and anointed the man's eyes.

7 *"I command you to go, and wash yourself in the Pool of Siloam"* [this word means "sent"].

So the man went, and washed, and came home seeing.

#160 The Healed Man's Neighbors Respond
JN 9.8-12

8 The man's neighbors, and those who saw that he used to be a beggar were saying, "Is this not the same man who used to sit and beg?" 9 Some were saying that he was. Others said, "No, he only looks like him."

But he himself was declaring, "I am the man."

10 "How then were your eyes opened?" they asked.

11 He replied, "The man they call Jesus made some mud and anointed my eyes. He told me to go to Siloam and wash. So I went and washed, and then I could see."

12 "Where is this man?" they asked him.

"I do not know," he said.

#161 The Pharisees Question the Healed Man
JN 9.13-17

13 They brought the man who was formerly blind to the Pharisees. 14 Now the day on which Jesus had made the mud and opened the man's eyes

was a Sabbath. 15 Therefore, the Pharisees also asked him how he had received his sight.

"He put mud on my eyes," the man replied, "and I washed, and now I continue to see."

16 Some of the Pharisees were saying, "This man is not from God for he does not keep the Sabbath." But others asked, "How can a sinner perform such signs?" So they were divided.

17 Then, they turned again to the blind man, "What have you to say about him? It was your eyes he opened."

The man said, "He is a prophet."

#162 The Pharisees Question the Healed Man's Parents
JN 9.18-23

18 The Pharisees still did not believe that the man had been blind and had received his sight until they sent for his parents.

19 "Is this your son?" they asked. "Is this the one you say was born blind? How is it that he is now seeing?"

20 "We know he is our son," the parents answered, "and we know he was born blind. 21 But how he can see now, or who opened his eyes, we do not know. Ask him. He is of age; he will speak for himself."

22 His parents said this because they were fearful of the Jewish leaders, who already had decided that anyone who confessed that Jesus was the Messiah would be excommunicated from the synagogue. 23 Because of this fear, they said, "He is of age; ask him."

#163 The Pharisees Question the Healed Man a Second Time
JN 9.24-34

24 They summoned the man who had been blind for the second time. "Give glory to God by telling the truth," they said. "We know this man is a sinner."

25 He replied, "I do not know if he is a sinner or not. One thing I do know. I was blind but now I see!"

26 Then, they asked him, "What did he do to you? How did he open your eyes?"

27 He answered, "I have told you already, and you did not listen. Why do you want to hear it again? Do you want to become his disciples too?"

28 Then, they reviled him, saying, "You are that fellow's disciple! But we are disciples of Moses! 29 We know for sure that God spoke decisively to Moses, but as for this fellow, we do not even know where he is from."

30 The man answered, "Now this is truly remarkable! You do not know where he comes from, yet he opened my eyes. 31 We do know that God does not make a practice of listening to sinners. He listens to the godly person who does his will. 32 Nobody has ever heard of opening the eyes of a man born blind. 33 If this man were not from God, he could do nothing."

34 To this they replied, "You were wholly in the grip of sin from your birth; how dare you lecture us!" And they threw him out of the synagogue.

#164 Jesus Explains Spiritual Sight versus Blindness
JN 9.35-41

35 Jesus heard that the Pharisees had excommunicated the healed man, and when he found him, he said, *"Do you believe in the Son of Man?"*

36 "Who is he, sir?" the man asked. "Tell me so that I may believe in him."

37 Jesus said, *"You have seen him in a way you will never forget; in fact, he is the one who is now speaking with you."*

38 Then, the man said, "Lord, I continue to believe," and he fell down and worshiped him.

39 Jesus said, *"I have come into this world for judgment, so that those who are not seeing will be able to see and those who are seeing might become blind."*

40 Some Pharisees who were with him heard him say this and asked, "What? Are we blind too?"

41 Jesus said, *"If you were blind, you would not be guilty of sin; but now that you claim you can see, you continue to abide in your sin."*

CHAPTER 25

Judea: Jesus' Final Teaching at Tabernacles--

"'I AM' the Door and the Good Shepherd"

#165 The Good Shepherd versus a Stranger
JN 10.1-6

1 *"Very truly I tell you, Pharisees, anyone who does not enter the sheep pen by the gate, but climbs in by some other way, is a thief and a robber. 2 The one who enters by the gate is the shepherd of the sheep. 3 The gatekeeper opens the gate for him, and the sheep listen to his voice. He calls his own sheep by name and leads them out. 4 When he has brought out all his own, he goes on ahead of them, and his sheep follow him because they know his voice. 5 But they will never follow a stranger; in fact, they will run away from him because they do not recognize a stranger's voice."*

6 Jesus used this figure of speech, but the Pharisees did not understand what he was telling them.

#166 "I AM the Door"
JN 10.7-10

7 Therefore Jesus said again, *"Very truly I tell you, I AM the door for the sheep. 8 All who have come before me are thieves and robbers, but the sheep have not*

listened to them. 9 I AM the door; whoever enters through me will be saved. They will come in and go out and find pasture.

10 *"The thief comes only to steal and kill and destroy; I myself have come that they may continually have eternal life, and have it in abundance."*

#167 "I AM the Good Shepherd"
JN 10.11-13

11 *"I AM the good shepherd. The good shepherd lays down his life for the sheep. 12 The hired hand is not the shepherd and does not own the sheep. So when he sees the wolf coming, he abandons the sheep and runs away. Then, the wolf attacks the flock and scatters it. 13 The man runs away because he is a hired hand and cares nothing for the sheep."*

#168 The Father Loves the Good Shepherd
JN 10.14-18

14 *"I AM the good shepherd; I know my sheep and my sheep know me, 15 just as the Father knows me and I know the Father, and I constantly lay down my life for the sheep.16 I have other sheep that are not of this sheep pen. I must bring them also. They too will listen to my voice, and they will become one flock under one shepherd.*

17 *"The reason my Father loves me is that I lay down my life, only to take it up again.18 No one takes it from me, but I lay it down of my own accord. I have the authority to lay it down, and I have the authority to take it up again. I received this command from my Father."*

#169 The Crowd Divides over Jesus again
JN 10.19-21

19 The Jews who heard these words were again divided. 20 Many of them were saying, "He is demon-possessed and raving mad. Why would anyone listen to him?" 21 But others were saying, "These are not the sayings of a man possessed by a demon. Can a demon open the eyes of the blind?"

CHAPTER 26

Judea: Jesus Trains and Sends Out 70 Workers for Ministry

#170 Jesus Selects and Prepares 70 Workers
LK 10.1-3

1 After this, the Lord appointed seventy others and sent them out, two by two, ahead of him to every town and place where he was about to go. 2 He told them, *"The harvest is plentiful, but the workers are few. Therefore, I command you to ask the Lord of the harvest to send out workers into his harvest field. 3 I command you to go now! I am sending you out like lambs among wolves."*

#171 Jesus Trains the 70 for Ministry
LK 10.4-9

4 *"I command you not to take a purse or bag or sandals, and do not greet anyone on the road. 5 When you enter a house, first say, 'Peace to this house.' 6 If someone who lives in peace is there, your peace will rest on them; if not, it will return to you.*

7 *"I command you to abide there, eating and drinking whatever they give you, for the worker deserves his wages. I command you not to move around from house to house. 8 When you enter a town and are welcomed, eat what is offered to you.*

9 *"I command you to heal the sick who are there and tell them, 'The kingdom of God has come near to you — permanently!'"*

#172 Jesus Prepares the 70 for Handling Rejection
LK 10.10-16 (Similar Text: MT 11.21-24)

10 *"I command that when you enter a town and are not welcomed, you go into its streets and say,* 11 *'We are wiping even the dust of your town from our feet as a warning to you. Yet be certain of this: The kingdom of God has come near you – permanently.'*

12 *"I tell you, it will be more tolerable on the day of judgement for Sodom than for that town.* 13 *Woe to you, Chorazin! Woe to you, Bethsaida! For if the miracles that were performed in you had been performed in Tyre and Sidon, they would have repented long ago, sitting in sackcloth and ashes.* 14 *But it will be more bearable for Tyre and Sidon at the judgment than for you.* 15 *And you, Capernaum, will you be lifted to the heavens? No, you will go down to Hades.*

16 *"Whoever listens to you listens to me; whoever rejects you, rejects me; but whoever rejects me, rejects him who sent me."*

#173 The 70 Return to Jesus with Great Joy
LK 10.17-20

17 The seventy returned with joy and said, "Lord, even the demons continue to submit themselves to us in your name."

18 He replied, *"I was looking at Satan fall like lightning from heaven.* 19 *I have given you permanent authority to continue to trample on snakes and scorpions and to overcome all the power of the enemy; absolutely nothing will ever harm you.* 20 *However, I command you not to keep rejoicing that the spirits keep submitting to you, but continually rejoice that your names are written permanently in heaven."*

#174 Jesus Joyfully Prays and Testifies
LK 10.21-23

21 At that time, Jesus was filled with joy through the Holy Spirit, and he prayed, *"I agree with you in praise, Father – Lord of heaven and earth – because you have hidden these things from the wise and learned and revealed them to little children. Yes, Father, for this was pleasing in your sight.*

22 *All things have been handed over to me by my Father. No one knows who the Son is except the Father, and no one knows who the Father is except the Son and those to whom the Son is choosing to reveal him."*

23 Then, he turned to his disciples and said privately, *"Blessed are the eyes that are seeing what you are seeing. 24 For I tell you that many prophets and kings ached to see what you are seeing, but they did not see it. And they ached to hear what you are hearing, but they did not hear it."*

CHAPTER 27

Judea: Jesus Tours the Region while Training His Followers in Discipleship Basics

---

#175 Jesus Teaches on the Greatest Commandment: Love for God
LK 10.25-28

25 On one occasion, an expert in the law stood up to test Jesus. "Teacher," he asked, "what must I do to inherit eternal life?"

26 *"What stands written in the Law?"* he replied. *"How do you read it?"*

27 He answered, "'Love the Lord your God with all your heart and with all your soul and with all your strength and with all your mind,' and 'Love your neighbor as yourself.'" (Duet. 6.4; Lev. 19.18)

28 Jesus answered, *"You have answered correctly. I command you to continually put this into practice, and you will live."*

#176 Jesus Teaches on Unconditional Love for Others:
"The Good Samaritan"
LK 10.29-37

29 The Law-expert wanted to justify himself, so he asked Jesus, "And who is my neighbor?"

30 Jesus answered, *"A man was traveling down from Jerusalem to Jericho, when he was suddenly attacked by robbers. They stripped him of his clothes, beat him to a pulp, and took off, leaving him half dead. 31 By chance, a priest was going down the same road, and when he took a good look at the man, he passed by on the other side. 32 In the same way, a Levite, when he came to that spot and looked at him, passed by on the other side.*

33 *"But a hated Samaritan, as he traveled, came to where the man was, and when he took a good look at him, he felt deep compassion for him.34 Having gone straight to him, he bandaged his wounds, lavishing oil and wine on them. Then, he put the man on his own donkey, brought him to an inn, and took care of him. 35 The next day, he took out two days' worth of wages and gave them to the innkeeper. 'You must look after him,' he said, 'and when I return, I myself will reimburse you for any extra expense you may have.'*

36 *"Which of these three do you think became a 'neighbor' to the man who fell into the hands of robbers?"*

37 The expert in the law replied, "The one who had mercy on him."

Jesus told him, *"I command you to go out and continue to do likewise."*

#177 Jesus Teaches on Abiding in His Word:
The Example of Mary and Martha
LK 10.38-42

38 As Jesus and his disciples were on their way, he came to a village where a woman named Martha opened her home to him

39 She had a sister called Mary, who was sitting at the Lord's feet, continuing to soak in what he said.

40 But Martha was completely distracted by all the preparations that had to be made. She came to him and asked, "Lord, do you not even care that my sister has left me to do the work all by myself? Tell her to help me!"

41 *"Martha, Martha,"* the Lord answered, *"you are worried and upset about so many things, 42 but few things are really necessary — indeed, only one is necessary. Mary has chosen what is better, and it will not be taken away from her."*

#178 Jesus Teaches His Disciples to Pray
LK 11.1-4 (Repeated Text: MT 6.9-13)

1 One day, Jesus was praying in a certain place. When he finished, one of his disciples said to him, "Lord, teach us to pray just as John taught his disciples."

2 So he said to them, *"When you pray, say,*

> *'Father, cause your name to always be honored as holy,*
> *Cause your sovereign reign to be fully acknowledged by all people.*
> 3 *Continually give us our daily allotment of bread, every day.*
> 4 *Forgive us our sins, for we also forgive everyone who sins against us.*
> *And do not lead us into temptation.'"*

#179 Jesus Teaches about Persistence in Prayer
LK 11.5-13 (Repeated Text: MT 7.7-12)

5 Then, Jesus said to them, *"Suppose you have a friend, and you go to him at midnight and say, 'Friend, lend me three loaves of bread;* 6 *a friend of mine on a journey has come to me, and I have no food to offer him.'*

7 *"Then imagine that the one inside answers, 'Do not bother me. The door is already locked, and my children and I are in bed. I cannot get up and give you anything.'*

8 *"I tell you, even though he will not get up and give you the bread because of friendship, because of your shameless persistence, he will surely get up and give you as much as you need.*

9 *"So I command you to keep on asking, and it will be given to you; keep on seeking, and you will find; keep on knocking, and the door will be opened to you.* 10 *For everyone who keeps on asking receives; the person who keeps on seeking finds; and to the one who keeps on knocking, the door will be opened.*

11 *"Which of you fathers, if your son asks for a fish, will give him a snake instead?* 12 *Or if he asks for an egg, will give him a scorpion?* 13 *Since even though you are evil, you know how to give good gifts to your children, how much more, therefore, will your Father in heaven give the Holy Spirit to those who ask him!"*

CHAPTER 28

Judea: Jesus Warns His Disciples Not to Emulate the Pharisees

---

#180 Miracle #27: The Pharisees Accuse Jesus of Demon Possession the Fourth Time, after he Heals a Demonized Mute Man
LK 11.14-26

14 Jesus was driving out a demon that caused a man to be mute. When the demon left, the man who had been mute spoke, and the crowd was struck with wonder. 15 But some of them said, "He is driving out demons by the power of Beelzebul, the prince of demons." 16 Others tested him by asking for a sign from heaven.

17 Jesus knew their thoughts and said to them, *"Any kingdom divided against itself will be ruined, and a house divided against itself is already starting to fall. 18 If Satan is divided against himself, how can his kingdom stand? I say this because you claim that I drive out demons by the power of Beelzebul. 19 Now if I drive out demons by Beelzebul, by whose power do your followers drive them out? So then, they will be your judges. 20 But because I am driving out demons by the finger of God, then the kingdom of God has overtaken you.*

21 *"When a strong man — fully set up in his armor — actively guards his own house, his possessions are safe and sound. 22 But when someone stronger attacks and overpowers him, he first takes away the armor that the man relied on and then divides*

up his plunder. 23 *Whoever is not with me is against me, and whoever does not gather with me scatters.*

24 *"When an impure spirit comes out of a person, it goes through arid places, seeking peace and rest, but does not find it. Then it says, 'I will return to the house I left.' 25 When it arrives, it finds the house swept clean and put in order. 26 Then, it takes seven other spirits more wicked than itself, and they go in and live there. Then, the final condition of that person is worse than the first."*

#181 The Blessing of Obedience
LK 11.27-28

27 As Jesus was saying these things, a woman in the crowd called out, "Blessed is the mother who gave you birth and blessed is she who nursed you."

28 He replied, *"Rather, blessed are those who continually listen to the word of God and continue obeying it."*

#182 The Sign of Jonah Revisited
LK 11.29-36

29 As the crowds were increasing, Jesus said, *"This is a wicked generation. It is seeking for a sign, but none will be given except the sign of Jonah. 30 Just as Jonah became a sign to the Ninevites, so also will the Son of Man be to this generation. 31 The Queen of the South will rise at the judgment with the people of this generation and condemn them, for she came from the ends of the earth to listen to Solomon's wisdom, but look – something greater than Solomon is here.*

32 *"The people of Nineveh will stand up at the judgment with this generation and condemn it, for they repented at the preaching of Jonah, but look – something greater than Jonah is here.*

33 *"No one lights a lamp and puts it in a place where it will be hidden or under a bowl. Instead, they place it on its lampstand, so that those who come in may see the light. 34 Your vision is the lamp of your body. When your vision is healthy, your whole body also is bright with light. But when your vision is unhealthy, your body also is full of darkness. 35 I command you to continually be sure, then, that the light within you is not darkness. 36 Therefore, if your whole body is full of light, and no part of it dark, it will be just as bright with light as when a lamp is shining its light on you."*

#183 The Hypocrisy of the Pharisees
LK 11.37-41

37 When Jesus had finished speaking, a Pharisee invited Jesus to eat with him, so he went in and reclined at the table. 38 But the Pharisee was shocked because he noticed that Jesus did not first wash before the meal.

39 Then, the Lord said to him, *"Now, then, you Pharisees make a practice of cleaning the outside of the cup and dish, but inside you are filled with enough greed to practice extortion and wickedness. 40 You foolish people! Did not the one who made the outside make the inside also? 41 Look! As for what is inside you, I command you to be generous to the poor, and everything will be clean for you."*

#184 Jesus Declares "Woe" upon the Pharisees and Scribes
LK 11.42-54 (Similar Text: MT 23.13-26)

42 *"Woe to you Pharisees, because you make a practice of giving God a tenth of your mint, rue, and all other kinds of garden herbs, but you continually neglect justice and the love of God. You should have practiced the latter without neglecting the former.*

43 *"Woe to you Pharisees, because you love the most honored seats in the synagogues and receiving respectful greetings in the marketplaces. 44 Woe to you, because you are like unmarked graves, which people freely walk over without even knowing it."*

45 One of the experts in the law answered him, "Teacher, when you say these things, you insult us also."

46 Jesus replied, *"And you experts in the law, woe to you, because you constantly load people down with burdens they can hardly carry, and you will not lift one finger to help them. 47 Woe to you, because you build tombs for the prophets, and it was your ancestors who killed them. 48 So you testify that you approve of what your ancestors did; they killed the prophets, and you build their tombs. 49 Because of this, God in his wisdom said, 'I will send them prophets and apostles, some of whom they will kill and others they will persecute.'*

50 *"Therefore, this generation will be held responsible for the blood of all the prophets that has been shed since the beginning of the world, 51 from the blood of Abel to the blood of Zechariah, who was killed between the altar and the sanctuary. Yes, I tell you, this generation will be held responsible for it all. 52 Woe to you, experts in the law, because you have taken away the key to knowledge. You have not entered, and you have hindered those who were entering."*

53 When Jesus went outside, the Pharisees and the teachers of the law began to oppose him fiercely and besiege him with questions, 54 waiting to catch him in something erroneous he might say.

#185 Jesus Gives a Final Warning about Hypocrisy
LK 12.1-7 (Similar Text: MT 10.27-31)

1 Meanwhile, when a crowd of many thousands had gathered so that they were trampling on one another, Jesus began to speak first to his disciples, saying, *"I command you to constantly guard against the yeast of the Pharisees, which is hypocrisy. 2 There is nothing that a person thinks is safely concealed that will not be disclosed; there is nothing hidden that will not be made known.3 What you have spoken secretly in the dark will be heard clearly in the daylight, and what you have secretly whispered in the ear in the inner rooms will be proclaimed from the rooftops.*

4 *"I command you, my friends, do not be afraid of those who kill the body; after that, they can do no more. 5 But I will show you whom you should fear; I command you all to all fear him who, after your body has been killed, has authority to throw you into hell. Yes, I command you, fear him.*

6 *"Are not five sparrows sold for two pennies? Yet not one of them is forgotten by God. 7 Indeed, the very hairs of your head are all numbered. I command you to stop being afraid; you are worth more than many sparrows."*

CHAPTER 29

Judea: Jesus Addresses More Crucial Discipleship Issues

#186 The Importance of Agreeing with Jesus
LK 12.8-12 (Similar Text: MT 10.19-20)

8 *"I tell you, whoever publicly confesses me before others, the Son of Man will also confess before the angels of God. 9 But whoever disowns me before others will be disowned before the angels of God. 10 And everyone who speaks a word against the Son of Man will be forgiven, but anyone who blasphemes against the Holy Spirit will not be forgiven.*

11 *"When you are brought before synagogues, rulers, and authorities, I command you all not worry about how you will defend yourselves or what you will say, 12 for the Holy Spirit will teach you at that time what you should say."*

#187 The Dangers of Greed
LK 12.13-21

13 Someone in the crowd said to him, "Teacher, I need you to tell my brother to divide the inheritance with me!"

14 Jesus replied, *"Man, who appointed me a judge or an arbiter between you?"* 15 Then, he said to them, *"I command you to always be vigilant! Stay on your guard against all kinds of greed; God's kind of life never consists in an abundance of possessions."*

16 And he told them the parable [of the Rich Fool]: *"The ground of a certain rich man yielded an abundant harvest. 17 He thought to himself, 'What shall I do? I have no place to store my crops.' 18 Then, he said, 'This is what I will do. I will tear down my barns and build bigger ones, and there I will store my surplus grain. 19 And I will say to myself, You have plenty of grain laid up for many years. Take life easy; eat, drink, and be merry.'*

20 *"But God said to him, 'You fool! This very night your life will be demanded from you. Then, who will get what you have prepared for yourself?' 21 This is how it will be with whoever stores up things for themselves but is not rich toward God."*

#188 Living with Confidence in God's Providence
LK 12.22-34 (Similar Text: MT 6.25-32)

22 Then, Jesus said to his disciples, *"Therefore, I command you, do not keep worrying about your life, what you will eat, or about your body and what you will wear. 23 For life is much more than food, and the body more than clothes. 24 I command you all to learn a lesson from the ravens. They do not continually sow or reap, and they have no storeroom or barn, yet God keeps on feeding them. And you are much more valuable than mere birds!*

25 *"Who can add a single hour to your life by non-stop worrying about it? 26 Because you cannot do this very little thing, why do you continue to worry about the rest? 27 I command you all to learn a lesson from the way wild flowers grow. They do not continue to labor or keep spinning all day. Yet I tell you, not even Solomon in all his splendor was dressed as beautifully as one of these flowers. 28 Because that is how God always clothes the grass of the field, which is here today and tomorrow is thrown into the fire; how much more will he clothe you — you of little faith!*

29 *"So I command you all not to keep setting your heart on what you will eat or what you will drink; you must not continue worrying about it. 30 For the pagan world is constantly seeking after all such things, and your Father always knows that you have an ongoing need for them."*

#189 The Joy of Giving
LK 12.31-34; Acts 20.35B

31 L *"I command you all to constantly pursue God's control over your life, and then these other things will be given to you as well. 32 I command you all to stop being*

afraid, little flock, for your Father has been delighted to give you the benefits of His sovereign reign. 33 So I command you all to do things like selling your possessions and giving the proceeds to the poor. I command you all to make purses for yourselves that will never wear out, a treasure in heaven that will never fail, where no thief comes near and no moth destroys. ᴬ*It is a greater blessing to continually give than it is to receive.*

34 ᴸ *"For where your treasure is, there your heart will be also."*

#190 Ready for Jesus' Return
LK 12.35-40

35 *"I command you to be fully dressed, to be ready for service, and to keep your lamps burning 36 like servants who keep waiting for their master to return from a wedding banquet, so that when he comes and knocks, they can immediately open the door for him.*

37 *"Those servants, whose master finds them watching when he comes, will be fully blessed. Truly I tell you, he will dress himself to serve, will have them recline at the table, and he will come and serve them. 38 Those servants whose master finds them ready – even if he comes in the middle of the night or toward daybreak – will be fully blessed.*

39 *"But I command you to understand this: If the owner of the house had known at what hour the thief was coming, he would not have let his house be broken into. 40 You also must be in a state of readiness because the Son of Man will come at an hour when you do not expect him."*

#191 The Parable of the Wise Manager
LK 12.41-48

41 Peter asked, "Lord, are you speaking this parable to us or to everyone?"

42 The Lord answered, *"Who then is the faithful and wise manager, whom the master will put in charge of his servants to give them their food allowance at the proper time? 43 The servant whom the master finds doing so when he returns will be truly blessed. 44 I speak the truth: he will put him in charge of all his possessions.*

45 *"But suppose the servant says to himself, 'My master is taking a long time in coming,' and he then begins to beat the other servants, both men and women, and to make a practice of eating and drinking and becoming drunk. 46 The master of that*

servant will come on a day when he does not expect him and at an hour when the servant is not aware. The master will then cut that servant in half and assign him a place with the unbelievers.

47 *"The servant who knows his master's will and does not prepare or does not do as the master desires will be punished with many blows.* 48 *But the one who does not know and does things deserving of punishment will be beaten with few blows. From everyone who has been given much, much will be demanded; and from the one who has been entrusted with much, much more will be required."*

#192 Jesus Causes Division in the World
LK 12.49-53

49 *"I have come to cast fire on the earth, and how I wish it were already kindled!* 50 *But I have a burial to undergo, and what pressure I remain under until it is completed!* 51 *Are you thinking that I came to bring peace on earth? No, I tell you, but division.*

52 *"From now on there will be five in one family divided against each other, three against two and two against three.* 53 *They will be divided father against son and son against father, mother against daughter and daughter against mother, and mother-in-law against daughter-in-law and daughter-in-law against mother-in-law."* (Ref. Micah 7.6)

#193 Jesus' Warning to Understand the Times
LK 12.54-59

54 Jesus said to the crowd, *"When you see a cloud rising in the west, immediately you say, 'It's going to rain,' and it does.* 55 *And when the south wind blows, you say, 'It's going to be hot,' and it is.* 56 *Hypocrites! You know how to interpret the appearance of the earth and the sky. How is it that you do not know how to interpret this present time?*

57 *"Why do you not judge for yourselves what is right?* 58 *As you are going with your adversary to the magistrate, try hard to be permanently reconciled on the way, or else your adversary may drag you off to the judge, and the judge will turn you over to the officer, and the officer will throw you into prison.* 59 *I tell you, you will not be released until you have paid the last penny."*

#194 Jesus Warns: "Repent or Perish!"
LK 13.1-9

1 Now some were present at that time who were announcing to Jesus the news about the Galileans whose blood Pilate had mixed with their sacrifices. 2 He answered, *"Do you think that these Galileans were worse sinners than all the other Galileans, just because they suffered this kind of death? 3 I tell you, no! But unless all of you practice repentance as your lifestyle, you too, will certainly perish. 4 Or those eighteen who died when the tower in Siloam fell on them — do you think they were more guilty than all the others sinners living in Jerusalem? 5 I tell you, no! But unless all of you practice repentance as your lifestyle, you, too, will certainly perish."*

6 Then, he told the parable [of the Fruitless Fig Tree]: *"A man had planted a fig tree that was growing in his vineyard, and he went to look for fruit on it but did not find any. 7 So he said to the man who took care of the vineyard, 'Look! For three years now I've been coming to look for fruit on this fig tree, and I never find any. Cut it down! Why should it use up the soil?'*

8 *"'Sir,' the man replied, 'leave it alone for one more year, and I will dig around it and fertilize it. 9 If it bears fruit next year, fine! If not, then cut it down.'"*

#195 Miracle 28: Jesus Heals a Crippled Woman on a Sabbath
LK 13.10-17

10 Jesus was teaching in one of the synagogues on a Sabbath, 11 and a woman was there who had been held in bondage by a spirit that made her weak for eighteen years. She was constantly bent over and could never straighten up at all. 12 When Jesus saw her, he called her forward and said to her, *"Woman, you are now set permanently free from your disabling weakness."*

13 Then, he put his hands on her, she was immediately straightened up, and she praised God. 14 Indignant because Jesus had healed on the Sabbath, the synagogue leader said to the people, "There are six days for work. So come and be healed on those days, not on the Sabbath."

15 The Lord answered him, *"You hypocrites! Do each of you not make a practice of untying your ox or donkey from the stall and leading it out to give it water on the Sabbath? 16 Then, should not this woman, a daughter of Abraham, whom Satan*

has kept bound — look at this! — for eighteen years, be set free on the Sabbath day from what bound her?"

17 When he said this, all his opponents were humiliated, and the entire crowd was rejoicing in all the glorious works that he was doing.

#196 Jesus Describes the Kingdom Using Parables
LK 13.18-21 (Repeated Text: MT 13.31-33)

18 Then, Jesus asked, *"What is the kingdom of God like? What can I compare it to? 19 It is like a tiny mustard seed that a man took and planted in his garden. It grew and became a tree, and the birds perched in its branches."*

20 Again, he asked, *"What can I compare the kingdom of God to? 21 It is like yeast that a woman took and mixed into about sixty pounds of flour until it worked its way all through the dough."*

CHAPTER 30

Jesus Ends His Judean Ministry at the Feast of Dedication

(Hanukkah)

#197 Jesus Travels to Jerusalem while Teaching along the Way
LK 13.22-29

22 Then, Jesus went through the towns and villages, teaching as he made his way to Jerusalem. 23 Someone asked him, "Lord, are only a few people going to be saved?"

He said to them, 24 *"I command you to make every ongoing effort to enter through the narrow door because many, I tell you, will try to enter and will not have the ability to do so. 25 Once the owner of the house gets up and closes the door, you will stand outside knocking and pleading, 'Sir, open the door for us.' But he will answer, 'I do not know you or where you come from.'*

26 *"Then you will say, 'We ate and drank with you, and you taught in our streets.' 27 But he will reply, 'I do not know you or where you come from. Away from me, all you evildoers!' 28 There will be weeping there and gnashing of teeth when you see Abraham, Isaac, Jacob, and all the prophets in the kingdom of God, but you yourselves will be thrown out.*

29 *"People will come from east and west and north and south, and they will take their places at the feast in the kingdom of God. 30 Indeed, those who are last who will be first, and first who will be last."*

#198 Jesus' First Lament over Jerusalem
LK 13.31-35 (Repeated Text: MT 23.37-39)

31 At that time, some Pharisees came to Jesus and said to him, "Leave this place and go somewhere else. Herod wants to kill you."

32 Jesus replied, *"Go tell that fox that I will continue driving out demons and healing people today and tomorrow, and on the third day I will reach my goal. 33 In any case, I must press on today and tomorrow and the next day, for surely no prophet can die outside Jerusalem!*

34 *"Jerusalem, Jerusalem, you who kill the prophets and stone those sent to you, how often I have longed to gather your children together, as a hen gathers her chicks under her wings, and you were not willing. 35 Look, your house is left to you desolate. I tell you, you will not see me again until you say, 'Blessed is he who comes in the name of the Lord.'"* (PS. 118.26A)

#199 Jesus' Miracles Prove that He IS the Messiah
JN 10.22-26

22 Then came the Festival of Dedication [Hanukkah] at Jerusalem. It was winter, 23 and Jesus was in the temple courts walking in Solomon's Colonnade. 24 The Jews who were there circled him, saying, "How long will you keep us in this suspense? If you are the Messiah, tell us plainly."

25 Jesus answered, *"I did tell you, but you continue not to believe me. The works that I am doing in my Father's name testify about me, 26 but you do not believe because you are not my sheep."*

#200 Jesus and the Father are One
JN 10.27-30

27 *"My sheep make a practice of listening to my voice; I know them, and they continually follow me. 28 I keep giving them eternal life, and they will never, ever perish; no one will ever snatch them out of my hand. 29 My Father, who has permanently*

given them over to me, is greater than all; no one is able to snatch them out of my Father's hand. 30 I myself and the Father are one."

#201 Another Failed Attempt to Stone Jesus for Blasphemy
JN 10.31-39

31 Again, Jesus' Jewish opponents took rocks in hand to stone him, 32 but Jesus said to them, *"I have shown you many good works from the Father. For which of these are you stoning me?"*

33 They answered, "We are not stoning you for any good work, but for blasphemy, because you, being a mere man, are making yourself out to be God."

34 Jesus answered them, *"Does it not stand written in your Law, 'I myself have said you are gods'? 35 If he called them 'gods,' to whom the word of God came – and Scripture cannot be set aside – 36 what about the one whom the Father dedicated as his very own and sent into the world? Why then do you accuse me of blasphemy because I said, 'I am God's Son'?*

37 *"If I am not doing the works of my Father, do not believe me. 38 But because I am doing the works of my Father, even though you do not believe me, I command you to believe the works, so that you may know and understand that the Father is in me, and I am in the Father."*

39 Again, they were trying to seize him, but he escaped out of their hands.

HIS MINISTRY IN PEREA

The Feast of Dedication ended in late December with another failed attempt to stone Jesus. With the death-plot against him, Jesus could not remain near Jerusalem. It was still not his appointed time to die, for about thirteen weeks remained until Passover. So Jesus crossed the Jordan River to the East and ministered in the Perean region.

Like his three tours of Galilee and his earlier tour of Judea, Jesus made a brief circuit through the region. The teams of two that he had sent out in the Fall had also visited the towns of Perea to prepare for his arrival. While Luke only records one of Jesus' miracles in the region, both Matthew and Mark wrote that Jesus engaged in mass healing ministry in Perea, and large crowds gathered around him. These three months were a fruitful season for Jesus. As John wrote: "Many people believed in Jesus in that place."

Along with effective evangelism, Luke emphasized the in-depth discipleship training that Jesus conducted in these weeks of intense ministry. He spoke some of his most famous parables in Perea, such as "The Prodigal Son."

Jesus continued to prepare his disciples for his death and resurrection, and the new life with him in the Spirit that would follow his ascension.

Chapters 31 to 33 cover the Perean ministry.

CHAPTER 31

Jesus Ministers in Perea after the Feast of Dedication

#202 Jesus Arrives in Perea for a Fruitful Time of Ministry
JN 10.40-42 (MT 19.1B-2; MK 10.1B-2)

40 ᴶThen, Jesus went back across ᴹᵀto the other side of the Jordan ᴶto the place where John had first been immersing in the early days. He remained there, 41 and many people—ᴹᵀlarge crowds—ᴶcame to him and ᴹᵀfollowed him, ᴹand as was his custom, he taught them ᴹᵀand he healed them there.

42 ᴶThey said, "Although John never performed a sign, everything that John said about this man was true." 43 And many people believed in Jesus in that place.

#203 Miracle 29: Jesus Heals again on the Sabbath, a Man with Edema
LK 14.1-6

1 One Sabbath, when Jesus went to share a meal in the house of a prominent Pharisee, he was being carefully observed.

2 Look! There in front of him was a certain man suffering from abnormal swelling of his body. 3 Jesus asked the Pharisees and experts in the law, *"Is it lawful to heal on the Sabbath, or not?"*

4 But they held their silence. So taking hold of the man, he healed him and sent him on his way. 5 Then, he asked them, *"If one of you has a child or an ox that falls into a well on the Sabbath day, will you not immediately pull it out?"*

6 And they were not able to say anything.

#204 Jesus Teaches about the Virtue of Humility
LK 14.7-14

7 Jesus noticed how the guests at a dinner carefully picked out the places of honor at the table for themselves, so he told them this parable. 8 *"When someone invites you to a wedding feast, I command you all not to take the place of honor, for a person more distinguished than you may have been invited. 9 If so, the host who invited both of you will come and say to you, 'Give this person your seat.' Then, thoroughly humiliated, you will have to take the lowliest place.*

10 *"But when you are invited to feast, I command you all to always take the least honored place, so that when your host comes, he will say to you, 'Friend, move up to a better place.' Then, you will be honored in the presence of all the other guests. 11 For all those who make a practice of exalting themselves will be humbled, and those who constantly humble themselves will be exalted."*

12 Then, Jesus said to his host, *"When you give a brunch or dinner, I command you all to stop inviting your friends, your brothers or sisters, your relatives, or your rich neighbors; if you do, they may invite you back and so you will be repaid. 13 But when you give a banquet, I command you to invite the poor, the crippled, the lame, the blind, 14 and you will be blessed. Although they cannot repay you, you will be repaid at the resurrection of the righteous."*

#205 Jesus' Parable of the Great Banquet
LK 14.15-24 (Similar Text: MT 22.1-14)

15 When one of those at the table with him heard this, he said to Jesus, "Blessed is the person who will eat at the feast in the kingdom of God."

16 Jesus replied, *"A certain man was preparing a great banquet and invited many guests. 17 At the time of the banquet, he sent his servant to tell those who had been invited, 'Come now, for everything is ready.' 18 But they all alike began making excuses. The first said, 'I have just bought a field, and I must go and see it. I beg you, please release me from this invitation.' 19 Another said, 'I have just bought five yoke*

of oxen, and I am on my way to try them out. I beg you, please release me from this invitation.' 20 *Still another said, 'I was just married, so I cannot come.'*

21 "*The servant came back and reported this to his master. Then, the owner of the house became angry and ordered his servant, 'I command you to go out quickly into the streets and alleys of the town and bring in the poor, the crippled, the blind, and the lame.'*

22 "*'Sir,' the servant said, 'what you ordered has been done, but there is still room.'* 23 *Then, the master told his servant, 'Go out to the roads and country lanes and compel them to come in, so that my house will be full.* 24 *I tell you, not one of those who were invited will have a taste of my banquet.'*"

#206 Jesus Describes the Cost of Discipleship
LK 14.25-35

25 A large crowd was traveling along with Jesus. Turning around to face them, he said, 26 "*If anyone comes to me and does not hate his father and mother, wife and children, brothers and sisters in comparison to his love for me – yes, even their own life – such a person simply cannot be my disciple.* 27 *And whoever does not continue to carry his cross and keep on following me cannot be my disciple.*

28 "*Say one of you wants to build a tower. Do you not first sit down and estimate the cost to see if you have enough money to complete it?* 29 *For if you lay the foundation and are not able to finish it, everyone who sees it will mock you,* 30 *saying, 'This person began to build and was not able to finish.'*

31 "*Or suppose a king is about to go to war against another king. Does he not first sit down and evaluate whether he is able to gain victory with ten thousand men over the one coming against him with twenty thousand men?* 32 *If he is not able, he will send a delegation while the other is still far away and will ask for the terms of peace.*

33 "*In the same way, those of you who do not give up everything you have cannot be my disciples.* 34 *Salt is good, but if it loses its saltiness, how can it be made salty again?* 35 *It is fit neither for the soil nor for the manure pile; it is thrown out. Whoever has ears to hear, I command him to continue hearing.*"

#207 Jesus' Parable of the Lost, then Found, Sheep
LK 15.1-7 (Repeated Text: MT 18.12-14)

1 Now the tax collectors and "sinful people" were all gathering around to listen carefully to Jesus. 2 But the Pharisees and the teachers of the law

grumbled among themselves, "This man makes a practice of welcoming sinners and sharing meals with them."

3 So Jesus told them this parable: 4 *"Suppose one of you has a hundred sheep and loses one of them. Does he not leave the ninety-nine in the open country and go searching after the lost sheep until he finds it? 5 And because he finds it, he joyfully puts it on his shoulders 6 and carries it home. Then, he calls his friends and neighbors together and says, 'You have to rejoice with me; I have found my sheep that was lost.' 7 I tell you that in the same way there will be more rejoicing in heaven over one sinner who repents than over ninety-nine righteous persons who do not need to repent."*

#208 Jesus' Parable of the Lost, then Found, Coin
LK 15.8-10

8 *"Or suppose a woman has ten silver coins and loses one. Does she not light a lamp, resume sweeping the house, and continue her careful search until she finds it? 9 And because she has found it, she calls her friends and neighbors together and says, 'You must rejoice with me; for I have found my lost coin.' 10 In the same way, I tell you, there is rejoicing in the presence of the angels of God over one repenting sinner."*

#209 Jesus' Parable of the Lost, then Found, Son
LK 15.11-24

11 Jesus continued, *"There was a man who had two sons. 12 The younger one said to his father, 'Father, I demand that you give me my share of the estate.' So he divided his property between the two sons.*

13 *"Not long after that, the younger son gathered up all he had, set off for a distant country, and there, he squandered his wealth in reckless living. 14 After he had spent everything, there was a severe famine in that whole country, and he found himself in constant, severe need. 15 So he hired himself out to a citizen of that country, who sent him out to his fields to feed pigs. 16 He continued longing to fill his stomach with the pods that the pigs were eating, but no one was giving him anything.*

17 *"When he came to his senses, he said, 'How many of my father's hired servants have more than enough food, and here I am starving to death! 18 I will rise up from here and go back to my father and say to him: 'Father, I have sinned against heaven and against you. 19 I am no longer worthy to be treated as your son; please make me like one of your hired servants.' 20 So he rose up and returned to his father.*

"But while he was still a long way off, his father saw him and was filled with compassion for him; he ran up to his son, threw his arms around him and kissed him. 21 The son said to him, 'Father, I have sinned against heaven and against you. I am no longer worthy to be treated as your son —'

22 *"But the father broke in and said to his servants, 'Quick! Bring the finest robe and put it on him. Put a ring on his finger and sandals on his feet. 23 Bring the fattened calf and kill it. We're going to have a feast and celebrate. 24 For this son of mine was dead and is alive again; he was lost but now is found.' So they began to celebrate."*

#210 Jesus' Parable of the Lost Older Brother
LK 15.25-32

25 *"Meanwhile, the older son was working in the field. When he came near the house, he heard music and dancing. 26 So he called one of the servants and asked him what was happening.*

27 *"'Your brother has returned,' the servant replied, 'and your father has killed the fattened calf because he has his son back safe and sound.'*

28 *"The older brother became angry and refused to go in. So his father went out and pleaded with him. 29 But he answered his father, 'Look! All these long years I've been slaving for you and never disobeyed your orders. Yet you never gave me even a young goat so I could celebrate with my friends. 30 But when this son of yours, who has squandered your property with prostitutes comes home, you kill the fattened calf for him!'*

31 *"'My son,' the father said, 'you are always with me, and everything I have is yours. 32 But we had to celebrate and be glad because this brother of yours was dead and is alive again; he was lost and is found.'"*

#211 Jesus' Parable of the Shrewd Manager
LK 16.1-13

1 Jesus told his disciples: *"There was a rich man whose manager was accused of wasting his assets. 2 So he called him in and asked him, 'What is this I am hearing about you? I command you to give me an account of your management because you cannot be manager any longer.'*

3 *"The manager said to himself, 'What am I going to do now? My master is firing me. I am not strong enough to dig, and I am too proud to beg. 4 I know what I will do so that, when I lose my job here, people will welcome me into their homes.' 5 So he*

called in each one of his master's debtors. He asked the first, 'How much do you owe my master?'

6 "'Nine hundred gallons of olive oil,' he replied.

"The manager told him, 'Take your bill, sit down quickly, and make it four hundred and fifty.'

7 "Then, he asked the second, 'And how much do you owe?'

"'A thousand bushels of wheat,' he replied.

"He told him, 'Take your bill and make it eight hundred.'

8 "The master commended the dishonest manager because he had acted shrewdly. For the people of this world are more shrewd in dealing with their own kind than are the people of the light. 9 I tell you, use worldly wealth to gain friends and connections for yourselves in heaven, so that when it is gone, you will be welcomed into eternal dwellings.

13 "No one can serve two masters. Either you will hate the one and love the other, or you will be devoted to the one and despise the other. You cannot serve both God and money."

#212 The Pharisees Respond to Jesus' Parable of the Shrewd Manager
LK 16.14-18

14 The Pharisees, who loved money, heard all this and were mocking Jesus. 15 He said to them, "You are the ones who are presenting yourselves as 'the righteous' in the eyes of others, but God knows your hearts. What people value highly is detestable in God's sight.

16 "The Law and the Prophets were proclaimed until John. Since that time, the good news of the kingdom of God is being preached, and everyone is forcing their way into it. 17 It is easier for heaven and earth to disappear than for the smallest stroke of a pen to drop out of the Law. 18 Anyone who divorces his wife and marries another woman commits adultery, and the man who marries a divorced woman commits adultery.

#213 Jesus' Story of the Rich Man and Lazarus
LK 16.19-31

19 "There was a rich man who was dressed in purple and fine linen and lived in luxury every day. 20 A beggar named Lazarus was laid at his gate; he was covered

with sores 21 and longing to eat the crumbs that fell from the rich man's table. Even the dogs came and licked the man's sores.

22 *"The time came when the beggar died and the angels carried him to Abraham's side. The rich man also died and was buried. 23 In Hades, where the rich man was in torment, he looked up and saw Abraham far away with Lazarus by his side. 24 So he called to him, 'Father Abraham, have mercy on me and send Lazarus to dip the tip of his finger in water and wet my tongue because I am in agony in this fire.'*

25 *"But Abraham replied, 'Son, remember that in your lifetime you received many good things, while Lazarus received bad things, but now he is comforted here and you are in agony. 26 And besides all this, a great chasm has been placed between us, so that those who want to go from here to you cannot, nor can anyone cross over from there to us.'*

27 *"The rich man answered, 'Then, I beg you, father, send Lazarus to my family 28 for I have five brothers. Let him warn them, so that they will not also come to this place of torment.'*

29 *"Abraham replied, 'They have Moses and the Prophets; they should listen to them.'*

30 *"'No, father Abraham,' he said, 'but if someone from the dead goes to them, they will repent.'*

31 *"He said to him, 'If they do not listen to Moses and the Prophets, they will not be persuaded, even if someone rises from the dead.'"*

#214 Jesus Warns His Disciples not to Offend Others
LK 17.1-4 (Similar Texts: MT 18.6-8, 15)

1 Jesus said to his disciples, *"Things that cause people to stumble are bound to come, but woe to the person through whom they come. 2 It would be better for them to be permanently thrown down to the bottom of the sea with a millstone tied around their necks, than to cause one of these little ones to sin. 3 I command you to constantly pay close attention to yourselves.*

4 *"If your brother or sister sins against you, I command you to rebuke them; and if they repent, forgive them. 5 Even if they sin against you seven times in a day, and come back to you seven times saying 'I repent,' I command you to forgive them."*

#215 Jesus Teaches about Faith and Obedience
LK 17.5-10

5 The apostles said to the Lord, "Increase our faith!"

6 He replied, *"If you have faith as tiny as a mustard seed, you can say to this mulberry tree, 'I command you to be uprooted and planted in the sea,' and it will obey you. 7 Suppose one of you has a servant plowing or looking after the sheep. Will he say to the servant when he comes in from the field, 'Come along now and sit down to eat'? 8 Will he not rather say, 'Prepare my supper now, prepare to wait on me while I eat and drink; after that, you may eat and drink'? 9 Will he honor the servant because he did what he was commanded to do?*

10 *"So, when you have done everything you were commanded to do, you also should say, 'We are unworthy servants; we have only completed the work we ought to have done.'"*

CHAPTER 32

Jesus Raises Lazarus from the Dead

#216 Jesus Remains in Perea while Lazarus Dies in Bethany
JN 11.1-6

1 Now a man named Lazarus was sick. He was from Bethany, the village of Mary and her sister, Martha. 2 Mary, whose brother Lazarus was laying sick, was the same one who later poured perfume on the Lord and wiped his feet with her hair. 3 So the sisters sent word to Jesus, "Lord, the one you constantly love is lying sick."

4 Because he heard this, Jesus said, *"This sickness will not result in death. Rather, it is for God's glory, so that God's Son may be glorified through it."*

5 Now Jesus truly loved Martha and her sister and Lazarus. 6 So when he heard that Lazarus was sick, he remained where he was for two more days.

#217 Jesus Informs His Disciples that Lazarus has Died
JN 11.7-16

7 Jesus said to his disciples, *"Let us go back to Judea."*

8 "But Rabbi," they said, "a short while ago the Jews were trying to stone you, and yet you are going back there?"

9 Jesus answered, *"Are there not twelve hours of daylight? Anyone who walks in the daytime will not stumble, for they see by this world's light. 10 When a person walks at night, they will stumble, for they have no light."* 11 After he had said this, he went on to tell them, *"Our friend Lazarus has fallen asleep, but I am going there to wake him up."*

12 His disciples replied, "Lord, because he is only sleeping, he will get better." 13 Jesus had been speaking of his death, but his disciples thought he meant natural sleep.

14 So then he told them plainly, *"Lazarus is dead, 15 and for your sake, I am glad I was not there, so that you may believe. But let us go to him."*

16 Then, Thomas (also known as Didymus) said to the rest of the disciples, "Let us also go that we may die with him."

#218 Jesus Tells Martha, I AM the Resurrection and the Life
JN 11.17-27

17 On his arrival, Jesus discovered that Lazarus had already been lying in the tomb for four days. 18 Bethany was less than two miles from Jerusalem. 19 Many Jews had come to Martha and Mary to comfort them in the loss of their brother. 20 When Martha heard that Jesus was coming, she went out to meet him, but Mary stayed at home.

21 "Lord," Martha said to Jesus, "if you had only been here, my brother would not have died. But you were not here! 22 Yet even now I know that God will give you whatever you ask."

23 Jesus said to her, *"Your brother will rise again."*

24 Martha answered, "I know he will rise again in the resurrection at the last day."

25 Jesus said to her, *"I AM the resurrection and the life. The one who believes in me will have eternal life, even though he dies, 26 and whoever has eternal life by believing in me will never die — forever. Do you believe this?"*

27 "Yes, Lord," she replied, "I have come to permanently believe that you are the Messiah, the Son of God, who is to come into the world."

#219 Jesus Comforts Mary
JN 11.28-37

28 After she had declared her faith, Martha called her sister Mary aside. "The Teacher is here," she said, "and is calling you."

29 When Mary heard this, she got up instantly and went straight to him. 30 Now Jesus had not yet entered the village, but he was still waiting at the place where Martha had met him. 31 Because the Jews had been with Mary in the house, comforting her, they saw how suddenly she got up and went out. They followed her, thinking that she was going to the tomb to mourn there. 32 As Mary reached the place where Jesus was and saw him, she fell at his feet and said, "Lord, if you had been here, my brother would not have died, but you were not here!"

33 When Jesus saw her weeping, and the Jews who had come along with her also weeping, he was deeply grieved in spirit and troubled. 34 *"Where have you laid him?"* he asked.

"Come and see, Lord," they replied.

35 Jesus wept. 36 Then, the Jews said, "Look! How he loved him!" 37 But some of them said, "Could not he who opened the eyes of the blind man have kept this man from dying?"

#220 Miracle 30: Jesus Raises Lazarus from the Dead
JN 11.38-44

38 Jesus was deeply moved once more as he came to the tomb. It was a cave with a stone lying across the entrance. 39 *"Remove the stone,"* he commanded.

"But, Lord," said Martha, the sister of the dead man, "by this time there will be a horrible odor, for it has been four days already."

40 Then, Jesus said, *"Did I not tell you that if you believe, you will see the glory of God?"*

41 So, they removed the stone.

Then, Jesus looked up and said, *"Father, I am thanking you that you have heard me. 42 I, myself knew that you always hear me, but I said this for the benefit of the people who are standing here, so that they may believe that you sent me."*

43 When he had said this, Jesus called out in a loud voice, *"Lazarus, I command you to come out now!"* 44 The dead man came out, his hands and

feet still wrapped with strips of linen and a cloth tied around his face. Jesus commanded them, *"Set him loose and let him go."*

#221 The Sanhedrin Plots to Kill Jesus
JN 11.45-53

45 Therefore, many of the Jews who had come to visit Mary and had seen what Jesus did believed in him. 46 Some of them went to the Pharisees and told them what Jesus had done. 47 Then, the chief priests and the Pharisees called a meeting of the Sanhedrin. "What are we doing?" they asked. "Here is this man performing many signs. 48 If we let him continue like this, everyone will believe in him, and then the Romans will come and take away both our temple and our nation."

49 Then, one of them, named Caiaphas, who was high priest that year, spoke up, "You know nothing at all! 50 Do you not understand that it is more advantageous for you that one man die on behalf of the people than for the whole nation to perish?"

51 He did not say this on his own, but as high priest that year he prophesied that Jesus was about to die for the Jewish nation. 52 And he would die not only for that nation, but also for the scattered children of God, to bring them all together and make them one. 53 So from that day on they made serious plans to take his life.

#222 Jesus Withdraws to Ephraim
JN 11.54

54 Therefore, Jesus no longer moved about openly among the people of Judea. Instead he withdrew to a region near the wilderness to a village called Ephraim. He remained there with his disciples.

CHAPTER 33

Perea: Jesus Makes His Final Journey to Jerusalem

#223 Miracle 31: Jesus Heals Ten Men at a Distance with Just a Word
LK 17.11-19

11 Now on his way to Jerusalem (through Perea), Jesus was traveling along the border between Samaria and Galilee. 12 As he was going into a village, ten men who had leprosy met him. They stood back at a distance 13 and called out in a loud voice, "Jesus, Master, have pity on us!"

14 Because Jesus saw them, he said, "*I command you to go and show yourselves to the priests.*" And while they were going along, they were cleansed. 15 Because he saw he was healed, one of them turned around and came back, giving glory to God in a loud voice. 16 He threw himself down at Jesus' feet as he thanked him, and he was a Samaritan.

17 Jesus questioned him, "*Were not all ten cleansed? Where are the other nine? 18 Has no one returned to give glory to God except this foreigner?*" 19 Then, he said to him, "*I command you to get up and go on your way; your faith has made you permanently whole.*"

#224 The Kingdom of God is within You
LK 17.20-21

20 Once, on being asked by the Pharisees when the kingdom of God would come, Jesus replied, *"The kingdom of God is not coming in a way that can be observed outwardly,* 21 *nor will people say, 'Look! It is here,' or 'There it is,' because the kingdom of God exists within you."*

#225 Yearning for Jesus' Final Coming
LK 17.22-25 (Repeated Text: MT 24.26-28)

23 Then, Jesus said to his disciples, *"The days are coming when you will keep yearning to see one of the days of the Son of Man, but you will not see it. 23 People will say to you, 'Look! There he is!' or 'Here he is!' I command you not to run off in pursuit of them. 24 For as the lightning that flashes and lights up the sky from one horizon to the other, so will the son of man be in his day. 25 But first he must suffer many things and be rejected by this generation."*

#226 Jesus Teaches about His Final Coming
LK 17.26-37 (Repeated Text: MT 24.37-42)

26 *"Just as it was in the days of Noah, so it will also be in the days of the Son of Man. 27 People were eating, drinking, marrying, and being given in marriage up to the day Noah entered the ark. Then, the flood came and destroyed them all. 28 It was just the same way in the days of Lot. People were eating and drinking, buying and selling, planting and building. 29 But the day Lot left Sodom, fire and sulfur rained down from heaven and destroyed them all.*

30 *"It will be just like this on the day the Son of Man is revealed. 31 On that day, no one who is on the housetop, with possessions inside, should go down to get them. Likewise, no one in the field should go back for anything.*

32 *"I command you to keep Lot's wife in mind constantly!*

33 *"Whoever tries to keep his life will lose it, and whoever loses his life will pre-serve it. 34 I tell you, on that night two people will be in one bed; one will be taken and the other left. 35 Two women will be grinding grain together; one will be taken and the other left*

37 *"Where, Lord?"* they asked. He replied, *"Where there is a dead body, there the vultures will gather."*

[Note: The SAGA omits verse 36, as do most ancient manuscripts.]

#227 Jesus' Prayer Parable of the Persistent Widow
LK 18.1-8

1 Then, Jesus told his disciples a parable to show them that they must always continue praying and never give up in discouragement.

2 He said, *"In a certain town there was a judge who neither feared God nor cared what people thought about him. 3 And there was a widow in that town who kept coming to him with the urgent plea, 'I implore you to give me justice against my adversary.' 4 For some time, he refused her. But finally, he said to himself, 'Even though I do not fear God or care what people think, 5 because this widow keeps bothering me, I will see that she receives justice, so that she will not eventually wear me out with her pesky persistence!'"*

6 Then, the Lord said, *"I command you to pay close attention to what the unjust judge is saying. 7 And will not God bring about justice for his chosen ones, who keep crying out to him day and night? Will he keep putting them off? 8 I declare to you, he will see that they get justice, and quickly! However, when the Son of Man comes, will he find faith on the earth?"*

#228 Jesus' Parable of the Pharisee and the Tax Collector
LK 18.9-14

9 Jesus told this parable to some people who were supremely confident of their own righteousness and made a habit of despising everyone else.

10 *"Two men went up to the temple to pray – one a Pharisee and the other a tax collector. 11 The Pharisee stood by himself and prayed, 'God, I thank you that I am not like other people – thieves, unrighteous, adulterers – or even like this tax collector. 12 I make a practice of fasting twice a week and giving a tenth of all I have.'*

13 *"But the tax collector stood at a distance. He would not even look up to heaven, but he was beating his breast and said, 'God, I am pleading with you to have mercy on me, a sinner.'*

14 *"I tell you that this man--the tax collector--rather than the other, went home in a permanent state of being justified before God. For all those who make a practice of exalting themselves will be humbled, and those who are making a practice of humbling themselves will be exalted."*

#229 Jesus Teaches on Divorce for the Third Time
MT 19.3-9 (Parallel Text: MK 10.3-12)

MT3 Some Pharisees came to him in order to test him. They asked, "Is it lawful for a man to divorce his wife for any reason at all?"

4 *"Have you not read,"* he replied, *"that at the beginning the Creator 'made them male and female,' 5 and said, 'for this reason a man will leave his father and mother and be bonded together with his wife, and the two will become one flesh'?* (Gen. 2.24) 6 *Therefore, what God has joined together, I command that people stop separating."*

7 "Why then," they asked, "did Moses command that a man give his wife a certificate of divorce and send her away?"

8 Jesus replied, *"Moses allowed men to divorce their wives because their hearts were so hard. But it was not this way from the beginning."*

MK Later on, in the house the disciples asked him again about this issue. 9 MT *"I tell you that anyone who divorces his wife, except for sexual immorality, and marries another woman is committing adultery. MKAnd if she divorces her husband and marries another man, she also commits adultery."*

#230 Jesus Teaches about Being Single
MT 19.10-12

10 The disciples said to Jesus, "Because this is the situation between a husband and wife, it is better not to marry."

11 Jesus replied, *"Not everyone can accept this word, but only those to whom it has been permanently given. 12 For there are eunuchs who were born that way, and there are eunuchs who have been made eunuchs by others, and there are those who choose to live like eunuchs for the sake of the kingdom of heaven. I command the person who can accept this calling to accept it."*

#231 Jesus Blesses the Children
MK 10.13-16 (Parallel Texts: MT 19.13-15; LK 18.15-17)

13 MPeople were bringing little children Land babies Mto Jesus for him to place his hands on them M and pray for them, Lbut when the disciples saw this, they rebuked them.

14 ^MWhen Jesus saw this, he was indignant. He ^Lcalled the children to him ^Mand said, *"I command you to allow the little children to come to me, and do not keep hindering them, for the kingdom of God belongs to those such as these. 15 Truly I tell you, anyone who will not receive the kingdom of God like a little child will never, ever enter it."*

16 And he took the children in his arms, placed his hands on them, and blessed them. ^{MT}When he had done so, he went on from there.

#232 Jesus and the Rich Young Ruler
MK 10.17-22 (Parallel Texts: MT 19.16-22; LK 18.18-23)

17 As Jesus started on his way, a man ran up to him and fell on his knees before him. "Good teacher," he asked, "what ^{MT}good thing ^Mmust I do to inherit eternal life?"

18 *"Why do you ^{MT}ask me about what is good and ^Mcall me good?"* Jesus replied. *"No one is good except God alone. ^{MT}If you want to enter eternal life, obey the commandments."*

The man inquired, "Which ones?"

19 ^M *"You know the commandments:*

> *'You shall not murder;*
> *You shall not commit adultery;*
> *You shall not steal;*
> *You shall not give false testimony;*
> *You shall not defraud;*
> *Honor your father and mother;* (Ex. 20.12-16; Dt. 5.16-20)
> ^{MT}*And, 'love your neighbor as yourself.'"* (Lev. 19.18)

20 ^M "Teacher," he declared, "all these I have kept since I was a boy. ^{MT}What do I still lack?"

21 ^MJesus looked at him and loved him. *"One thing you lack,"* he said. ^{MT} *"If you want to be perfect, ^MI command you to go, sell everything you have, and give it to the poor, and you will have treasure in heaven. Then, I command you to come and continually follow me."*

22 At this, the man's face fell. He went away sadly because he had great wealth.

#233 The Peril of Riches and the Rewards of Faithfulness
MK 10.23-31 (Parallel Texts: MT 19.23-30; LK 18.24-30)

23 Jesus looked around and said to his disciples, ^{MT} *"I tell you the truth.* ^M*How hard it is for the rich to enter the kingdom of God!"*

24 The disciples were astonished at his words. But Jesus said again, *"Children, how hard it is to enter the kingdom of God! 25 It is easier for a camel to go through the eye of a needle than for someone who is rich to enter the kingdom of God."*

26 ^{MT}When the disciples heard this, ^Mthey were even more befuddled, and they said to each other, "Who then can be saved?"

27 Jesus looked at them and said, *"With man this is impossible, but not with God; all things are eminently possible with God."*

28 Then, Peter spoke up, "We have left everything ^Lwe had ^Mto follow you! ^{MT}What, then, will there be for us?"

Jesus said to them, *"I tell you the truth. At the renewal of all things, when the Son of Man sits on his glorious throne, you who have followed me will also sit on twelve thrones, judging the twelve tribes of Israel. 29 ^MNo one who has left home or fields ^Lor wife ^Mor brothers or sisters or mother or father or children for me and the gospel 30 will fail to receive a hundred times as much in this present age: homes, brothers, sisters, mothers, children and fields — along with persecutions — and in the age to come, eternal life. 31 But many who are first will be last, and the last first."*

#234 Jesus' Parable of the Workers in the Vineyard
MT 20.1-16

1 *"For the kingdom of heaven is like a man who went out first thing in the morning to hire workers for his vineyard. 2 He agreed to pay them a denarius for the day and sent them into his vineyard. 3 At nine in the morning, he went out and saw others standing around in the marketplace. 4 He told them, 'You also go and work in my vineyard, and I will pay you whatever is right.' 5 So they went. He went out again at noon and at three in the afternoon, and he did the same thing. 6 At five in the afternoon, he went out and found still others standing around. He asked them, 'Why have you been standing here all day long doing nothing?'*

7 *"'Because no one has hired us,' they answered. He said to them, 'You also go and work in my vineyard.' 8 When evening came, the owner of the vineyard said to his manager, 'Call the workers and pay them their wages, beginning with those hired last, and moving on to the first.'*

9 *"The workers who were hired at five in the afternoon came and each received a denarius. 10 So when those came who were hired first, they expected to receive more. But each one of them also received a denarius. 11 When they received it, they began to complain against the landowner.*

12 *"'These who were hired last worked only one hour,' they said, 'and you have made them equal to us who have borne all the burden of the work and the heat of the day.'*

13 *"But he answered one of them, 'I am not being unjust to you, friend. Did you not agree to work for a denarius? 14 Take your pay and go. I want to give the one who was hired last the same as I gave you. 15 Do I not have the right to do what I want with my own money? Or are you envious because I am generous?'*

16 *"So the last will be first, and the first will be last."*

#235 Jesus Teaches about His Death the Third Time
MK 10.32-34 (Parallel Texts: MT 20.17-19; LK 18.31-34)

32 ᴹThey were on their way up to Jerusalem. Because Jesus was leading the way out in front, the disciples were in a state of astonishment, while those who followed were afraid. Jesus took the Twelve aside again and began to tell them what was going to happen to him.

33 *"We are going up to Jerusalem, and* ᴸ*everything that stands written by the prophets about the Son of Man will be fulfilled. He* ᴹ*will be* ᴹᵀ*betrayed* ᴹ*by being delivered over to the chief priests and the teachers of the law. They will condemn him to death and will hand him over to the Gentiles, 34 who will mock him, spit on him, flog him, and kill him* ᴹᵀ*by crucifying him.* ᴹ*Three days later, he will rise* ᴹᵀ*to life."*

ᴸThe disciples did not understand any of this. Its meaning was thoroughly hidden from them, so they did not know what he was talking about.

#236 Jesus Commands Servant-Leadership
MT 20.20-28 (Parallel Texts: MK 10.35-45)

20 ᴹᵀThen, the mother of Zebedee's sons came to Jesus with her sons, ᴹJames and John, and they asked a favor of him while kneeling before him. They said, "Teacher, we want you to do for us whatever we ask."

21 ᴹᵀ *"What is it you want* ᴹ*me to do for you?"* he asked.

ᴹᵀShe [they] said, "Command that one of these two sons of mine may sit at your right and the other at your left in your kingdom ᴹglory."

22 Jesus said to them: *"You have no idea what you are asking for yourselves. Are you able to drink the cup that I myself am going to drink, ^Mor be immersed with the immersion I am being immersed with?"*

"We can," they answered.

23 Jesus said to them, *"You will indeed drink from my cup, and be immersed with the immersion I am immersed with, ^{MT} but to sit at my right or left is not for me to grant. These places belong to those for whom they have been permanently prepared by my Father."*

24 When the ten heard about this, they were indignant with the two brothers. 25 Jesus called them together and said, *"You know that ^Mthose who are regarded as ^{MT}the rulers of the Gentiles make a practice of lording it over them, and their high officials constantly exercise authority over them. 26 But I command that it will not be this way among you. Instead, whoever really wants to become great among you must be your servant, 27 and whoever wants to be first among you must be your slave, 28 just as the Son of Man did not come to be served, but to serve, and to give his life as a ransom for many."*

#237 Miracle 32: Jesus Heals Blind Bartimaeus and his Companion
MT 20.29-34 (Parallel Texts: MK 10.46-52; LK 18.35-43)

29 ^MThen, they came to Jericho. ^{MT}As Jesus and his disciples were leaving [the ancient section of] Jericho ^Land approaching [the new part of] Jericho, ^{MT}a large crowd followed them. 30 Two blind men, ^Mincluding Bartimaeus (which means "son of Timaeus"), ^{MT} were sitting by the roadside, ^Mbegging. ^LWhen Bartimaeus heard the crowd going by, he asked what was happening. They told him, "Jesus of Nazareth is passing by."

^{MT}When they heard that Jesus was going by, they shouted out, "Lord ^LJesus, ^{MT}Son of David, have mercy on us."

31 ^MMany ^{MT}in the crowd ^Lwho were leading the way ^{MT}rebuked them and told them to be quiet, but they shouted all the louder, "Lord, Son of David, have mercy on us!"

32 Jesus stopped ^Mand called for them. So they shouted to the blind men, "Take courage! On your feet! He's calling you!"

Tossing his cloak away, Bartimaeus jumped to his feet and came to Jesus, with the other man.

^{MT}Jesus asked, *"What do you want me to do for you two?"*

33 "Lord, ^MRabbi," the blind men ^{MT}answered, "we want our sight."

34 Jesus had compassion on them and touched their eyes. He said, ᴸ *"I command you to receive your sight.* ᴹGo — *your faith has made you permanently whole."*

ᴹᵀImmediately, they received their sight and followed Jesus ᴹalong the road, ᴸpraising God. When all the people saw this, they also praised God.

#238 Jesus Saves Another Tax Collector, Zachaeus
LK 19.1-10

1 Jesus entered [the newer section of] Jericho and was passing through it. 2 Look at this! A man was there by the name of Zachaeus; he was a chief tax collector and was wealthy. 3 He was earnestly seeking to see who Jesus was, but because he was short, he was unable to see over the crowd. 4 So having run ahead, he climbed up a sycamore-fig tree to see him because Jesus was about to pass that way.

5 When Jesus reached that spot, he looked up and said to him, *"Zachaeus, I command you to come down immediately. It is necessary for me to stay at your house today."*

6 So, he hopped down at once and joyfully received him. 7 Because all the people saw this they began to mutter, "He has gone to hang out with a sinful man."

8 But Zachaeus stood up and said to the Lord, "Look, Lord! Right now I am giving half of my possessions to the poor, and if I have cheated anybody out of anything, I will certainly pay back four times the amount."

9 Jesus said to him, *"Today, salvation has come to this house because this man, too, is a son of Abraham."* 10 *For the Son of Man came to seek and to save those who are in a state of destruction."*

#239 Jesus' Parable about Faithfulness until His Final Coming
LK 19.11-28

11 While they were listening to this, he proceeded to tell them a parable because he was near Jerusalem and the people supposed that the kingdom of God was going to appear at once. 12 He said, *"A man of royal birth went to a distant region to have himself appointed king and then to return. 13 So, he called ten of his servants and gave them ten minas [three months of wages]. He commanded them, 'Do business with this money until I come back.'*

14 *"But his subjects hated him and sent a delegation after him to say, 'We do not want this man to rule over us.' 15 He was made king, however, and returned home. Then, he called the servants to whom he had given the money in order to find out what kind of profit they had made with it. 16 The first one came and said, 'Master, your mina has earned ten more.'*

17 *"'Well done, my good servant!' his master replied. 'Because you have been trustworthy in a very small matter, I command that you take authority over ten cities.'*

18 *"The second came and said, 'Master, your mina has earned five more.'*

19 *"His master answered, 'I command that you take authority over five cities.'*

20 *"Then, another servant came and said, 'Master, here is your mina; I have kept it safely laid away in a piece of cloth. 21 I was afraid of you because you are a hard man. You take out what you did not put in and reap what you did not sow.'*

22 *"His master replied, 'I am judging you by your own words, you wicked servant! You knew that I am a hard man, taking out what I did not put in and reaping what I did not sow? 23 Why then did you not put my money on deposit, so that when I came back, I could have collected it with interest?'*

24 *"Then, he said to those standing by, 'I command you to take his mina away from him and give it to the one who has ten minas.'*

25 *"'But Master,' they said, 'he already has ten!'*

26 *"He replied, 'I tell you that to everyone who has, more will be given, but as for the one who has nothing, even what they have will be taken away. 27 But those enemies of mine who did not want me to reign over them, bring them here and kill them in front of me.'"*

28 After Jesus had spoken this, he went walking on ahead—going up to Jerusalem.

#240 Jesus Arrives in Bethany
JN 11.55-12.1, 9-11

55 When the time for the Jewish Passover had drawn near, many went up from the country areas to Jerusalem for their ceremonial cleansing before the Passover. 56 They kept looking for Jesus, and as they stood in the temple courts, they were asking one another, "What do you think? That there is surely no way he will come to the Feast?"

57 For the chief priests and the Pharisees had given standing orders that anyone who found out where Jesus was should inform them, so that they might arrest him.

12.1 Six days before the Passover, Jesus came to Bethany, where Lazarus was--whom Jesus had raised from the dead. 9 A large crowd of Jews found out that Jesus was there and came, not only because of him, but also to see Lazarus, whom he had raised from the dead.

10 So the chief priests also plotted to kill Lazarus 11 because he was the reason many of the Jews were going over to Jesus and were believing in him.

#241 Mary Anoints Jesus in Advance for Burial
JN 12.2-8; MK 14.3-9 (Parallel Text: MT 26.6-13)

MT14.3 While MTJesus Mwas in Bethany, Ja dinner was given in his honor. Martha served, while Lazarus was among those Mreclining at the table Jwith Jesus Min the home of Simon the Leper.

JMary Mcame with an alabaster jar of very expensive perfume, made Jof about a pint Mof pure nard. She shattered the jar and poured the perfume on his head, Jthen anointed Jesus' feet, and wiped his feet with her hair. And the house was filled with the fragrance of the perfume.

4 Some MTof the disciples who were present Mwere saying indignantly to one another, "Why this waste of perfume?"

5 JOne of his disciples, Judas Iscariot, who was later to betray him, complained, "Why was this perfume not sold and given to the poor? It was worth Mmore Jthan a year's wages!" He did not say this because he cared about the poor, but because he was a thief; as keeper of the moneybag, he used to help himself to what was put into it. MAnd they rebuked her harshly.

6 MTAware of this, Jesus said to them, M *"I command you to let her be. Why are you causing trouble for her? She has done a beautiful, good thing to me. 7 You will always have with the poor with you, and you can help them any time you want. But you will not always have me. 8 She did what she could. JIt was intended that she would save this perfume for the day of my burial. MShe poured perfume on my body beforehand to prepare it.*

9 *"Truly I tell you, wherever MTthis Mgospel is proclaimed throughout the world, what she has done will also be spoken of, as a memorial to her."*

Stage VIII of the life of Jesus Christ:

JESUS' FINAL WEEK IN THE FLESH — HIS PASSION

We come at last to the heart of Jesus' life and the gospel — his death, resurrection, ascension, and what followed. Jesus (and all the Scriptures) made these saving works the cornerstone of his ministry.

Consider how the four gospel writers made this emphasis plain. The gospels show us that Jesus ministered for about 40 months, or 1,200 days. The gospel writers collectively devoted 65% of their content to the first 1,193 of those days. Then, they lavished the remaining 35% of their narrative (Saga Chapters 34 to 49) upon just seven days! In other words, Matthew, Mark, Luke, and John gave literally 100 times more attention to the final week of Jesus' life — Passion Week-- than the rest of his ministry.

Even within Passion Week, the gospel writers devoted ten times more content to the 24 hours surrounding Jesus' death than the other days of the week. (Nine Chapters in The Jesus Saga are devoted to these 24 hours.) This means that the day Jesus died received hundreds of times more emphasis in the gospels than the other days of his life.

Thus, the most important part of Jesus' life from the gospel point of view is his death and resurrection. We must pay close attention here. Everything that preceded Passion Week in the Scriptures was intended to prepare us to understand what Jesus accomplished when he died and rose again on our behalf, as the Lord and Savior of the world he created.

Every day of Passion Week built in intensity. We have arranged this Stage to move through each day in progression. Dear reader, open your inner eyes wide, and tune your heart to hear the Spirit's voice in the testimony he inspired about the way Jesus died and rose for you. Our Lord revealed the love, grace, and truth of the Trinity in these events to the very limits of his finite humanity.

Chapters 34 to 47 cover Passion Week.

CHAPTER 34

His Passion

Sunday: Jesus Presents Himself as the Messiah to Israel

#242 A Colt is Prepared for Jesus
MK 11.1-7 (Parallel Texts: MT 21.1-7; LK 19.29-35; JN 12.12)

ᴶThe next day, the huge crowd that had come for the Feast heard that Jesus was on his way to Jerusalem.

MK 11.1 As they approached Jerusalem and came to Bethphage and Bethany at the Mount of Olives, Jesus sent two of his disciples, 2 saying to them, *"I command you to go to the village ahead, and just as you enter it, you will find* ᴹᵀ*a donkey and a colt* ᴹ*tied there* ᴹᵀ*with her, which no one has ever ridden.* ᴹᵀ*You must untie them and bring them here to me.* 3 ᴹ*If anyone asks you, 'Why are you doing this?' say, 'The Lord needs* ᴹᵀ*them* ᴹ*and will send them back here shortly.'"*

ᴹᵀThis took place to fulfill what was spoken through the prophet:

> "Say to Daughter Zion,
> 'See, your king comes to you,
> gentle and riding on a donkey,
> and on a colt, the foal of a donkey.'" (Zech. 9.9)

4 ^MThey went and ^{MT}found the animals as Jesus had directed them; ^Ma colt stood outside in the street, tied at a doorway. As they untied it, 5 some people standing there asked, "What are you doing, untying that colt?" 6 They answered as Jesus had told them, ^Lsaying, "The Lord has need of it." And the people let them go.

7 So, they brought ^{MT} the donkey and ^Mthe colt to Jesus. Throwing their garments on them, ^Lthey set Jesus on the colt, ^Mand he rode.

#243 Jesus is Acclaimed as the Messiah on the Road into Jerusalem
LK 19.36-40; JN 12.16-19 (Parallel Texts: MT 21.8-9; MK 11.8-10; JN 12.13-15)

36 ^LAs he went along, ^{MT}a very large crowd of ^Lpeople were spreading their cloaks on the road, ^Mwhile others ^Jwent out to meet him, ^Mspreading the palm branches they had cut in the fields.

37 When he came near the place where the road goes down the Mount of Olives, the whole crowd of disciples – those ^{MT}who had gone ahead of him and those who had followed – ^Lbegan to praise God joyfully with loud voices for all the miracles they had seen, saying:

^{MT}Hosanna to the Son of David!
Blessed is the coming kingdom of our father, David!
38 ^LBlessed is the king who comes in the name of the Lord! (Ps 118.26)
Peace in heaven and glory in the highest!

39 Some of the Pharisees in the crowd said to Him, "Teacher, you must rebuke your disciples!"

40 He replied, *"I tell you, even if they fall silent, the stones will certainly cry out."*

^JAt first, his disciples did not comprehend all this. It was after Jesus had been glorified that they realized that these things stood written about him and had been done to him. 17 Now, the crowd that was with him when he called Lazarus from the tomb and raised him from the dead was continuing to witness about it. 18 Many more people went out to meet him because they had heard that he had performed this sign, and Lazarus was still alive.

19 So the Pharisees said to one another, "We all see that this is getting us nowhere. Look how the whole world has gone after him!"

#244 Jesus' Second Lament over Jerusalem
LK 19.41-44

41 As he approached Jerusalem and saw the city, he wept over it 42 and said, *"If you had only known on this day the things that would give you real peace, but they have been hidden from your eyes now. 43 The days will come when your enemies will build an embankment against you and encircle you and press in against you on every side. 44 They will smash you to the ground, you and the children within your walls. They will not leave one stone standing on another because you did not recognize the perfect timing of God's arrival to visit you [in me]."*

#245 Jesus Ministers in the Temple
MT 21.10-11, 14-17 (Parallel Text: MK 11.10-11)

10 When Jesus entered Jerusalem, the whole city was stirred up and asked, "Who is this?"

11 The crowds answered, "This is Jesus, the prophet from Nazareth in Galilee."

14 ᴹHe went into the Temple and looked around carefully at everything. ᴹᵀThe blind and the lame came to him, and he healed them there. 15 But when the chief priests and the teachers of the law saw the wonderful things he did, and they saw the children shouting in the temple courts, "Hosanna to the Son of David," they were fuming with indignation.

16 "Are you hearing what these children are saying?" they asked him.

"Yes," replied Jesus, *"have you never read, "From the lips of children and infants you, Lord, have called forth your praise'?"* (Ps. 8.2)

17 And ᴹbecause it was already late, ᴹᵀhe left them and went out of the city to Bethany ᴹwith the Twelve, ᴹᵀwhere he spent the night.

CHAPTER 35

His Passion

Monday: Jesus Takes Authority Over the Temple

#246 Miracle 33: Jesus Takes Authority over a Fruitless Fig Tree
MK 11.12-14 (Parallel Text: MT 21.18-19)

12 ^{MT}Early in the morning ^Mon the next day, as they were leaving Bethany ^{MT}on the way back to the city, ^MJesus was hungry. 13 Seeing a fig tree in leaf in the distance ^{MT}by the road, ^Mhe went to find out if it had any fruit. When he reached it, he found nothing but leaves because it was not the season for figs.

14 Then, he said to the tree, *"I command that no one ever eat fruit from you again."* His disciples heard him say this. ^{MT}The tree immediately withered.

#247 Jesus Takes Authority over the Temple by Cleansing it
MK 11.15-18; LK 19.47-48 (Parallel Texts: MT 21.12-13; LK 19.45-46)

15 On reaching Jerusalem, Jesus entered the temple courts and began driving out those who were buying and selling there. He overturned the tables of

the moneychangers and the benches of those selling doves 16 and would not allow anyone to carry merchandise through the temple courts.

17 And as he taught them, he said, *"Does it not stand written, 'My house will be called a house of prayer for all nations?'* (Is. 56.7) *But you have made it 'a den of robbers.'"* (Jer. 7.11)

18 The chief priests and the teachers of the law heard this and began looking for a way to kill Jesus, for they feared him because the whole crowd was amazed at his teaching. 47 ᴸEvery day he was teaching at the temple. But the chief priests, the teachers of the law, and the leaders among the people were trying to destroy him. 48 Yet they could not find any way to do it because all the people hung on his words.

#248 The Seeking Greeks and Jesus' Death
JN 12.20-26

20 Now there were some Greeks among those who went up to worship at the festival. 21 They came to Philip, who was from Bethsaida in Galilee, with a request. "Sir," they said, "we would like to see Jesus." 22 Philip went to tell Andrew; Andrew and Philip in turn told Jesus.

23 Jesus replied, *"The hour has come for the Son of Man to be glorified. 24 Very truly I tell you, unless a kernel of wheat falls to the ground and dies, it remains only a single seed. But if it dies, it produces many seeds. 25 Anyone who loves his life will lose it, while anyone who hates his life in this world will keep it for eternal life. 26 Whoever serves me must follow me; and where I am, my servant also will be. My Father will honor the one who serves me."*

#249 The Father Speaks from Heaven in Affirmation of His Son's Death
JN 12.27-33

27 *"Now my soul has become deeply troubled, so that it is in a state of turmoil, and what shall I say? 'Father, save me from this hour'? No, it was for this very reason I came to this hour. 28 Father, glorify your name!"*

Then, a voice came from heaven, *"I have both glorified it already, and will certainly glorify it again."*

29 The crowd that was there and heard it said it had thundered; others said an angel had spoken to him in a way he would never forget.

30 Jesus said, *"This voice was for your benefit, not mine. 31 Now is the time for judgment on this world; now the prince of this world will be thrown out. 32 And when I am lifted up from the earth, I will actively draw all people to myself."*

33 He said this to show the kind of death he was going to die.

#250 The Crowd's Response and Jesus' Warning
JN 12.34-36 (Parallel Text: MK 11.19)

34 The crowd spoke up, "We have heard from the Law that the Messiah remains forever, so how can you say, 'The Son of Man must be lifted up'? Who is this 'Son of Man'?"

35 Then, Jesus told them, *"You are going to have the light only a little while longer. I command you to continue walking while you have the light before darkness overcomes you. Whoever walks in the dark does not know where he is going. 36 I command you to believe in the light while you have the light, so that you may become children of light."*

When ᴹevening came ᴶand he had finished speaking, Jesus ᴹand his disciples left the city, ᴶand he hid himself from the Pharisees.

CHAPTER 36

His Passion

Tuesday: Jesus' Final Day of Public Teaching

#251 Jesus Teaches about the Power of Praying in Faith
MK 11.20-25 (Parallel Text: MT 21.20-22)

20 In the morning [on Tuesday], as they went along, they saw the fig tree withered from the roots. 21 ^{MT}When the disciples saw this, they were amazed. They asked, "How did the fig tree wither so quickly?"

^MPeter remembered and said to Jesus, "Rabbi, look! The fig tree you cursed has permanently dried up!"

22 *"I command you all to continue to hold on tenaciously to your faith in God,"* Jesus answered. 23 ^{MT} *"I speak the truth—if you continue to have faith and do not doubt, not only will you do what was done to the fig tree, ^Mbut if anyone says to this mountain, 'I command you to go, throw yourself into the sea,' and does not doubt in their heart, but keeps on believing that what they say will really happen, it will certainly be done for them. 24 Therefore I tell you, whatever you persist in asking for in prayer, I command you to continue believing that you have received it, and it will be yours.*

25 *"And when you stand praying, if you are holding on to anything against any-one, I command you to forgive them, so that your Father in heaven may also forgive your sins."*

#252 Jesus' Authority is Questioned
MK 11.27-33 (Parallel Text: MT 21.23-27; LK 20.1-8)

27 They arrived again in Jerusalem, and while Jesus was walking in the temple courts, ᴸteaching the people and preaching the gospel, ᴹthe chief priests, the teachers of the law, and the elders came to him.

28 "By what authority are you doing these things?" they asked. "And who gave you authority to do this?"

29 Jesus replied, *"I will ᴹᵀalso ask you one question. Answer me, and I will tell you by what authority I am doing these things. 30 John's immersion – ᴹᵀwhere did it come from? ᴹWas it from heaven, or of human origin? I command you to tell me!"*

31 They discussed it among themselves and said, "If we say, 'From heaven,' he will ask, 'Then why did you not believe him?' 32 But if we say, 'Of human origin,' ᴹᵀwe are afraid of the people, ᴸfor they will all stone us. They are convinced that John was a prophet."

33 ᴹSo they answered Jesus, "We do not know."

Jesus said, *"Neither will I tell you by what authority I am doing these things."*

#253 Jesus Rebukes the Leaders with the Parable of Two Sons
MT 21.28-32

28 *"What do you think? There was a man who had two sons. He went to the first and said, 'Son, go and work today in the vineyard.'*

29 *"'I will not,' he answered, but later he changed his mind and went.*

30 *"Then, the father went to the other son and said the same thing. He answered, 'I will, sir,' but he did not go.*

31 *"Which of the two did what his father wanted?"*

"The first," they answered.

Jesus said to them, *"Truly I tell you, the tax collectors and the prostitutes are entering the kingdom of God ahead of you. 32 For John came to you to show you the way of righteousness, and you did not believe him, but the tax collectors and the prostitutes did. Even after you saw this, you refused to repent and believe him."*

#254 Jesus Rebukes the Leaders with the Parable of the Wicked Tenants
MT 21.33-46 (Parallel Texts: MK 12.1-12; LK 20.9-19)

33 *"Listen to another parable: There was a landowner who planted a vineyard. He put a wall around it, dug a winepress in it, and built a watchtower. (Is. 5.2) Then, he rented the vineyard to some farmers and moved to another place. 34 When the harvest time approached, he sent his servants to the tenants to collect* ^M*some of* ^MT*the fruit* ^M*of his vineyard.*

35 *"The tenants seized his servant, beat him, and sent him away empty-handed. Then, he sent another servant to them; they beat this man on the head and treated him shamefully. He sent still another, and they killed this one. 36* ^MT *He sent many others; some they beat, and others they killed.*

37 *"Last of all,* ^M*he had only one left to send to them,* ^MT*his son,* ^M*whom he loved.* ^L*'Perhaps* ^MT*they will respect my son,' he said.*

38 *"But when the tenants saw the son,* ^L*they talked the matter over with each other, and said,* ^MT*'This is the heir. Come, let's kill him and take his inheritance.' 39 So they took him and threw him out of the vineyard and killed him. 40 "Therefore, when the owner of the vineyard comes, what will he do to those tenants?"*

41 "He will bring those wretches to a wretched end," they replied.

^M *"He will come and kill those tenants* ^MT*and he will rent the vineyard to other tenants, who will give him his share of the crop at harvest time."*

^L When the people heard this, they said, "May this never be!"

42 Jesus said to them, *"Have you never read in the Scriptures:*

> *'The stone the builders rejected*
> *has become the cornerstone;*
> *the Lord has done this,*
> *and it is marvelous in our eyes?' (Ps. 118.22-23)*

43 *"Therefore, I tell you that the kingdom of God will be taken away from you and given to a people who will produce its fruit. 44 Anyone who falls on this stone will be broken to pieces; anyone on whom it falls will be crushed."*

45 When the chief priests and the Pharisees heard Jesus' parables, they knew he was talking about them. 46 They looked for a way to arrest him, but they were afraid of the crowd because the people held that he was a prophet.

#255 Jesus Rebukes the Leaders with the Parable of
the Rejected Marriage Banquet
MT 22.1-14 (Similar Text: LK 14.15-24)

1 Jesus spoke to them again in parables, saying, 2 *"The kingdom of heaven is like a king who prepared a wedding banquet for his son. 3 He sent his servants to those who had been invited to the banquet to tell them to come, but they refused to come. 4 Then, he sent some more servants and said, 'Tell those who have been invited that I have prepared my dinner. My oxen and fattened cattle have been butchered, and everything is ready. Come to the wedding banquet.'*

5 *"But they paid no attention and went off—one to his field, another to his business. 6 The rest seized his servants, mistreated them, and killed them. 7 The king was enraged. He sent his army and destroyed those murderers and burned their city. 8 Then, he said to his servants, 'The wedding banquet is ready, but those I invited did not deserve to come. 9 So go to the street corners and invite anyone you can find to the banquet.'*

10 *"The servants went out into the streets and gathered all the people they could find, the bad as well as the good, and the wedding hall was filled with guests. 11 But when the king came in to see the guests, he noticed a man there who was not wearing wedding clothes. 12 He asked, 'How did you get in here without wedding clothes, friend?' The man was speechless.*

13 *"Then, the king told the attendants, 'Tie him hand and foot, and throw him outside, into the darkness, where there will be weeping and gnashing of teeth.'*

14 *"For many are invited, but few are chosen."*

#256 The Pharisees and Herodians Question Jesus
About Paying Imperial Tribute to Caesar
MT 22.15-22 (Parallel Texts: MK 12.13-17; LK 20.20-26)

15 Then the Pharisees went out and laid plans to trap him in his words. 16 [L]Keeping a close watch on him, they sent spies who pretended to be honest. They hoped to catch Jesus in something he said so they might hand him over to the power and the authority of the governor. [MT]They sent their disciples to him along with the Herodians.

"Teacher," they said, "we know that you are a man of integrity and that you [L]speak and teach what is right; [MT]the way of God in accordance with the truth. You aren't swayed by others, because you pay no attention to who they are.

17 "Tell us then, what is your opinion? Is it right to pay the imperial tax to Caesar or not? ^MShould we pay or shouldn't we?"

18 ^LBut Jesus saw through their duplicity ^Mand hypocrisy. ^{MT}Knowing their evil intent, he said,

"You hypocrites, why are you trying to trap me? 19 I command you to show me the coin used for paying the tax. ^M*Bring me a denarius and let me look at it."*

^{MT}They brought him a denarius, 20 and he asked them, *"Whose image is this? And whose inscription?"*

21 "Caesar's," they replied.

Then he said to them, *"So I command you to give back to Caesar what is Caesar's, and to God what is God's."*

22 When they heard this they were amazed ^Mat him. ^LThey were unable to trap him in what he had said there in public. And astonished at his answer, they became silent. ^{MT}So they left him and went away.

#257 The Sadducees Question Jesus about the Resurrection
LK 20.27-39 (Parallel Texts: MT 22.23-33; MK 12.18-27)

27 ^{MT}That same day ^Lsome of the Sadducees, who say there is no resurrection, came to Jesus with a question. 28 "Teacher," they said, "Moses wrote for us that if a man's brother dies and leaves a wife but no children, the man must marry the widow and raise offspring for his brother. (Duet. 25.5)

29 Now, there were seven brothers ^{MT}among us. ^LThe first one married a woman and died childless. 30 The second and 31 then, the third married her, and in the same way the seven died, leaving no children. 32 Finally, the woman died too. 33 Now then, at the resurrection whose wife will she be, because ^{MT}all of ^Lthe seven were married to her?"

34 Jesus replied, ^{MT} *"You are in error because you do not know the Scriptures or the power of God.* ^L*The people of this age marry and are given in marriage. 35 But those who are considered worthy of taking part in the age to come, and in the resurrection from the dead, will neither marry nor be given in marriage, 36 and they can no longer die for they are like the angels. They are God's children because they are children of the resurrection.*

37 *"But* ^{MT}*about the resurrection of the dead, have you never read what God said to you? In the account of the burning bush, even Moses showed that the dead rise, for he says of the Lord,* ^{MT'}*I AM* ^L*the God of Abraham, and the God of Isaac, and the God of Jacob.'*

38 *"He is not the God of the dead, but of the living, for to him, all are alive.* ^M*You are badly mistaken!"*

39 ^MT When the crowd heard this, they were astonished at his teaching. ^L Some of the teachers of the law responded, "Well said, Teacher!"

#258 An Expert in the Law Questions Jesus about the Greatest Commandment
MK 12.28-34A (Parallel Text: MT 22.34-40)

28 ^MT Hearing that Jesus had silenced the Sadducees, the Pharisees congregated. ^M A teacher of the law, ^MT who was an expert in the law, ^M came and heard them debating. Noticing that Jesus had given them a good answer, he ^MT tested him with this question, "Teacher, ^M of all the commandments, which is the most important, ^MT the greatest commandment in the Law?"

29 Jesus answered, ^M *"The most important one is this, 'Hear, O Israel: The Lord our God, the Lord is one. 30 Love the Lord your God with all your heart and with all your soul and with all your mind and with all your strength.'* (Duet. 6.4-5)

31 *"The second is this, 'Love your neighbor as yourself.'* (Lev. 19.18) *There is no commandment greater than these.* ^MT *All the Law and the Prophets hang on these."*

32 ^M "Well said, Teacher," the man replied. "You are right in saying that God is one and there is no other but him. 33 To love him with all your heart, with all your understanding, and with all your strength, and to love your neighbor as yourself is more important than all burnt offerings and sacrifices."

34A When Jesus saw that he had answered wisely, he said to him, *"You are not far from the kingdom of God."*

#259 Jesus Questions the Pharisees about David's Relationship to the Messiah in Ps. 110
MT 22.41-46 (Parallel Texts: MK 12.34B-37; LK 20.40-44)

41 While the Pharisees were gathered together, Jesus asked them, 42 *"What do you think about the Messiah? Whose son is he?"*

"The son of David," they replied.

^M *"How is it that you teachers of the law say that Christ is the son of David?* 43 ^{MT}*How is it, then, that David, speaking by the Spirit, calls him 'Lord'?* ^L*For he says in the Book of Psalms:*

> 44 ^{MT}*The Lord said to my Lord:*
> *'Sit at my right hand*
> *until I put your enemies*
> *under your feet.'* (Ps. 110.1)

45 *"Given that David* ^M*himself* ^{MT}*calls him 'Lord,' how then can he be his son?"*

46 No one could say a word in reply, and from that day on, no one dared to ask him any more questions. ^MBut the large crowd listened to him with delight.

#260 Jesus Warns the People not to Emulate the Pharisees and Scribes
MT 23.1-12 (Parallel Texts: MK 12.38-40; LK 20.45-47)

1 ^LWhile all the people were listening, ^{MT}Jesus said to the crowds and to his disciples, 2 ^L *"I command you all to continually be careful concerning the teachers of the Law.* ^{MT}*The teachers of the law and the Pharisees sit in Moses' seat.* 3 *So you all must be careful to do everything they tell you.*

"But I command you all not to do what they are doing, for they are not practicing what they preach. 4 *They tie up heavy, cumbersome loads and put them on other people's shoulders, but they themselves are not willing to lift a finger to move them.* ^M*They devour widows' houses and make lengthy prayers just for show. Such men will be punished most severely.*

5^{MT} *"Everything they do is done for people to see. They make their phylacteries wide and the tassels on their garments long;* 6 *they adore the place of honor at banquets and the most important seats in the synagogues;* 7 *they* ^M*delight to walk around in flowing robes and* ^{MT}*love to be greeted with respect in the marketplaces and to be called 'Rabbi' by others.*

8 *"But I command you all not to be called 'Rabbi,' for you have one Teacher, and you are all brothers.* 9 *And I command you all not to call anyone on earth 'father,' for you have one Father, and he is in heaven.* 10 *I command you all not to be called 'Leader,' for you have one Leader, the Messiah.* 11 *The greatest among you will be your servant.* 12 *For those who exalt themselves will be humbled, and those who humble themselves will be exalted.*

#261 Jesus' First Four (of Seven) Woes upon the Pharisees and Scribes
MT 23.13-24

13 *"Woe to you, teachers of the law and Pharisees, you hypocrites! You continually shut the door of the kingdom of heaven in people's faces. You yourselves are not entering, nor will you let those enter who are trying to do so.*

[Note: The content of MT 23.14 is not found in the most reliable, earlier manuscripts of Matthew. Thus, we do not include it in this publication.]

15 *"Woe to you, teachers of the law and Pharisees – you hypocrites! You continue traveling over land and sea to win a single convert, and when you have succeeded, you turn them into twice as much a child of hell as you are.*

16 *"Woe to you, blind guides! You say, 'If anyone swears by the temple, it means nothing; but anyone who swears by the gold of the temple is bound by that oath.' 17 You blind fools! Which is greater: the gold or the temple that makes the gold sacred? 18 You also say, 'If anyone swears by the altar, it means nothing; but anyone who swears by the gift on the altar is bound by that oath.' 19 You foolish, blind men! Which is greater-- the gift or the altar that makes the gift holy?*

20 *"Therefore, anyone who swears by the altar is swearing by it and by everything on it. 21 And anyone who swears by the temple is swearing by it and by the one who is dwelling in it. 22 And anyone who swears by heaven is swearing by God's throne and by the one who sits on it.*

23 *"Woe to you, teachers of the law and Pharisees – you hypocrites! You continually give a tenth of your spices: mint, dill, and cumin. But you have neglected the more important matters of the law: justice, mercy, and faithfulness. You should have practiced the latter, without neglecting the former. 24 You blind guides! You strain out a gnat but swallow a camel."*

#262 Jesus' Final Three (of Seven) Woes upon the Pharisees and Scribes
MT 23.25-36

25 *"Woe to you, teachers of the law and Pharisees – you hypocrites! You constantly clean the outside of the cup and dish, but inside they are always full of greed and self-indulgence. 26 Blind Pharisee! I command you all to first clean the inside of the cup and dish, and then the outside also will be clean.*

27 *"Woe to you, teachers of the law and Pharisees – you hypocrites! You are like permanently whitewashed tombs, which shine with beauty on the outside but on the inside are full of the bones of the dead and everything unclean. 28 In the same way,*

on the outside you appear to people as righteous, but on the inside, you are full of hypocrisy and wickedness.

29 *"Woe to you, teachers of the law and Pharisees — you hypocrites! You continue to build tombs for the prophets and decorate the graves of the righteous. 30 And you say, 'If we had lived in the days of our ancestors, we would not have taken part with them in shedding the blood of the prophets.' 31 So you are testifying against yourselves that you are the descendants of those who murdered the prophets. 32 Go ahead, then, I command you all to complete what your ancestors started!*

33 *"You snakes! You brood of vipers! How will you escape being condemned to hell? 34 Therefore, I myself am sending you prophets and sages and teachers. Some of them you will kill and crucify; others you will whip in your synagogues and persecute from town to town. 35 And so upon you will come all the righteous blood that has been shed on earth, from the blood of righteous Abel to the blood of Zechariah son of Berekiah, whom you murdered between the temple and the altar. 36 Truly I tell you, all this will come on this generation."*

#263 Jesus Rejoices in a Poor Widow Who Gave Everything
MK 12.41-44 (Parallel Text: LK 21.1-4)

41 ^MJesus sat down opposite the place where the offerings were kept, and ^Las he looked up, ^Mhe watched ^Lthe rich in ^Mthe crowd putting their money into the temple treasury. Many rich people kept throwing in large amounts. 42 ^LBut he also saw ^Ma poor widow come and toss in two very small copper coins, worth only a few cents.

43 Calling his disciples to him, Jesus said, *"Truly I tell you, this poor widow has put more into the treasury than all the others. 44 They all gave ^Ltheir gifts ^Mout of their wealth; but she, out of her poverty, put in everything — all she had to live on."*

#264 The Apostle John Describes Israel's Rejection of Jesus
JN 12.37-43

37 Even after Jesus had performed so many signs with permanent effects in their presence, they were still refusing to believe in him. 38 This was to fulfill the word of Isaiah the prophet:

"Lord, who has believed our message
and to whom has the arm of the Lord been revealed?" (Is. 53.1)

39 For this reason they were not able to believe because, as Isaiah says elsewhere:

40 "He has permanently blinded their eyes
and hardened their hearts,
so they can neither see with their eyes,
nor understand with their hearts,
nor turn—and I would heal them." (Is. 6.10)

41 Isaiah said this because he saw Jesus' glory and spoke about him.

42 Yet at the same time, many even among the leaders believed in him. But because of the Pharisees, they would not openly acknowledge their faith for fear they would be put out of the synagogue, 43 for they loved human praise more than praise from God.

#265 Jesus' Final Public Message
JN 12.44-50

44 Then, Jesus cried out, *"Whoever continues to believe in me does not believe in me only, but also in the one who sent me. 45 The one who sees me for who I really am is seeing the one who sent me. 46 I have come permanently into the world as light, so that no one who believes in me should make their home in darkness.*

47 *"If anyone hears my words but does not keep them, I myself do not judge that person. For I did not come to judge the world, but to save the world.*

48 *"There is a judge for the one who rejects me and does not accept my words; the very words I have spoken will judge them at the last day. 49 For I did not speak on my own initiative, but the Father who sent me commanded me to say all that I have spoken. 50 I know that his command imparts eternal life. So whatever I say is just what the Father has permanently entrusted me to say."*

#266 Jesus' Public Ministry Ends with His Third Lament over Jerusalem
MT 23.37-39 (Repeated Text: LK 13.31-35)

37 *"Jerusalem, Jerusalem, you who kill the prophets and stone those sent to you, how often I have longed to gather your children together, as a hen gathers her chicks*

under her wings, and you were not willing. 38 Look, your house is left to you desolate. 39 For I tell you, you will not see me again until you say, 'Blessed is he who comes in the name of the Lord.'" (Ps. 118.26A)

CHAPTER 37

His Passion

Tuesday: Jesus' Private Teaching to His Disciples—The "Olivet Discourse"

#267 The Setting and Key Command of the Discourse
MT 24.1-5 (Parallel Texts: MK 13.1-6; LK 21.5-8)

1 ᴹᵀJesus left the temple and was walking away when his disciples came up to him to call his attention to its buildings. ᴸSome of his disciples were discussing how the temple was permanently adorned with beautiful stones and with gifts dedicated to God. ᴹOne of them said to Jesus, "Look, Teacher! What massive stones! What magnificent buildings!"

2 ᴹᵀ *"Do you see all these ᴹgreat buildings?"* he asked. ᴸ *"As for what you see here,* ᴹᵀ*truly I tell you,* ᴸ*the time will come when* ᴹᵀ*not one stone here will be left on another; every one will be thrown down."*

3 As Jesus was sitting on the Mount of Olives, ᴹopposite the temple, Peter, James, John, and Andrew ᴹᵀcame to him privately. "Tell us," they said, "when will this happen, and what will be the sign of your coming and of the end of the age?"

4 Jesus answered, *"I command you all to continue watching out that no one deceives you. 5 For many will come in my name, claiming, 'I am the Messiah,' and* ^L*'the time is near,'* ^{MT}*and will deceive many.* ^L*I command you all not to follow after them."*

#268 Jesus Prophesies the Destruction of Jerusalem
MT 24.15-22 (Parallel Texts: MK 13.14-20; LK 21.20-24)

^L *"When you see Jerusalem being surrounded by armies, you will know that its desolation is near.*

15 ^{MT}*"So when you see standing in the holy place 'the abomination that causes desolation,' spoken of through the prophet Daniel (Dan 9.27, 11.31, 12.11) — let the reader understand — 16 then, I command those who are in Judea to flee to the mountains,* ^L*those in the city get out, and those in the country not to enter the city.* 17 ^{MT}*I command no one on the housetop to go down to take anything out of the house. 18 Let no one in the field go back to get their cloak.* ^L*For this is the time of punishment in fulfillment of all that has been written.*

19 ^{MT}*"How dreadful it will be in those days for pregnant women and nursing mothers! 20 Pray that your flight will not take place in winter or on the Sabbath. 21 For then there will be great distress, unequaled from the beginning,* ^M*when God created the world* ^{MT}*until now — and never to be equaled again. 22 If those days had not been cut short, no one would survive, but for the sake of the elect, those days will be shortened.*

^L *"There will be great distress in the land and wrath against this people. They will fall by the sword and will be taken as prisoners to all the nations. Jerusalem will be trampled underfoot by the Gentiles until the times of the Gentiles are fulfilled."*

#269 Four of the Conditions Preceding Jesus' Final Coming
MT 24.6-14 (Parallel Texts: MK 13.7-13; LK 21.9-19)

"Birth Pains"

6 *"You will hear of wars and rumors of wars, but see to it that you are not alarmed* ^L*or frightened.* ^{MT}*Such things must happen* ^L*first,* ^{MT}*but the end is still to come. 7 Nation will rise against nation, and kingdom against kingdom. There will be famines and* ^L*great* ^{MT}*earthquakes* ^L*and pestilences* ^{MT}*in various places,* ^L*and fearful events and great signs from heaven. 8* ^{MT}*All these are the beginning of 'birth pains.'"*

Universal, World-wide Persecution

9 ᴸ *"But before all of this, they will lay hands on you,* ᴹᵀ*and you will be delivered over to be persecuted and put to death, and you will be hated by all nations because of me.* ᴹ*You will be handed over to the local councils and flogged in the synagogues.* ᴸ*They will put you in prison, and you will be brought before kings and governors, and all on account of me. This will result in your being witnesses to them.*

"But I command you all to make up your mind not to worry beforehand how you will defend yourselves. For I will give you words and wisdom that none of your adversaries will be able to resist, ᴹ*for it is not you but the Holy Spirit speaking."*

Apostasy, False Prophets, and Deception

10 ᴹᵀ *"At that time, many will turn away from the faith and will betray and hate each other.* ᴸ*You will be betrayed even by parents, brothers, relatives, and friends, and they will put some of you to death. All men will hate you because of me. But not a hair of your head will perish. By standing firm you will gain life.*

11 ᴹᵀ *"Many false prophets will appear and deceive many people. 12 Because of the increase of wickedness, the love of most will grow cold, 13 but the one who stands firm to the end will be saved."*

Gospel will First Reach all Nations

14 *"And this gospel of the kingdom will* ᴹ*first* ᴹᵀ*be preached in the whole world as a testimony to all nations, and then the end will come."*

#270 Three More of the Conditions Preceding Jesus' Final Coming
MT 24.23-31 (Parallel Texts: MK 13.21-27; LK 21.25-27)

False Christs, including the Anti-Christ

23 *"At that time, if anyone says to you, 'Look, here is the Messiah!' or, 'There he is!' – do not believe it. 24 For false messiahs and false prophets will appear and perform great signs and wonders to deceive, if possible, even the elect. 25* ᴹ*I command you to remain on your guard.* ᴹᵀ*See, I have told you ahead of time.*

26 *"So if anyone tells you, 'There he is, out in the wilderness,' do not go out, or, 'Here he is, in the inner rooms,' do not believe it. 27 For as lightning that comes*

from the east is visible even in the west, so will be the coming of the Son of Man. 28 Wherever there is a carcass, vultures will gather.

Signs and Distress in the Stars and Sky

29 *"Immediately after the distress of those days*
'the sun will be darkened,
and the moon will not give its light;
the stars will fall from the sky,
and the heavenly bodies will be shaken.'

ᴸ *"Nations on the earth will be in anguish and perplexity at the roaring and toss-ing of the sea. Men will faint from terror and be apprehensive of what is coming on the world, for the heavenly bodies will be shaken.*

The "Sign of the Son of Man" Visible in the Sky Throughout the World

30 ᴹᵀ *"Then, the sign of the Son of Man in heaven will appear. And then, all the peoples of the earth will mourn when they see the Son of Man coming on the clouds of heaven with power and great glory. 31 And he will send his angels with a loud trumpet call, and they will gather his elect from the four winds, from one end of the heavens to the other."*

#271 Only the Father Knows the Day or Hour, so Jesus Commands Vigilance
MT 24.32-44 (Parallel Texts: MK 13.28-32; LK 21.28-33)

32 ᴹᵀ *"Now learn this lesson from the fig tree ᴸand all the trees. ᴹᵀAs soon as its twigs become tender and its leaves come out, you ᴸcan see for yourselves ᴹᵀand know that summer is near. 33 Even so, when you see all these things, you know that ᴸthe kingdom of God ᴹᵀis near, right at the door. ᴸWhen these things begin to take place, I command you to stand up and lift up your heads because your redemption is drawing near.*

34 ᴹᵀ *"Truly I tell you, this generation will certainly not pass away until all these things have happened. 35 Heaven and earth will pass away, but my words will never pass away. 36 But about that day or hour no one knows, not even the angels in heaven, nor the Son, but only the Father.*

37 *"As it was in the days of Noah, so it will be at the coming of the Son of Man.
38 For in the days before the flood, people were eating and drinking, marrying and
giving in marriage, up to the day Noah entered the ark; 39 and they knew nothing
about what would happen until the flood came and took them all away. That is how it
will be at the coming of the Son of Man. 40 Two men will be in the field; one will be
taken and the other left. 41 Two women will be grinding with a hand mill; one will be
taken and the other left.*

42 *"Therefore, I command you all to keep watch because you do not know on what
day your Lord will come. 43 But understand this: If the owner of the house had known
at what time of night the thief was coming, he would have kept watch and would not
have let his house be pillaged. 44 So, you also must be ready because the Son of Man
will come at an hour when you do not expect him."*

#272 Jesus Commands Readiness for His Coming Using Two Parables
MT 24.45-51; MK 13.33-37; LK 21.34-36

MT 24.45 *"Who then is the faithful and wise servant whom the master has put in
charge of the servants in his household to give them their food at the proper time? 46
It will be good for that servant whose master finds him doing so when he returns. 47
Truly I tell you, he will put him in charge of all his possessions.*

48 *"But suppose that servant is wicked and says to himself, 'My master is staying away a long time,' 49 and he then begins to beat his fellow servants and to eat
and drink with drunkards. 50 The master of that servant will come on a day when the
servant does not expect him and at an hour of which the servant is not aware. 51 He
will cut him to pieces and assign him a place with the hypocrites, where there will be
weeping and gnashing of teeth.*

MK 13.33 *"I command you all to be on guard! Be alert! You do not know when
that time will come. 34 It's like a man going away: He leaves his house and puts his
servants in charge, each with their assigned task, and tells the one at the door to keep
watch.*

35 *"Therefore, I command you all to keep watch because you do not know when
the owner of the house will come back, whether in the evening, or at midnight, or when
the rooster crows, or at dawn. 36 If he comes suddenly, do not let him find you sleeping. What I say to you, I say to everyone: 'Watch!'*

LK 21.34 *"I command you all to be careful, or your hearts will be weighed down with
carousing, drunkenness, and the anxieties of life, and that day will close on you suddenly
like a trap. 35 For it will come for all those who live on the face of the whole earth. 36 I*

command you all to always be on the watch, and to pray that you may be able to escape all that is about to happen, and that you may be able to stand before the Son of Man."

#273 Jesus Commands Readiness for His Coming:
The Parable of "The Ten Virgins"
MT 25.1-13

1 *"At that time, the kingdom of heaven will be like ten virgins who took their lamps and went out to meet the bridegroom. 2 Five of them were foolish, and five were wise. 3 The foolish ones took their lamps but did not take any oil with them. 4 The wise ones, however, took oil in jars along with their lamps. 5 The bridegroom was a long time in coming, and they all became drowsy and fell asleep.*

6 *"At midnight the cry rang out, 'Here's the bridegroom! Come out to meet him!'*

7 *"Then, all the virgins woke up and trimmed their lamps. 8 The foolish ones said to the wise, 'Give us some of your oil; our lamps are going out.'*

9 *"'No way,' they replied, 'because there may not be enough for both us and you. Instead, go to those who sell oil and buy some for yourselves.'*

10 *"But while they were on their way to buy the oil, the bridegroom arrived. The virgins who were ready went in with him to the wedding banquet. And the door was shut. 11 Later, the others also came. 'Lord, Lord,' they said, 'open the door for us!'*

12 *"But he replied, 'Truly I tell you, I do not know you.'*

13 *"Therefore, I command you all to remain on guard because you do not know the day or the hour."*

#274 Jesus Commands Readiness for His Coming:
The Parable of "The Talents"
MT 25.14-30 (Similar Text: LK 19.12-27)

14 *"Again, it will be like a man going on a journey, who called his servants and entrusted his wealth to them. 15 To one, he gave five talents worth of wealth; to another, two talents; and to another, one talent — each was given according to his own ability. Then, the man left on his journey.*

16 *"The man who had received five talents went at once and put his money to work, gaining five talents more. 17 So also did the one with two talents, who gained two more. 18 But the man who had received one talent went off, dug a hole in the ground and hid his master's money safely away.*

19 *"After a long time, the master of those servants returned and settled accounts with them. 20 The man who had received five talents brought the other five. 'Master,' he said, 'you entrusted me with five talents. See, I have gained five more.'*

21 *"His master replied, 'Well done, good and faithful servant! You have proved faithful with a few things; I will put you in charge of many things. Come and share in your master's joy!'*

22 *"The man with two talents also came. 'Master,' he said, 'you entrusted me with two talents; see, I have gained two more.'*

23 *"His master replied, 'Well done, good and faithful servant! You have proved faithful with a few things; I will put you in charge of many things. Come and share in your master's joy!'*

24 *"Then, the man who had received one bag of gold came. 'Master,' he said, 'I knew that you are a tough man, harvesting where you have not sown and gathering where you have not scattered seed. 25 So, out of my fear I went out and hid your gold safely in the ground. See, here is what belongs to you.*

26 *"His master replied, 'You wicked, lazy servant! So you knew that I harvest where I have not sown and gather where I have not scattered seed? 27 Well then, you should have put my money on deposit with the moneylenders, so that when I returned I would have received it back with some earnings.*

28 *"So the man took the talent from him and gave it to the one who has ten talents. 29 For whoever has produced earnings will be given more, and they will have an abundance. Whoever does not have any earnings, even what they have will be taken from them. 30 And he threw the worthless servant outside, into the darkness, where there will be weeping and gnashing of teeth."*

#275 Jesus Commands Readiness for His Coming: The Final Judgment
MT 25.31-46

31 *"When the Son of Man comes in his glory and all the angels with him, then he will sit on his glorious throne. 32 All the nations will be assembled before him, and he will separate the people one from another, as a shepherd separates the sheep from the goats. 33 He will put the sheep on his right and the goats on his left.*

34 *"Then, the King will say to those on his right, 'Come, you who are blessed by my Father; take your inheritance, the kingdom prepared for you from the creation of the world. 35 For I was hungry and you gave me something to eat, I was thirsty and you gave me something to drink, I was a stranger and you invited me in, 36 I needed*

clothes and you clothed me, I was sick and you looked after me, and I was in prison and you came to visit me.'

37 *"Then, the righteous will answer him, 'Lord, when did we see you hungry and feed you, or thirsty and give you something to drink? 38 When did we see you a stranger and invite you in, or needing clothes and clothe you? 39 When did we see you sick or in prison and go to visit you?'*

40 *"The King will reply, 'Truly I tell you, whatever you did for one of the least of these brothers and sisters of mine, you did personally for me.'*

41 *"Then, he will say to those on his left, 'Depart from me, you who are cursed, into the eternal fire prepared for the devil and his angels. 42 For I was hungry and you gave me nothing to eat, I was thirsty and you gave me nothing to drink, 43 I was a stranger and you did not invite me in, I needed clothes and you did not clothe me, and I was sick and in prison and you did not look after me.'*

44 *"They also will answer, 'Lord, when did we see you hungry or thirsty or a stranger or needing clothes or sick or in prison, and did not help you?'*

45 *"He will reply, 'Truly I tell you, whatever you did not do for one of the least of these, you did not do personally for me.'*

46 *"Then, they will go away to eternal punishment, while the righteous enjoy eternal life."*

#276 Tuesday Ends with the Sanhedrin's Final Rejection of Jesus
MT 26.1-5 (Parallel Texts: MK 14.1-2; LK 22.1-2)

1 ᴸNow the Feast of Unleavened Bread, called Passover, was approaching. ᴹᵀWhen Jesus had finished speaking all these words, he said to his disciples, 2 *"As you know, the Passover is two days away, and the Son of Man will be delivered over to be crucified."*

3 Then, the chief priests and the elders of the people assembled in the palace of the high priest, whose name was Caiaphas. 4 ᴸThey were looking for some way to be rid of Jesus, ᴹᵀso they plotted among themselves to arrest Jesus secretly and to kill him.

5 They said, "But not during the festival, or there may be a riot among the people."

CHAPTER 38

His Passion

Wednesday: Day of Betrayal and Conspiracy

#277 Judas Iscariot Conspires to Betray Jesus
LK 22.3-6 (Parallel Texts: MT 26.14-16; MK 14.10-11)

3 Then, Satan entered Judas, called Iscariot, one of the Twelve. 4 And Judas went to the chief priests and the officers of the temple guard and discussed with them how he might betray Jesus ᴹto them.

ᴹᵀHe asked, "What are you willing to give me if I hand him over to you?"

5 ᴸThey were delighted and agreed to give him money. ᴹᵀSo they counted out thirty silver coins for him. 6 ᴸHe consented, and ᴹᵀfrom then on, Judas ᴸwatched for an opportunity to hand Jesus over to them when no crowd was present.

CHAPTER 39

His Passion

Thursday: The Last Supper

#278 Jesus' Disciples Prepare the Supper for Him
MK 14.12-16 (Parallel Texts: MT 26.17-19; LK 22.7-13)

12 On the first day of the Festival of Unleavened Bread, when it was customary to sacrifice the Passover lamb, Jesus' disciples asked him, "Where do you want us to go and make preparations for you to eat the Passover?"

13 So, he sent two of his disciples, [L]Peter and John, [M]commanding them, *"Go into the city, and a man carrying a jar of water will meet you. Follow him [L]to the house that he enters.* 14 [M]*Say to the owner of the house he enters, 'The Teacher says,* [MT]*My appointed time is near. I am going to celebrate the Passover with my disciples at your house.* [M]*Where is my guest room, where I may eat the Passover with my disciples?'*

15 *"He will show you a large room upstairs, furnished and ready. I command you to make preparations for us there."*

16 The disciples left, went into the city, and found things just as Jesus had told them. So, they prepared the Passover.

#279 A Supper Argument about Who Is the Greatest
LK 22.14-16; 24-30 (Parallel Texts: MT 26.20; MK 14.17)
(Similar Text: MK 10.35-45)

14 ᴹᴷAs evening came, Jesus arrived with the Twelve. ᴸAt suppertime, Jesus and his apostles reclined at the table. 15 He said to them, *"I have eagerly desired to eat this Passover with you before I suffer. 16 For I tell you, I will not eat it again until it finds fulfillment in the kingdom of God."*

24 A dispute flared up among them as to which of them was considered to be greatest. 25 Jesus said to them, *"The kings of the Gentiles lord it over them, and those who exercise authority over them call themselves 'Benefactors.' 26 But I command you all not to be like that. Instead, the greatest among you should be like the youngest, and the one who rules like the one who serves. 27 For who is greater-- the one who is at the table or the one who serves? Is it not the one who is at the table? But I am among you as one who serves.*

28 *"You are those who have stood by me in my trials. 29 And I confer on you a kingdom — just as my Father conferred one on me — 30 so that you may eat and drink at my table in my kingdom and sit on thrones, judging the twelve tribes of Israel."*

#280 Jesus Washes His Disciple's Feet
JN 13.1-11

1 It was just before they ate the Passover Meal. Because Jesus knew that the hour had come for him to leave this world and go to the Father, having loved his own who were in the world, he loved them to the very end. 2 The evening meal had begun, and the devil had already prompted Judas, the son of Simon Iscariot, to make his final decision to betray Jesus.

3 Because Jesus knew that the Father had given all things into his hands, and he knew that he had come from God and was returning to God, 4 he rose up from the meal, took off his outer clothing, and wrapped a towel around his waist. 5 After that, he poured water into a basin and began washing his disciples' feet and drying them with the towel that was wrapped around him.

6 He came to Simon Peter, who said to him, "Lord, are you going to wash my feet?"

7 Jesus replied, *"You do not realize what I myself am doing now, but later you will understand."*

8 "No," said Peter, "there's no way you will ever wash my feet."

Jesus answered, *"Unless I wash you, you have no fellowship with me."*

9 "Then, Lord," Simon Peter replied, "not just my feet, but my hands and my head as well!"

10 Jesus answered, *"Those who have washed are still clean and need only to wash their feet; their whole body is clean. And all of you are clean, although not every one of you."*

11 For he knew who was going to betray him, and that was why he said not everyone was clean.

#281 Jesus Explains and Applies His Foot Washing Lesson
JN 13.12-20

12 When Jesus had finished washing the disciples' feet, he put on his clothes and returned to his place. *"Do you understand what I have done for you?"* he asked them. 13 *"You call me 'Teacher' and 'Lord,' and it is well that you do so, for so I am.*

14 *"Now that I, myself, your Lord and Teacher, have washed your feet, you also should continue to wash one another's feet. 15 I have given you an example that you should continually emulate, doing for others as I have done for you. 16 Very truly I tell you, no servant is greater than his master is, nor is a messenger greater than the one who sent him is. 17 Because you know these things, you will be truly blessed if you keep doing them.*

18 *"I am not referring to all of you; I know those I have chosen. But this is to fulfill this passage of Scripture: 'He who shared my bread has turned against me.'* (Ps. 41.9)

19 *"I am telling you now before it happens, so that when it does happen you will believe that I AM who I am. 20 Very truly I tell you, whoever accepts anyone I send accepts me, and whoever accepts me accepts the one who sent me."*

#282 Jesus Identifies Judas as the Betrayer
JN 13.21-30 (Parallel Texts: MT 26.21-25; MK 14.18-21; LK 22.21-23)

21 [J]After he had said this, [M]while they were reclining at the table eating, [J]Jesus was troubled in spirit and testified, *"Very truly I tell you, one of you is going to betray me —* [M]*one who is eating with me."*

They began to feel deep sorrow, and one by one, they said, "Surely it is not I?"

"It is one of the twelve," Jesus replied. ^{MT}"*One who has dipped his hand into the bowl with me will betray me. The Son of Man will go just as it stands written about him. But woe to that man who betrays the Son of Man. It would have been better for him not to have been born.*"

22 ^JHis disciples stared at one another, at a loss to know which of them he meant. ^LThey began to question among themselves which of them it might be who would do this.

23 ^JOne of them, the disciple whom Jesus loved, was reclining next to him. 24 Simon Peter motioned to this disciple and said, "Ask him which one he means."

25 Leaning back against Jesus' chest, he asked him, "Lord, who is it?"

26 Jesus answered, "*It is the one to whom I will give this piece of bread after I have dipped it in the dish.*" Then, dipping the piece of bread, he gave it to Judas, the son of Simon Iscariot.

^{MT}Judas, the one who would betray him, said, "Surely not I, Rabbi?"

Jesus answered, "*Yes, it is you.*"

27 ^JAs soon as Judas took the bread, Satan entered into him. So, Jesus told him, "*What you are about to do, I command you to do quickly.*"

28 But no one at the meal understood why Jesus said this to him. 29 Because Judas had responsibility for the money, some thought Jesus was telling him to buy what was needed for the festival or to give something to the poor. 30 As soon as Judas had eaten the bread, he went out. And it was night.

#283 Jesus' New Love Command
JN 13.31-32, 34-35

^J31 When Judas was gone, Jesus said, "*Now the Son of Man is glorified and God is glorified in him. 32 Because God is glorified in him, God will glorify the Son in himself, and will glorify him at once.*

34 *I give you a new command: You must continue loving one another. As I have loved you, so I command you to continually love one another. 35 If you continue loving one another, everyone will know that you are my disciples because of this.*"

#284 Jesus Predicts Peter's Threefold Denial
MT 26.31-35 (Parallel Texts: MK 14.27-31; LK 22.31-34; JN 13.33, 36-38)

JN 13.33 ¹ *"My children, I will be with you only a little longer. You will look for me, and just as I told the Jews, so I tell you now: where I am going, you cannot come.*

36 Simon Peter asked him, "Lord, where are you going?"

Jesus replied, *"Where I am going, you cannot follow now, but you will follow later."*

37 Peter asked, "Lord, why can I not follow you now? I will lay down my life for you."

MT 26.31 ᴹᵀThen, Jesus told them, *"This very night you will all fall away on account of me, for it is written: 'I will strike the shepherd, and the sheep of the flock will be scattered.' (Zech. 13.7)*

32 *"But after I have risen, I will go ahead of you into Galilee."*

33 Peter replied, "Even if all fall away on account of you, I never will."

ᴸ *"Simon, Simon, Satan has asked to sift all of you as wheat. But I have prayed for you, Simon, that your faith may not fail. And when you have turned back, I command you to strengthen your brothers."*

But he replied, "Lord, I am ready to go with you to prison and to death."

ᴶJesus answered, *"Will you really lay down your life for me?"* 34 ᴹᵀ*Truly I tell you, this very night, before the rooster crows* ᴹ*twice--* ᴹᵀ*you will* ᴸ*deny me by* ᴹᵀ*disowning me three times."*

35 But Peter declared, "Even if I have to die with you, I will never disown you." And all the other disciples said the same.

#285 Jesus Declares that Isaiah 53 was Written about Himself
LK 22.35-38

35 Then, Jesus asked them, *"When I sent you out without wallet, bag, or sandals, did you lack anything?"*

"Nothing," they answered.

36 He said to them, *"But now if you have a wallet, I command you to take it, and also a bag; and if you do not have a sword, sell your cloak and buy one. 37 It stands written: 'And he was numbered with the transgressors' (Isaiah 53.12); and I tell you that this must be fulfilled in me. Yes, what stands written about me is reaching its fulfillment."*

38 The disciples said, "See, Lord, here are two swords."

"That's enough!" he replied.

#286 Jesus Institutes 'The Lord's Supper'
MK 14.22-25 (Parallel Texts: MT 26.26-29; LK 22.17-20; I Cor. 11.23-26)

(Note: The superscript ID for the I Cor. text is [P], for Paul.)

[P] For I received from the Lord what I also passed on to you.

The Lord Jesus, on the night he was betrayed [L]took the [3rd] cup [of the Passover meal], gave thanks, and said, *"Take this and divide it among you."*

22 [M]While they were eating, Jesus took bread, and when he had given thanks, he broke it and gave it to his disciples, saying, *"Take it* [MT]*and eat;* [M]*this is my body,* [P/L]*which has been given permanently for you. I command you to continue doing this in remembrance of me."*

23 In the same way, after supper, he took a cup, saying, 24 *"This is the new covenant in my blood,* [M]*which is poured out for many* [MT]*for the forgiveness of sins.* [P]*I command you to continue doing this, every time you are drinking it, in remembrance of me."*

[M]And when he had given thanks, he gave it to them, and they all drank from it.

25 Jesus said, *"Truly I tell you, I will never, ever drink again from the fruit of the vine until that day when I drink it new* [MT]*with you in my Father's kingdom —* [M]*the kingdom of God."*

CHAPTER 40

His Passion

Thursday: Jesus' "Farewell Discourse"

#287 Jesus is the Way to the Father, the Truth that Reveals Him and the Life
JN 14.1-11

1 *"I command you to stop letting your hearts become troubled. You believe in God; I command you also to continue believing in me.*

2 *"My Father's house has many rooms; if that were not so, I would not have told you that I am going there to prepare a place for you. 3 And if I go and prepare a place for you, I will come back and take you to be with me, that you also may be where I myself am. 4 You know the way to the place where I am going."*

5 Thomas said to him, "Lord, we do not know where you are going, so how can we know the way?"

6 Jesus answered, *"I myself am the way and the truth and the life. No one comes to the Father except through me. 7 Because you have come to know me, you will know my Father as well. From now on, you do know him and have conclusively seen him."*

8 Philip said, "Lord, show us the Father and that will be enough for us."

9 Jesus answered, *"Have you not come to know me, Philip, even after I have been among you such a long time? Anyone who has really seen me and understood*

me has seen the Father, too. How can you say, 'Show us the Father?' 10 Do you not believe that I am in the Father, and that the Father is in me? The words I say to you I do not speak from myself. Rather, it is the Father, who is living in me, who is doing his work. 11 I command you to keep believing me when I say that I am in the Father and the Father is in me, or at least continue to believe based on the evidence of the works themselves."

#288 Jesus Gives the "Anything in My Name" Prayer Promise
JN 14.12-14

12 *"Very truly I tell you, whoever believes in me will do the works I am doing, and they will do even greater things than these, because I am going to the Father. 13 And I will do whatever you ask in my name, so that the Father may be glorified in the Son. 14 Whatever you ask for in my name, I will certainly do it."*

#289 Jesus Promises the Holy Spirit to His Disciples
JN 14.15-26

15 *"If you love me, you will keep my commands. 16 And I will ask the Father, and he will give you another Advocate just like me to help you and be with you forever; 17 the Spirit of truth. The world cannot accept him because it neither sees him nor knows him. But you know him, for he is living with you, and he will be in you.*

18 *"I will not leave you as orphans; I will come to you. 19 Before long, the world will not see me anymore, but you will see me. Because I live eternally, you also will have eternal life. 20 On that day — when the Spirit comes to make his home in you — you will realize that I am living in the consciousness of my union with my Father, and you are likewise living in the same union in me, and I am alive in you.*

21 *"Whoever is holding on firmly to my commands and keeping them is the one who loves me. The one who loves me will be loved by my Father, and I too will love them and reveal myself to them."*

22 Then Judas [not Judas Iscariot] said, "But, Lord, why do you intend to show yourself to us and not to the world?"

23 Jesus replied, *"Anyone who is loving me will obey my teaching. My Father will love them, and we will come to them and make our home with them. 24 Anyone who does not love me will not obey my teaching. The words you hear are not my own; they belong to the Father who sent me. 25 I have spoken these things while still with you. 26 But the Advocate — the Holy Spirit, whom the Father will send in my*

name – will teach you all things and will remind you of everything I have said to you."

#290 Jesus Gives His Own Peace to His Disciples
JN 14.27-31; 16.33; LK 22.39 (Parallel Texts: MT 26.30; MK 14.26)

27 *"I am leaving my kind of peace with you; my peace I am giving to you. I am not giving to you as the world gives. I command you to stop letting your hearts be troubled, and stop being afraid.*

16.33 "I have spoken these things to you so that you may continue to have peace in me. In this world, you will continue to experience trouble and difficulty. But I command you always to be courageous, for I have permanently overcome the world.

28 *"You heard me say, 'I am going away and I am coming back to you.' If you were loving me right now, you would be glad that I am going to the Father, for the Father is greater than I am. 29 I have told you now--before it happens--so that when it does happen, you will believe.*

30 *"I will not say much more to you, for the prince of this world is coming. He has no hold over me, 31 but he comes so that the world may learn that I always love the Father, and so I do exactly what my Father has commanded me. Come now; let us leave."*

M, MTWhen they had sung a hymn, LJesus went out as usual to the Mount of Olives, and his disciples followed him.

#291 Jesus Commands His Disciples, "Abide in Me"
JN 15.1-8

1 *"I AM the true vine, and my Father is the keeper of the vineyard. 2 He cuts off every branch in me that bears no fruit, while every branch that does bear fruit he cleanses by pruning, so that it will be even more fruitful. 3 You are already clean because of the word I have spoken to you.*

4 *"I command you to live in the consciousness of your union with me, as I also live in the consciousness of my union with you. Just as no branch can bear fruit by itself, unless it continues to live securely in the vine, so neither can you bear fruit unless you keep living in conscious dependence upon me. 5 I AM the vine; you are the branches. The person who constantly makes their home in me and I them – that person will continue to bear much fruit; for apart from me, you can do nothing. 6 If a person does not live in the consciousness of their union with me, they will be like a*

branch that is thrown away and withers; such branches are gathered together, thrown into the fire, and burned.

7 *"If you continue to live in conscious dependence upon me, and my words make their home in you, you may ask for whatever you desire, and it will be done for you. 8 This is how my Father is glorified – that you keep bearing abundant fruit – and so show yourselves to be my disciples."*

#292 Jesus Commands His Disciples, "Abide in My Love"
JN 15.9-17

9 *"Just as the Father has loved me, so I have also loved you. Now I command you to live in the constant awareness of my love. 10 If you keep my commands, you will live in the consciousness of my love, just as I have perfectly kept my Father's commands and continue to remain in the consciousness of his love. 11 I have told you this so that my joy may be in you, and that your joy may be full to overflowing, and complete.*

12 *"My command is this: continue loving each other as I have first loved you. 13 Greater love has no one than this--to lay down one's life for one's friends. 14 You are my friends if you do as I command. 15 I no longer call you servants because a servant does not know what his master is doing. Instead, I have called you friends, for everything that I heard from my Father I have made known to you.*

16 *"You did not choose me, but I, myself, chose you and appointed you so that you might go and continue bearing fruit – fruit that will last – and so that whatever you ask in my name, the Father will give you. 17 This is my command: continue loving each other."*

#293 Jesus Prepares His Disciples to Endure the World's Hatred
JN 15.18-16.6

18 *"Because the world hates you, do not forget that it perfected its hatred of me first. 19 If you belonged to the world – and you do not – it would love you as its own. As it is, you do not belong to the world, but I have chosen you out of the world. That is why the world is hating you.*

20 *"Remember what I told you: 'A servant is not greater than his master.' Since they persecuted me, they will persecute you also. If they obeyed my teaching, they will obey yours also. 21 They will do all these things to you because of my name, for they do not know the one who sent me.*

22 *"If I had not come and spoken to them, they would not be guilty of sin, but now they have no excuse for their sin. 23 Whoever hates me hates my Father as well. 24 If I*

had not done among them the works no one else did, they would not be guilty of sin. As it is, they have seen and yet they have hated both my Father and me. 25 But this is to fulfill what is written in their Law: 'They hated me without reason.' (Ps. 35.19; 69.4)

26 *"When the Advocate comes, whom I will send to you from the Father — the Spirit of truth who goes out from the Father — he will testify about me. 27 And I command you also to continue to witness, for you have been with me from the beginning.*

16.1 *"I have told you these things so that you will not fall away. 2 They will put you out of the synagogue; in fact, the time is coming when anyone who kills you will think they are offering a service to God. 3 They will do such things because they have not known the Father or me.*

4 *"I have told you this so that when the time comes you will remember that I clearly warned you about them in advance. I did not tell you this from the beginning because I was with you, 5 but now I am going to him who sent me. Yet, none of you asks me, 'Where are you going?' 6 Instead, you are filled with grief because I have said these things."*

#294 Jesus Promises the Ministry of the Holy Spirit
JN 16.7-15

7 *"Very truly I tell you, it is to your great advantage that I am going away. Unless I go away, the Advocate will not come to you; however, if I go, I will send him to you. 8 When he comes to you, he will convict the world concerning sin and righteousness and judgment: 9 about sin because people do not believe in me; 10 about righteousness because I am going to the Father, where you can see me no longer; 11 and about judgment because the prince of this world now stands condemned.*

12 *"I have much more to say to you, more than you can now bear. 13 But when he, the Spirit of truth, comes, he will guide you into all the truth. He will not speak on his own; he will speak only what he hears, and he will tell you what is yet to come. 14 He will glorify me because he will take from what belongs to me, and he will make it known to you. 15 All that belongs to the Father is mine. This is why I said the Spirit will take what is mine, and he will make it known to you."*

#295 Jesus Promises the Joy of His Risen Presence
JN 16.16-22

16 Jesus went on to say, *"In a little while you will see me no more, and then after a little while you will see me."*

17 At this, some of his disciples said to one another, "What does he mean by saying, 'In a little while you will see me no more, and then after a little while you will see me,' and 'Because I am going to the Father?'" 18 They kept asking, "What does he mean by 'a little while'? We do not understand what he is saying."

19 Jesus saw that they wanted to ask him about this, so he said to them, *"Are you asking one another what I meant when I said, 'In a little while you will see me no more, and then after a little while you will see me'?*

20 *"Very truly I tell you, you will weep and mourn, and the world will rejoice. You will grieve, but then your grief will transform into joy. 21 A woman giving birth to a child has pain because her time has come, but when her baby is born, she forgets the anguish because of her joy that a child is born into the world.*

22 *"So it is with you; Now is your time of grief, but I will see you again and your hearts will rejoice, and no one will be able to take away your joy."*

#296 Jesus Promises the Joy of Answered Prayer
JN 16.23-32

23 *"In that day, you will no longer ask me anything. Very truly I tell you, whatever you ask the Father in my name, he will give you. 24 Until now, you have not asked for anything in my name. I command you to continue asking and you will receive so that your joy will become permanently full.*

25 *"Although I have been speaking figuratively, a time is coming when I will no longer use this kind of language, but will tell you plainly about my Father. 26 In that day, you will ask in my name, and I am not saying that I will ask the Father on your behalf. 27 For the Father himself loves you because you have loved me fully, and you have permanently believed that I came from God. 28 I came from the Father and entered the world; now I am leaving the world and going back to the Father."*

29 Then, Jesus' disciples said, "Now you are speaking clearly and without figures of speech. 30 Now we can see that you know all things and that you do not even need anyone to ask you questions. This makes us believe that you came from God."

31 *"Do you now believe?"* Jesus replied. 32 *"A time is coming, and in fact has now come, when you will be scattered, each to your own home. You will leave me all alone. Yet I am not alone, for my Father is always with me."*

CHAPTER 41

His Passion

Thursday: Jesus Offers His High Priestly Prayers

#297 Jesus Prays for His Father to be Glorified
JN 17.1-5

1 After Jesus said this, he looked toward heaven and prayed, *"Father, the hour has fully come. Glorify your Son, that your Son may glorify you. 2 For you granted him permanent authority over all people so that he might give eternal life to all those you have permanently given him. 3 Now this is eternal life: that they know you, the only true God, and Jesus Christ, whom you have sent. 4 I have glorified you on earth by finishing the work you permanently gave me to do. 5 And now, Father, glorify me in your presence with the glory I had with you before the world began."*

#298 Jesus Prays for His Disciples' Protection and Sanctification
JN 17.6-19

6 *"I have revealed your name — you — to those whom you gave me out of the world. They were yours; you gave them to me and they have permanently kept your word. 7 Now they come to fully know that everything you have permanently given to me comes from you. 8 For I permanently gave them the words you gave me and they*

accepted them. They knew with certainty that I came from you, and they believed that you sent me.

9 *"I am praying for them. I am not praying for the world, but for those you have permanently given me, for they are yours.* 10 *All I have is yours, and all you have is mine. And I have been permanently glorified through them.*

11 *"I will remain in the world no longer, but they are still in the world, and I am coming to you. Holy Father, protect them by the power of your name, the name you permanently gave me, so that they may be one as we are one.* 12 *While I was with them, I protected them and kept them safe by that name you gave me. None has been lost except the one doomed to destruction, so that Scripture would be fulfilled.*

13 *"I am coming to you now, but I say these things while I am still in the world so that they may have the full measure of my joy within them permanently.* 14 *I have permanently given them your word, and the world has hated them, for they are not of the world any more than I am of the world.* 15 *My prayer is not that you take them out of the world, but that you protect them from the evil one.* 16 *They are not of the world, even as I am not of it.* 17 *Sanctify them by the truth; your word is truth.* 18 *Just as you sent me into the world, I have sent them into the world.* 19 *I am sanctifying myself on their behalf, that they too may be sanctified by the truth."*

#299 Jesus Prays for Unity with the Trinity and Each Other
JN 17.20-26

20 *"My prayer is not for them alone. I pray also for those who will believe in me through their message,* 21 *that all of them may be one, Father, just as you are in me and I am in you. May they also be in us so that the world may believe that you have sent me.*

22 *"I have permanently given them the glory that you permanently gave me, that they may be one as we are one —* 23 *I in them and you in me — so that they may be permanently unified so that the world will know that you sent me and that you have loved them just as you have loved me.*

24 *"Father, I want those whom you have permanently given me to be with me where I am and to continue seeing my glory, the glory you permanently gave me because you loved me before the creation of the world.*

25 *"Righteous Father, though the world does not know you, I know you, and they know that you have sent me.* 26 *I have made you and your name known to them, and I will continue to make you known in order that the love you have for me may be in them and that I myself may be in them."*

#300 Jesus Prays the First Time at Gethsemane
MK 14.32-36 (Parallel Texts: MT 26.36-39; LK 22.40-44; JN 18.1)

[J]When Jesus had finished praying, he left with his disciples and crossed the Kidron Valley. On the other side, there was an Olive grove. 32 [MT]They went to a place called Gethsemane, and Jesus said to his disciples, *"I command you to sit here while I* [MT]*go over there and* [M]*pray."*

33 He took Peter, James, and John along with him, and he began to feel deeply distressed and troubled. 34 *"My soul is overwhelmed with sorrow to the point of death,"* he said to them. *"I command you to stay here and continue watching.* [L]*I command you to continue to pray that you will not enter into temptation."*

35 [M]Going a little farther, [L]he withdrew about a stone's throw beyond them and knelt; then, [MT]he fell on his face [M]to the ground and prayed that, if possible, the hour might pass from him.

36 [M] *"Abba,* [MT]*my* [M]*Father,"* he said, *"everything is possible for you.* [MT]*If it is possible –* [L]*if you are willing –* [M]*take this cup from me. Yet not as I, myself, am willing, but what you will-- [L]cause your will to be done."*

[L]An angel from heaven appeared to him and strengthened him. And being in agony, he kept praying even more earnestly, and his sweat was like drops of blood falling to the ground.

#301 Jesus Prays the Second and Third Time at Gethsemane
MK 14.37-42 (Parallel Texts: MT 26.40-46; LK 22.45-46)

37 He rose from prayer and [M]returned to his disciples and found them sleeping, [L]exhausted from sorrow. *"Why are you sleeping?"* he said to them. [M] *"Simon,"* he said to Peter, *"are you asleep? Could* [MT]*you men* [M]*not keep watch* [MT]*with me* [M]*for one hour?* 38 [L]*I command you to rise and* [M]*watch and continue to pray so that you will not fall into temptation. The spirit is willing, but the flesh is weak."*

39 [M]Once more, [MT]a second time, [M]he went away and prayed the same thing. [MT] *"My Father, if it is not possible for this cup to be taken away unless I drink it, may your will be done."*

40 [M]When he came back, he again found them sleeping because their eyes were heavy. They did not know what to say to him. [MT]So he left them and went away once more and prayed the third time, saying the same thing.

41 [M]Returning the third time, he said to them, *"Are you still sleeping and resting? Enough! The hour has come. Look, the Son of Man is delivered into the hands of sinners.* 42 *I command you to rise. Let us go! Here comes my betrayer."*

CHAPTER 42

His Passion

Friday: Jesus' Arrest in the Garden of Gethsemane

#302 Judas Guides the Soldiers and Leaders to Jesus
JN 18.2-9 (Parallel Texts: MT 26.47; MK 14.43; LK 22.47)

2 ᴹJust as he was speaking, Judas, one of the Twelve, appeared. Now Judas, who betrayed him, knew the place because Jesus had often met there with his disciples. 3 So Judas came to the garden, guiding a ᴹᵀlarge ᴶdetachment of soldiers and some officials from the chief priests, the Pharisees, ᴹᵀand the elders of the people. ᴶThey were carrying torches, lanterns, and weapons — ᴹᵀswords and clubs.

4 ᴶJesus, knowing all that was going to happen to him, went out and asked them, *"Who are you seeking?"*

5 "Jesus of Nazareth," they replied.

"I AM," Jesus said. [And Judas the traitor was standing there with them.] 6 When Jesus said, *"I AM,"* they stepped back and fell to the ground.

7 Again he asked them, *"Who are you seeking?"*

"Jesus of Nazareth," they said.

8 Jesus answered, *"I told you that I AM. Because you are looking for me, I command you to let these men go."*

9 This happened so that the words he had spoken would be fulfilled: *"I have not lost one of those you gave me."* (JN 17.12)

#303 Miracle 34: Jesus Heals Malchus, After Judas Betrays Jesus
MT 26.48-54 (Parallel Texts: MK 14.44-47; LK 22.48-51; JN 18.10-11)

48 [MT]Now the betrayer had arranged a signal with them: "The one I kiss is the man; arrest him [M]and lead him away under guard."

49 [MT]Going at once to Jesus, Judas said, "Greetings, Rabbi!"

[L]He approached Jesus to kiss him, but Jesus asked him, *"Judas, are you betraying the Son of Man with a kiss?"*

[MT]Judas kissed him.

50 Jesus said, *"Friend, do what you came to do."* Then, the men stepped forward, seized Jesus, and arrested him. 51 With that, one of Jesus' companions, [J]Simon Peter, [MT]reached for his sword, drew it out, and struck the servant of the high priest, cutting off his [J]right [MT]ear. [J]The servant's name was Malchus. 52 Jesus commanded Peter, [L] *"No more of this."* And he touched the man's ear and healed him.

[MT]Jesus said to Peter, *"Put your sword back in its place, for all who draw the sword will die by the sword. 53 [J]Shall I not drink the cup the Father has permanently given me? [MT]Or do you think I cannot call on my Father, and he will at once put at my disposal more than twelve legions of angels? 54 But how then would the Scriptures be fulfilled that say it has to happen in this way?"*

#304 The Disciples Abandon Jesus and Flee into the Night
MK 14.48-52 (Parallel Texts: MT 26.55-56; LK 22.52-53)

48 [L]Then, Jesus said to the Chief Priests, the officers of the temple guard, and the elders, who had come for him, [M] *"Am I leading a rebellion that you have come out with swords and clubs to capture me? 49 Every day I was with you, teaching in the temple courts, and you did not arrest me. [L]But this is your hour, when darkness reigns. [MT]This has all taken place because [M]the Scriptures must be fulfilled."*

50 Then, [MT]all the disciples [M]abandoned him and fled.

51 A young man wearing nothing but a linen garment was following Jesus. When they seized him, 52 he left his garment behind and fled naked.

CHAPTER 43

His Passion

Friday: Jesus' Three-Phase Jewish Trial

#305 Phase I of the Jewish Trial: Before Annas
JN 18.12-14, 19-23

12 ᵀWhen the detachment of soldiers with its commander and the Jewish officials arrested Jesus, they bound him 13 and brought him first to Annas, who was the father-in-law of Caiaphas, the high priest that year. 14 Caiaphas was the one who had counseled the Jewish leaders that it would be best if one man died for the people. 19 Meanwhile, the high priest questioned Jesus about his disciples and his teaching.

20 *"I have spoken openly to the world without changing my message,"* Jesus replied. *"I always taught in synagogues or at the temple, where all the Jews come together. I said nothing in secret. 21 Why question me? Ask those who heard me. Surely they know what I said."*

22 When Jesus said this, one of the officials nearby slapped him in the face. "Is this the way you answer the high priest?" he demanded.

23 *"If I said something wrong,"* Jesus replied, *"I command you to testify as to what is wrong. But since I spoke the truth, why are you beating me?"*

#306 Jesus is Led to Caiaphas' House for Questioning
MK 14.53, 55-59 (Parallel Texts: MT 26.57, 59-61; LK 22.54A; JN 18.24)

53 ᴶThen, Annas sent him, still bound, to Caiaphas the high priest. ᴹᵀSo, those who arrested ᴹJesus took him to the high priest, and representatives from all the chief priests, the elders, and the teachers of the law came together. 55 The chief priests and the whole Sanhedrin were searching for evidence against Jesus so that they could put him to death, but they could not find any. 56 Many testified falsely against him, but their statements did not agree.

57 ᴹᵀFinally two came forward, ᴹstood up, and gave this false testimony against him. 58 "We heard him say, 'I myself will destroy this temple made with human hands and in three days will build another, not made with hands.'"

59 Yet, their testimony still did not agree.

#307 Phase II: Before Caiaphas — The Charge of Blasphemy
MK 14.60-65 (Parallel Texts: MT 26.62-68; LK 22.63-65)

60 Then, the high priest stood up before them and asked Jesus, "Are you not going to answer? What is this testimony that these men are bringing against you?"

61 But Jesus was holding his silence and gave no answer.

The high priest spoke to him, ᴹᵀ "I charge you under oath by the living God. Tell us, ᴹare you the Messiah, the Son of ᴹᵀGod, ᴹthe Blessed One?"

62 *"I AM,"* said Jesus, ᴹᵀ *"It is as you say. And I say to all of you: in the future* ᴹ*you will see 'the Son of Man'* (Dan. 7.13) *'sitting at the right hand of the Mighty One'* (Ps. 110.1) *and 'coming on the clouds of heaven.'"* (Dan. 7.13)

63 The high priest tore his clothes. ᴹᵀ "He has spoken blasphemy. ᴹWhy do we need any more witnesses?" he asked. 64 You have heard the blasphemy. What do you think?"

They all condemned him as worthy of death.

65 Then, some began to ᴹᵀspit in his face; ᴸthe men who were guarding Jesus began mocking and beating him. They blindfolded him, struck him with their fists, ᴹᵀand slapped him, saying, "Prophesy to us, Christ. Who hit you?" ᴸAnd they said many other insulting things to him. ᴹThen, the guards took him and beat him.

#308 Peter Gains Entry to Caiaphas' Courtyard
JN 18.15-18 (Parallel Texts: MT 26.58; MK 14.54B-55; LK 22.54B)

15 Simon Peter and another disciple were following Jesus from afar [MT]up to the courtyard of the High Priest. Because the other disciple was known to the high priest, he went with Jesus into the high priest's courtyard, 16 but Peter had to stand waiting outside at the door. The other disciple, who was known to the high priest, came back, spoke to the servant girl on duty there, and brought Peter in.

17 "You are not one of this man's disciples, are you?" she asked Peter, assuming that he was not.

He replied, "I am not."

18 It was cold, so when the servants and officials [L]had kindled a charcoal fire in the middle of the courtyard, [J]they stood around the fire to keep warm. Peter also took a place standing with them, and he was warming himself. [L]When they sat down together, Peter [MT]sat down with the guards to see the outcome.

#309 Peter Denies Jesus Three Times
MK 14.66-72 (Parallel Texts: MT 26.69-75; LK 22.56-62; JN 18.25-27)

66 While Peter was [MT]sitting out [M]below in the courtyard, one of the servant girls of the high priest came by. 67 When she saw Peter warming himself [L]there in the firelight, she gazed intently at his face. "This man was with him," she said. [M] "You also were with that Nazarene, Jesus [MT]of Galilee. [J]You are not one of his disciples too, are you?"

68 [M]But he denied it [MT]before them all. [J] "I am not. [L]Woman, I do not know him. [M]I do not know or understand what you are talking about," he said, and went out into the entryway.

69 [MT]When he went out to the gateway, another [M]servant girl saw him there, she said again to those standing around, "This fellow is one of them; [MT]he was with Jesus of Nazareth." 70 [L]Someone else said, "You are also one of them."

70 [M]Again, he denied it [MT]with an oath: "Man, I am not! I do not know the man."

After a little while, [L]about one hour later, [M]those standing near [MT]went to Peter. [J]One of the High Priest's servants, a relative of the man whose ear Peter had cut off, challenged Peter, saying, "Did I not see you with him in the olive grove? ^MSurely you are one of them, ^{MT}for your accent gives you away; ^Myou are a Galilean."

71 He began to call down curses ^{MT}on himself, ^Mand he swore to them, "I do not know this man you are talking about."

72 ^LJust as he was speaking, ^Mthe rooster crowed. ^LThe Lord turned and looked straight at Peter. ^MThen, Peter remembered the word Jesus had spoken to him: "Before the rooster crows ^Ltoday, ^Myou will disown me three times."

^{MT}And he went outside ^Mand broke down, and continued to weep ^{MT}bitterly.

[Note: Some early manuscripts of Mark include a reference at the end of 14.68, *"and the rooster crowed."* Those manuscripts also add the word *"twice"* to 14.72: *"Before the rooster crows twice you will disown me three times."* We have chosen not to include these less reliable manuscript references in the SAGA text.]

#310 Phase III of the Jewish Trial:
Jesus is Officially Condemned to Death by the Sanhedrin
LK 22.66-71 (Parallel Texts: MT 27.1; MK 15.1A)

66 ^MVery early in the morning ^Lat daybreak, the council [Sanhedrin] of the elders of the people, both the chief priests and the teachers of the law, met together, and Jesus was led before them.

67 "Since you are the Messiah," they said, "tell us."

Jesus answered, *"If I did tell you, you would not truly believe me, 68 and if I asked you a question, you would not answer honestly. 69 But from now on, the Son of Man will be seated at the right hand of the mighty God."* (Ps. 110.1; Dan. 7.13)

70 They all asked, "Then are you the Son of God?"

He replied, *"I AM as you are saying."*

71 Then, they said, "Why do we need any more testimony? We have heard it from his own lips."

^MTherefore, the whole Sanhedrin reached ^{MT}the decision to put Jesus to death.

CHAPTER 44

His Passion

Friday: Jesus' Three-Phase Roman Trial

#311 Jesus is Led to the Roman Governor Pilate
JN 18.28-32 (Parallel Texts: MT 27.2; MK 15.1B; LK 23.1)

28 ^MThey bound Jesus, ^Land the entire assembly rose and led him ^Jfrom Caiaphas to the palace of the Roman governor, ^{MT}and they handed him over to Pilate, the governor. By now, it was early morning and to avoid ceremonial uncleanness, they did not enter the palace because they wanted to be able to eat the Passover. 29 So, Pilate came out to them and asked, "What charges are you bringing against this man?"

30 "If he were not a criminal," they replied, "we would not have handed him over to you."

31 Pilate said, "Then, take him yourselves and judge him according to your own law."

"But we do not have the right to execute anyone," they objected.

32 This took place to fulfill what Jesus had said about the kind of death he was going to die.

#312 Judas Commits Suicide and a Field is Bought in His Name
MT 27.3-10 (Parallel Text: Acts 1.18-19)

3 ^{MT}When Judas, who had betrayed him, saw that Jesus was condemned, he was seized with remorse and returned the thirty pieces of silver to the chief priests and the elders. 4 "I have sinned," he said, "for I have betrayed innocent blood."

"What is that to us?" they replied. "That is your responsibility."

5 So, Judas threw the money into the temple and left. Then, he went away and hanged himself. ^AThere, he fell headlong, his body burst open, and all his intestines spilled out.

6 ^{MT}The chief priests picked up the coins and said, "It is against the law to put this into the treasury, because it is blood money." 7 They decided to use the money to buy the potter's field as a burial place for foreigners. ^AIn this way Judas bought a field with the reward he got for his wickedness. 8 Everyone in Jerusalem heard about this, so they called the field in their language 'Akeldama,' which is "Field of Blood." ^{MT}That is why it has been called the "Field of Blood" to this day.

9 Then, what was spoken by Jeremiah the prophet was fulfilled: "They took the thirty pieces of silver, the price set on him by the people of Israel, 10 and they used them to buy the potter's field, as the Lord commanded." (Zech. 11.12-13; Jer. 18.2,11; 32.6-9)

#313 Phase I of the Roman Trial: Before Pilate
JN 18.33-38 (Parallel Texts : MT 27.11-14; MK 15.2-5; LK 23.2-5)

^LAnd they began to accuse Jesus, saying, "We have found this man subverting our nation. He opposes payment of taxes to Caesar, and he claims to be Christ, a King."

33 ^JPilate then went back inside the palace and summoned Jesus. ^{MT}He stood before the governor, and the governor ^Jasked him, "Are you the king of the Jews?"

34 ^L *"Yes, it is as you say,"* Jesus replied. ^J *"Are you saying this as your own idea, or did others talk to you about me?"*

35 "Am I a Jew?" Pilate replied. "Your own people and chief priests handed you over to me. What have you done?"

36 Jesus said, *"My kingdom is not of this world. If it were, my servants would have been fighting to prevent my arrest by the Jewish leaders. But now my kingdom is not from here, this world."*

37 "You are a king, then?" said Pilate.

Jesus answered, *"You are saying that I am a king. In fact, the reason I was born and came into the world is to testify to the truth. Everyone who is born of the truth listens to me."*

38 "What is truth?" retorted Pilate.

With this, he went out again to the Jews gathered there and ᴸannounced to the Chief Priests and the crowd, ᴶ "I find no basis for a charge against him."

ᴹThe chief priests accused him of many things. ᴹᵀWhen he was being accused by the chief priests and the elders, he gave no answer. ᴹSo again ᴹᵀPilate asked him, "Do you not hear the testimony they keep bringing against you? ᴹAre you not going to answer? See how many things they are accusing you of?"

ᴹᵀBut Jesus made no reply—not even to a single charge—to the great amazement of Pilate.

ᴸAnd they insisted, "He is stirring up the people all over Judea by his teaching. He started in Galilee and has come all the way here."

#314 Phase II of the Roman Trial: Before Herod Antipas
LK 23.6-12

6 Because he heard this, Pilate asked if the man was a Galilean. 7 When he learned that Jesus was under Herod's jurisdiction, he sent him to Herod, who was also in Jerusalem at that time.

8 When Herod saw Jesus, he was greatly pleased because he had been wanting to see him for a long time. From what he had heard about him, he hoped to see him perform some kind of sign. 9 He was asking him many questions, but Jesus gave him no answer. 10 The chief priests and the teachers of the law were standing there, vehemently accusing him.

11 Then, Herod and his soldiers ridiculed and mocked him. Dressing him in an elegant robe, they sent him back to Pilate. 12 That day Herod and Pilate became friends; they had been enemies toward each other before this.

Phase III of the Roman Trial: Before Pontius Pilate

#315 Pilate Declares Jesus' Innocence,
But the Crowd Demands Barabbas Be Released
LK 23.13-16, 18-19; MT 27.15-21 (Parallel Texts : MK 15.6-11; JN 18.39-40)

13 Pilate called together the chief priests, the rulers, and the people, 14 and he said to them, "You brought me this man as one who was inciting the people to rebellion. I have examined him in your presence and have found no basis for your charges against him. 15 Neither has Herod, for he sent him back to us, as you can see; he has done nothing to deserve death. 16 Therefore, I will punish him and then release him."

^{MT}Now it was the governor's custom at the Feast to release a prisoner chosen by the crowd. At that time, they had a notorious prisoner named Barabbas, ^Lwho had been thrown into prison for an insurrection in the city and for murder.

^{MT}So when the crowd had gathered, ^Mthey came up and asked Pilate to do for them what he usually did. Pilate said to them, ^J "It is your custom for me to release to you one prisoner at the time of Passover. ^{MT}Which one do you want me to release to you? Barabbas or ^Mthe King of the Jews, ^{MT}Jesus, who is called Christ?" For he knew that it was out of envy that ^Mthe chief priests ^{MT}had handed Jesus over to him.

While Pilate was sitting on the judge's seat, his wife sent him this message: "Do not have anything to do with that innocent man, for I have suffered a great deal today in a dream because of him."

But the chief priests and the elders persuaded the crowd to ask for Barabbas and to have Jesus executed. The governor asked, "Which of the two do you want me to release to you?" ^LWith one voice they ^Jshouted back, "No, not him! ^LAway with this man! Release Barabbas to us!"

#316 Pilate Has Jesus Flogged and Appeals
the Second Time to the Crowd for His Release
JN 19.1-6 (Parallel Texts : MT 27.22-23; MK 15.12-14; LK 23.20-22)

1 Then, Pilate took Jesus and had him scourged. 2 The soldiers twisted together a crown of thorns and put it on his head. They wrapped him in a purple robe 3 and went up to him again and again, saying, "Hail, king of the Jews!" And they kept on hitting him in the face. 4 Once more Pilate came out

and said to the Jews gathered there, "Look, I am bringing him out to you to let you know that I find no basis for a charge against him."

5 When Jesus came out wearing the crown of thorns and the purple robe, Pilate said to them, "Look at the man!"

[L]Wanting to release Jesus, Pilate appealed to them again. [MT] "What shall I do then with Jesus, [M]the one you call the King of the Jews, [MT]who is called Christ?"

6 As soon as the chief priests and their officials saw him, [L]they kept shouting, "Crucify Him! Crucify Him!"

For the third time, Pilate spoke to them, "Why? What crime has this man committed? I have found no grounds for the death penalty in him."

[MT]But they kept shouting all the louder, "Crucify him!"

So Pilate answered, "You take him then and crucify him. I myself find no basis for a charge against him."

#317 Pilate Conducts His Second Private Interview of Jesus
JN 19.7-12

7 The Jewish leaders insisted, "We have a law, and according to that law, he must die because he made himself out to be the Son of God."

8 When Pilate heard this, he was even more afraid, 9 and he went back inside the palace. "Where do you come from?" he asked Jesus, but Jesus gave him no answer. 10 "Are you refusing to speak to me?" Pilate said. "Do you not understand that I myself have the power to free you, and I myself have the power to crucify you?"

11 Jesus answered, *"You would have no power over me if it had not been given to you from above, so it remains in force. Therefore, the one who handed me over to you is guilty of a greater sin."*

12 From then on, Pilate kept seeking to set Jesus free, but the Jewish leaders kept shouting, "If you let this man go, you are no friend of Caesar. Anyone who claims to be a king openly opposes Caesar."

#318 Pilate Ends Jesus' Trial with the Death Sentence
JN 19.13-16 (Parallel Texts : MT 27.24-26; MK 15.15; LK 23.23-25)

13 [J]When Pilate heard this, he brought Jesus out and sat down on the judge's seat at a place known as the "Stone Pavement." [Which in Aramaic is "Gabbatha."] 14 It was mid-morning on the day of Preparation of the Passover.

"Look! This is your king," Pilate said to the Jews.

15 But they shouted, "Take him away! Take him away! Crucify him!"

"Shall I crucify your king?" Pilate asked.

"We have no king but Caesar," the chief priests answered.

^{MT} When Pilate saw that he was achieving no resolution and a riot was erupting instead, he took water and washed his hands in front of the crowd. Then, he said, "I am innocent of this man's blood. I command you all to see to it."

All the people shouted, "Let his blood be upon us and on our children!"

^LSo Pilate decided to grant their demand. ^MWanting to please the crowd, Pilate released Barabbas, ^Lthe man who had been thrown into prison for insurrection and murder—the one they asked for—and surrendered Jesus to their will. 16 ^JSo Pilate finally handed him over to them to be crucified.

CHAPTER 45

His Passion

Friday: Jesus Bears His Cross to Golgotha

#319 Jesus is Beaten and Mocked by a Company of Roman Soldiers
MT 27.27-30 (Parallel Text: MK 15.16-19)

27 ᴹᵀThen, the governor's soldiers took Jesus ᴹand led him away into the palace [that is, ᴹᵀthe Praetorium] and gathered ᴹtogether ᴹᵀthe entire company of soldiers around him. 28 They stripped him and put a ᴹpurple-ᴹᵀscarlet robe on him 29 and then twisted together a crown of thorns and set it on his head. They put a staff in his right hand. Then, they knelt in front of him ᴹand began to call out to him, ᴹᵀmocking him.

"Hail, king of the Jews!" they said.

30 They spit on him and took the staff and struck him on the head again and again. ᴹFalling on their knees, they paid homage to him.

#320 Jesus Mourns for Jerusalem on the Road to Golgotha
LK 23.26-32 (Parallel Texts: MT 27.31-34; MK 15.20-23; JN 19.17)

ᴶSo the soldiers took charge of Jesus. ᴹWhen they had mocked him, they took off the purple robe and put his own clothes on him. Then, they led him out to crucify him. ᴶHe was carrying his own cross as he headed out for the place of "The Skull," which is called "Golgotha" in Aramaic. 26 ᴸAs the soldiers led him along, they seized ᴹa certain man from Cyrene, Simon, the father of Alexander and Rufus, ᴸwho was on his way in from the country, and they laid the cross on him ᴹand forced him ᴸto carry it behind Jesus.

27 A large number of people were following him, including women who mourned and wailed for him. 28 Jesus turned and said to them, *"Daughters of Jerusalem, I command you to stop weeping for me; you must continue weeping for yourselves and for your children. 29 For the time will come when you will say, 'Blessed are the childless women, the wombs that never bore, and the breasts that never nursed!'*

30 *"Then, they will say to the mountains, 'Fall on us!' and to the hills, 'Cover us!'* (Hos. 10.8) 31 *Since people do these things when the tree is green, what will happen when it is dry?"*

32 Two other men, both criminals, were also led out with him to be executed. They came to the place called Golgotha. ᴹᵀThere, they offered Jesus wine to drink, mixed with myrrh, but after tasting it, he refused to drink it.

CHAPTER 46

His Passion

Friday: Jesus' Death on the Cross

#321 Jesus is Crucified, as He Prays, *"Father, Forgive Them"* [Saying #1]
JN 19.18-24 (Parallel Texts: MT 27.35-38; MK 15.24-27; LK 23.33-34, 38)

18 ^LWhen they came to the place called The Skull, ^Jthey crucified him there, along with him two other ^Lcriminals — ^Mbandits — one on the right side, one on the left, ^Jand Jesus in the middle. ^MIt was the third hour [about 9:00 AM] when they crucified him.

^LJesus continued praying, *"Father, forgive them, for they do not know what they are doing."*

19 Pilate had a notice prepared and fastened to the cross. ^{MT}They placed the written charge against him above his head. ^JIt stood written: ^{MT} "THIS IS ^JJESUS OF NAZARETH, THE KING OF THE JEWS." 20 Many of the Jews read this sign, for the place where Jesus was crucified was near the city, and the sign was written in Aramaic, Latin, and Greek.

21 The chief priests of the Jews protested to Pilate, "Do not write 'The King of the Jews,' but that this man *claimed* to be king of the Jews."

22 Pilate answered, "What I have permanently written, I have written permanently."

23 When the soldiers crucified Jesus, they took his clothes, dividing them into four shares, one for each of them, with the undergarment remaining. This garment was seamless, woven in one piece from top to bottom.

24 "Let's not tear it," they said to one another. "Let's decide by lot who will get it." ᴹSo they cast lots to see what each would get.

ᴶThis happened that the scripture might be fulfilled that said,

> "They divided my clothes among them
> and cast lots for my garment." (Ps. 22.18)

So this is what the soldiers did. ᴹᵀAnd sitting down, they were keeping watch over him there.

#322 Jesus is Mocked by the Crowd, While Promising Paradise to a Penitent Thief [Saying #2]
MK 15.29-30; LK 23. 35-37, 39-43 (Parallel Texts: MT 27.39-44; MK 15.31-32)

MK 15.29-30 ᴹThose who passed by hurled insults at him, shaking their heads, and saying, "So! You who are going to destroy the temple and build it in three days, come down from the cross and save yourself, ᴹᵀsince you are the Son of God!"

LK 23.35 In the same way, ᴸthe people stood watching, ᴹᵀand the chief priests, the teachers of the Law, and the elders mocked him, ᴸand the rulers sneered at him.

They said, "He saved others; but he cannot save himself! He's the King of Israel! Let ᴹthis Christ ᴹᵀcome down now from the cross that we may ᴹsee and ᴹᵀbelieve in him. He trusts in God. Let God rescue him now, if he delights in him (Ps. 22.8), for he said, 'I AM the son of God.' ᴸLet him save himself if he is God's Messiah, the Chosen One."

36 The soldiers also came up and mocked him. They offered him wine vinegar 37 and said, "Since you are the king of the Jews, save yourself."

ᴹIn the same way, the bandits who were crucified with him were also heaping insults on him. 39 One of the criminals who hung there continued to hurl blasphemies at him, "Are you not the Messiah? Save yourself and us!"

40 But then the other criminal rebuked him. "Do not you fear God," he said, "since you are under the same sentence? 41 We are punished justly, for we are receiving what our deeds deserve. But this man has done nothing

wrong." 42 Then, he said, "Jesus, I plead with you to remember me when you come into your kingdom."

43 Jesus answered him, *"Truly I tell you, today you will be with me in paradise."*

#323 Jesus' Third Saying on the Cross: The Formation of His New Spiritual Family
JN 19.25-27

25 ᴶNear the cross of Jesus stood his mother, his mother's sister, Mary the wife of Clopas, and Mary Magdalene. 26 When Jesus saw his mother there and the disciple whom he loved standing nearby, he said to her, *"Woman, here is your son,"* 27 and to the disciple, *"Here is your mother."* From that time on, this disciple took her into his home.

#324 Jesus' Fourth Saying on the Cross: *"My God, My God! Why Have You Forsaken Me?"*
MK 15.33-36 (Parallel Texts: MT 27.45-49; LK 23.44-45A)

33 At ᴹᵀabout ᴹthe sixth hour [noon], darkness came over the whole land until the ninth hour [3:00 PM], ᴸfor the sun stopped shining. 34 ᴹAt ᴹᵀabout ᴹthe ninth hour [3:00 PM] Jesus cried out in a loud voice, *"Eloi, Eloi, lema sabachthani?"* This means, *"My God, my God, why have you forsaken me?"* (Ps. 22.1)

35 When some of those standing nearby heard this, they said, "Listen, he's calling Elijah."

36 ᴹᵀImmediately, ᴹone of them ran and got a sponge, filled it with wine vinegar, put it on a staff, and offered it to him. ᴹᵀThe rest said, ᴹ "Now leave him alone. Let's see if Elijah comes ᴹᵀto save him, ᴹto take him down."

#325 The Death of Jesus: His Fifth, Sixth, and Seventh Sayings on the Cross
JN 19.28-30 (Parallel Texts: MT 27.50; MK 15.37; LK 23.46)

28 ᴶLater, knowing that everything had now been permanently finished, and so that Scripture would be fulfilled, Jesus said, *"I am thirsting."*

29 A jar of wine vinegar was sitting near, so they soaked a sponge in it, put the sponge on a stalk of the hyssop plant, and lifted it to Jesus' lips.

30 When he had received the drink, Jesus said, *"It has been permanently accomplished (finished)."* ᴸJesus cried out ᴹᵀagain ᴸwith a loud voice, *"Father, into your hands I commit my spirit."* (Ps. 31.5) Then, he bowed his head and gave up his last breath.

#326 A Variety of Witnesses Testify to Jesus' Death
MT 27.51-56 (Parallel Texts: MK 15.38-41; LK 23.45B, 47-49)

51 At the moment [when Jesus died], the curtain of the temple was ripped in two from top to bottom. The earth shook, huge rocks split, 52 and the tombs broke open. The bodies of many holy people who had died were raised to life. 53 They came out of the tombs after Jesus' resurrection and went into the holy city and appeared to many people.

54 When the centurion, ᴹwho stood there in front of Jesus, ᴹᵀand those with him who were guarding Jesus ᴹheard his cry and saw how he died, ᴹᵀthe earthquake, and all that had happened, they were terrified, ᴸand they praised God, exclaiming, "Surely ᴸthis was a righteous man—ᴹᵀthe Son of God!"

ᴸWhen all the people who had gathered to witness this sight saw what had taken place, they beat their breasts as they went away. 55 ᴹᵀMany women were there, watching from a distance. ᴹIn Galilee, these women had followed him and cared for his needs. ᴹᵀThen, they had followed Jesus from Galilee to care for his needs. 56 Among them were Mary Magdalene, Mary the mother of James and Joses, ᴹSolome, ᴹᵀand the mother of Zebedee's sons. ᴹMany other women who had come up with him to Jerusalem were also there.

CHAPTER 47

His Passion

Friday: Jesus' Burial in the Garden Tomb

#327 Jesus' Death is Officially Certified
JN 19.31-37

31 ᴶNow it was the day of Preparation, and the next day was to be a special Sabbath. Because the Jewish leaders did not want the bodies left on the crosses during the Sabbath, they asked Pilate to have the legs broken and the bodies taken down. 32 Therefore, the soldiers came and broke the legs of the first man who had been crucified with Jesus, and then those of the other. 33 But when they came to Jesus and found that he was already dead, they did not break his legs. 34 Instead, one of the soldiers pierced Jesus' side with a spear, bringing a sudden flow of blood and water.

35 The man who saw it has given his permanent testimony, and his testimony remains true. He knows that he tells the truth, and he testifies so that you also may believe.

36 These things happened so that the scripture would be fulfilled: "Not one of his bones will be broken," (Num. 9.12) and, as another scripture says, "They will look on the one they have pierced." (Zech. 12.10)

#328 Joseph of Arimathea Receives Possession of Jesus' Body
MK 15.42-45 (Parallel Texts: MT 27.57-58; LK 23.50-52; JN 19.38)

42 ᴹIt was Preparation Day [that is, the day before the Sabbath]. As evening approached, 43 ᴸa man named Joseph, who came from the Judean town ᴹof Arimathea, ᴹᵀa rich man ᴹand a prominent member of the Council, went boldly to Pilate and asked for Jesus' body.

ᴸNow Joseph was a good and upright man who had not consented to their decision. ᴹHe was waiting for the kingdom of God, ᴹᵀfor he himself had become a disciple of Jesus, ᴶbut secretly because he feared the other Jewish leaders.

44 ᴹPilate was surprised to hear that Jesus was already dead. Summoning the centurion, he asked him if Jesus had already died. 45 When he learned from the centurion that it was so, he gave the body to Joseph. ᴶSo with Pilate's permission, Joseph came and took the body away.

#329 Jesus is Buried in Joseph's New Garden Tomb
JN 19.39-42 (Parallel Texts: MT 27.59-60; MK 15.46; LK 23.53-54)

39 ᴹSo, Joseph took down the body. ᴶHe was accompanied by Nicodemus, the man who earlier had visited Jesus at night. Nicodemus brought a mixture of about seventy-five pounds of myrrh and aloes. 40 Taking Jesus' body, the two of them wrapped it, with the spices, in strips of ᴹᵀclean ᴶlinen. This was done in accordance with Jewish burial customs.

41 At the place where Jesus was crucified, there was a garden, and in the garden was ᴹᵀ[Joseph's] own new tomb that he had cut out of the rock, ᴶin which no one had ever been laid. 42 Because it was the Jewish Day of Preparation and because the tomb was nearby, they laid Jesus there. Then, Joseph rolled a big stone in front of the entrance to the tomb, and they went away.

#330 Faithful Women and Roman Guards Watch over Jesus' Tomb
MT 27.61-66 (Parallel Texts: MK 15.47-16.1; LK 23.55-56)

61 ᴸThe women who had come with Jesus from Galilee followed Joseph and saw the tomb and how Jesus' body was laid in it. ᴹᵀMary Magdalene and the other Mary, ᴹthe mother of Joses, ᴹᵀwere sitting opposite the tomb. ᴸThen, they went home and prepared spices and perfumes. But they rested on the Sabbath in obedience to the commandment. When the Sabbath was over,

Mary Magdalene, Mary the mother of James, and Salome bought more spices so that they might anoint Jesus' body.

62 ^{MT}The next day, after Preparation Day, the chief priests and the Pharisees went to Pilate. 63 "Sir," they said, "we remember that while he was still alive that deceiver said, 'After three days I will rise again.' 64 So give the order for the tomb to be made secure until the third day. Otherwise, his disciples may come and steal the body and tell the people that he has been raised from the dead. This last deception will be worse than the first."

65 "Take a guard," Pilate answered. "Go, make the tomb as secure as you know how."

66 So they went and made the tomb secure by putting a seal on the stone and posting the guard.

HIS RESURRECTION AND ETERNAL MINISTRY

Jesus' earthly life ended with his victory cry: *"It is permanently finished!"*

Now, we discover something even more wonderful in The JESUS SAGA — the final stage of Jesus' life and ministry begins in the Bible and continues forever!

There are two phases of Jesus' incarnation. The first lasted 33 years in Jesus' flesh and blood body. The second phase lasts forever in Jesus' spiritual, resurrection body. Jesus is the same person in both phases, but the characteristics of his physical body are different. Jesus showed himself to be alive in a new resurrection body with many convincing proofs in his eleven appearances over 40 days recorded in the gospels. At the eleventh appearance, he ascended back to the Father in heaven.

But there is more — MUCH more! Jesus' earthly ministry did not end at his ascension; it merely became invisible to our mortal eyes. Rather than removing

Jesus' presence from the earth, the ascension made Jesus more accessible to us in every place and time through His Spirit. Jesus continues to speak and act on this earth in his ascension, even more actively than he did during the first phase of his incarnation, for a flesh and blood body no longer limits him. Jesus is alive and working throughout the whole earth now in his Spirit.

The final chapters of The JESUS SAGA focus on what Jesus has said and done after his ascension. They show us that Jesus is now at the controls of the universe, the Living Head of his body, the Church; he is the King of Kings and Lord of Lords. He is directing the events of history on earth and in heaven according to his loving master plan.

The words and deeds of this risen, ascended Jesus, as recorded in the New Testament, continue the ministry he began in the four gospels, right up to the last words in the Bible, which contain Jesus' final commands and promise to each of us. Chapters 48 to 52 cover this final, eternal stage of Jesus' life and ministry.

The JESUS SAGA has begun, but it will never end. Hallelujah!

CHAPTER 48

Resurrection and Eternal Ministry:

Easter Sunday--The Discovery of the Empty Tomb

#331 Faithful Women Discover the Empty Tomb
Acts 1.3; MT 28.1-4 (Parallel Texts: MK 16.2-4; LK 24.1-3; JN 20.1)

After his suffering, Jesus revealed himself to the apostles and gave many convincing proofs that he was alive. He appeared to them over a period of forty days and spoke about the kingdom of God. (Acts 1.3)

1 ᴹᵀAfter the Sabbath, ᴶon the first day of the week, very early in the morning—while it was still dark—Mary Magdalene, ᴹᵀthe other Mary, ᴹSalome, ᴸand the other women took the spices they had prepared and left for the tomb.

2 There was a violent earthquake, for an angel of the Lord came down from heaven and, going to the tomb, rolled back the stone and sat on it. 3 His appearance was like lightning, and his clothes were white as snow. 4 The guards were so afraid of him that they shook and became like dead men.

ᴹᵀAt dawn, ᴹjust after sunrise, as they were on their way to the tomb, the women asked each other, "Who will roll the stone away from the entrance of the tomb?" But when they looked up, they saw that the stone, which was very large, had been rolled away. ᴸWhen they entered, they did not find the body of the Lord Jesus.

#332 Angels Appear to the Women, Saying, "He is Risen"
LK 24.4-8 (Parallel Texts: MT 28.5-8; MK 16.5-8)

4 ᴹAs they had entered the tomb, ᴸwhile they were wondering about the absence of Jesus' body, suddenly two men in clothes that gleamed like lightning stood beside them, ᴹincluding a young man dressed in a white robe who sat down on the right side, and they were alarmed.

5 In their fright, the women bowed down with their faces to the ground, but the men said to them, ᴹᵀ"Stop being afraid, for I know ᴹthat you are looking for Jesus, who was crucified. He has risen! He is not here. ᴹᵀCome and ᴹsee the place where he lay. Why do you look for the living among the dead?

6 "Remember how he told you, while he was still with you in Galilee, 7 *'The Son of Man must be delivered over to the hands of sinners, be crucified and on the third day be raised again.'* ᴹNow go ᴹᵀquickly and ᴹtell his disciples and Peter. ᴹᵀHe has risen from the dead and ᴹis going ahead of you into Galilee. There you will see him, just as he told you."

8 ᴸThen, they remembered his words. ᴹTrembling and bewildered, the women went out ᴹᵀand hurried away as ᴹthey fled from the tomb, ᴹᵀafraid yet filled with joy; they ran to tell his disciples. ᴹThey said nothing to anyone along the way because they were afraid.

#333 The Women Report to the Apostles;
Peter and John Visit the Empty Tomb
JN 20.2-9 (Parallel Texts: LK 24.9-11)

ᴸWhen they arrived back from the tomb, the women told these things to the Eleven and to all the others. It was Mary Magdalene, Joanna, Mary the mother of James, and the others with them who told this to the apostles. But the apostles did not believe the women, because their words seemed like nonsense to them.

2 ᴶMary Magdalene had come running to Simon Peter and the other disciple, the one Jesus loved, and said, "They have taken the Lord out of the tomb, and we do not know where they have put him!"

3 So Peter and the other disciple ᴸrose and ᴶstarted for the tomb. 4 Both were running, but the other disciple outran Peter and reached the tomb first. 5 He bent over and looked in at the strips of linen lying there but did not go in.

6 Then, Simon Peter came along behind him and, ᴸbending over, ᴶwent straight into the tomb. He saw the strips of linen lying there, 7 as well as the

cloth that had been wrapped around Jesus' head. The cloth was still lying in its place, separate from the linen.

8 Finally, the other disciple, who had reached the tomb first, also went inside. He saw and believed. 9 They still did not understand from Scripture that Jesus had to rise from the dead.

ᴸPeter went away, wondering to himself what had happened.

CHAPTER 49

Resurrection and Eternal Ministry:

Easter Sunday--Five Resurrection Appearances of Jesus

#334 Jesus' First Resurrection Appearance, to Mary Magdalene
JN 20.10-18 (Parallel Text: MK 16.9-11)

ᴹWhen Jesus rose early on the first day of the week, he appeared first to Mary Magdalene, out of whom he had driven seven demons.

10 ᴶThe disciples [Peter and John] went back [from the tomb] to where they were staying. 11 And Mary stood outside the tomb, continuing to cry. As she was weeping, she bent over to look into the tomb, 12 and she saw two angels in white, seated where Jesus' body had been, one at the head and the other at the foot.

13 They asked her, "Woman, why are you crying?"

"They have taken my Lord away," she said, "and I do not know where they have laid him." 14 At this, she turned around and saw Jesus standing there, but she did not realize that it was Jesus.

15 He asked her, *"Woman, why are you crying? Who are you seeking for?"*

Thinking he was the gardener, she said, "Sir, if you have taken him away, tell me where you have laid him, and I will take him."

16 Jesus said to her, *"Mary."*

She turned toward him and cried out in Aramaic, "Rabboni!" [which means "teacher"]

17 Jesus said, *"I command you to stop holding on to me, for I have not yet permanently ascended to the Father. I command you instead to go to my brothers and tell them that I am ascending to my Father and your Father, to my God and your God."*

18 Mary Magdalene went ᴹout ᴶto the disciples—ᴹthose who had been with him and who were mourning and weeping—ᴶand she announced to them, "I have really seen the Lord. I will never forget the sight!"

And she told them that he had said these things to her. ᴹWhen they heard that Jesus was alive and that she had seen him, they did not believe it.

#335 Jesus' Second Resurrection Appearance, to the Women
MT 28.9-10

9 Look! Jesus met the group of women [on the way back to the tomb]. *"Greetings,"* he said. They came to him, clasped his feet, and worshiped him. 10 Then Jesus said to them, *"I command you to stop being afraid. Rather, I command that you go tell my brothers to go to Galilee; for there they will see me."*

#336 The Sanhedrin Bribes the Guards to Spread Lies
MT 28.11-15

11 While the women were on their way, some of the guards went into the city and announced to the chief priests everything that had happened. 12 When the chief priests had met with the elders and devised a plan, they gave the soldiers a large sum of bribe-money, 13 telling them, "You are to say, 'His disciples came during the night and stole him away while we were asleep.' 14 If this report reaches the governor, we will satisfy him and keep you out of trouble."

15 So because the soldiers had gladly grabbed the money, they did as they were instructed. And this story has been widely told among the Jews to this very day.

#337 Jesus' Third Resurrection Appearance, to Two Disciples on the Road to Emmaus
LK 24.13-32

13 Now that same day, two of them were going to a village called Emmaus about seven miles from Jerusalem. 14 They were talking with each other about everything that had happened. 15 While they were talking and discussing these things with each other, Jesus himself came up and walked along with them. 16 but they were kept from recognizing him.

17 He asked them, *"What are you discussing together as you walk along?"*

They stood still, their faces gloomy and sad. 18 One of them, named Cleopas, asked him, "Are you the only one visiting Jerusalem who does not know the things that have happened there in these days?"

19 *"What things?"* he asked.

"About Jesus of Nazareth," they replied. "He was a prophet, powerful in word and deed before God and all the people. 20 The chief priests and our rulers handed him over to be sentenced to death, and they crucified him, 21 but we had hoped that he was the one who was going to redeem Israel. And what is more, it is the third day since all this took place.

22 In addition, some of our women shocked us. They went to the tomb early this morning 23 but did not find his body. They came and told us that they had seen a vision of angels, who said he was alive. 24 Then, some of our companions went to the tomb and found it just as the women had said, but they did not see Jesus."

25 He said to them, *"How foolish you are, and how slow to believe all that the prophets have spoken! 26 Was it not necessary for the Messiah to suffer these things and then enter his glory?"*

27 And beginning with Moses and all the Prophets, he explained to them what was said in all the Scriptures concerning himself.

28 As they approached the village to which they were going, Jesus continued on as if he were going farther. 29 But they urged him strongly, "Stay with us, for it is nearly evening; the day is almost over." So he went in to stay with them.

30 When he was at the table with them, he took bread, gave thanks, broke it, and began to give it to them. 31 Then, their eyes were opened and they recognized him, but he vanished from their sight.

32 They asked each other, "Were not our hearts burning within us while he was talking with us on the road and opening the Scriptures to us?"

#338 Jesus' Fourth Resurrection Appearance, to the Apostle Peter in Private
LK 24.33-34; I Cor. 15.3-5

33 [The two disciples] rose and returned immediately to Jerusalem. They found the Eleven and those gathered together with them there. 34 They were saying, "It is true! The Lord has risen, and appeared to Peter."

Paul's Witness in I Cor. 15.3-5

3 For I delivered to you as of the highest importance what I also received, that Christ died for our sins according to the Scriptures, 4 and that he was buried, and that he was raised on the third day according to the Scriptures, 5 **and that he appeared to Cephas (Peter)**, and to the Twelve.

#339 Jesus' Fifth Resurrection Appearance, to the Apostles in the Upper Room
LK 24.35-49 (Parallel Text: JN 20.19-23)

ᴶOn the evening of that first day of the week, the disciples were together with the doors locked for fear of the Jews. 35 ᴸThe two told what had happened on the way [to Emmaus] and how they recognized Jesus when he broke the bread. 36 While they were talking about this, Jesus himself ᴶcame and ᴸstood in the midst of them and said to them, *"Peace be with you."*

37 They were startled and frightened, thinking they were seeing a ghost. 38 He said to them, *"Why are you troubled, and why do doubts rise in your minds? 39 I command you all to look at my hands and my feet. It is I myself! I command you to touch me and see; a ghost does not have flesh and bones as you see I have."*

40 When he had said this, he showed them his hands and feet ᴶand side. The disciples were overjoyed when they saw the Lord. 41 ᴸAnd while they still did not believe it because of joy and amazement, he asked them, *"Do you have anything here to eat?"*

42 They gave him a piece of broiled fish, 43 and he took it and ate it in their presence.

44 ᴶAgain, Jesus said to them, *"Peace be with you. ᴸThis is what I told you while I was still with you: Everything must be fulfilled that is written about me in the Law of Moses, the Prophets, and the Psalms."*

45 Then, he opened their minds so they could understand the Scriptures. 46 He told them, *"This is what is written: The Messiah will suffer and rise from the dead on the third day, 47 and repentance for the forgiveness of sins will be preached in his name to all nations, beginning at Jerusalem. 48 You are witnesses of these things. 49 I am going to send you what my Father has promised, but I command you to stay in the city until you have been clothed with power from on high. ᴶAs the Father has sent me, I am sending you."*

And with that, he breathed on them and said, *"I command you to receive the Holy Spirit. If you cause anyone's sins to be forgiven, they will be forgiven. If you do not cause them to be forgiven, they will not be forgiven."*

CHAPTER 50

Resurrection and Eternal Ministry:

Six More Resurrection Appearances of Jesus over 40 Days

#340 Jesus' Sixth Resurrection Appearance, to Thomas and the Apostles
JN 20.24-31

24 Now Thomas [also known as Didymus, the Twin], one of the Twelve, was not with the disciples when Jesus came. 25 So the other disciples kept on telling him, "We have seen the Lord!"

But he answered them, "Unless I see the nail marks in his hands and actually put my finger where the nails were and stab my hand into his side, there is absolutely no way that I will believe."

26 A week later, Jesus' disciples were in the house again, and Thomas was with them. Although the doors were still locked, Jesus came and stood in their midst and said, *"Peace be with you!"*

27 Then, he said to Thomas, *"I command you to put your finger here; see my hands. Reach out your hand and stab it into my side. I command you to stop making yourself an unbeliever, and believe."*

28 Thomas said to him, "My Lord and my God!"

29 Then, Jesus told him, *"Because you have seen me, you have permanently believed; blessed are those who have believed, in spite of not seeing."*

30 Jesus performed many other signs in the presence of his disciples, signs that are not permanently recorded in this book. 31 But these stand written so that you may believe that Jesus is the Messiah, the Son of God, and that because you believe, you may continue to have eternal life in his name.

#341 Miracle 35: Jesus' Seventh Resurrection Appearance, Part I: Jesus Serves Breakfast to Seven Disciples by the Sea of Galilee
JN 21.1-14

1 Afterward Jesus revealed himself again to his disciples by the Sea of Galilee. It happened this way: 2 Simon Peter, Thomas (also known as Didymus), Nathanael from Cana in Galilee, the sons of Zebedee, and two other disciples were together.

3 "I am going out to fish," Simon Peter told them, and they said, "We will go with you." So they went out and climbed into the boat, but that night they caught nothing. 4 Early in the morning, Jesus stood on the shore, but the disciples did not recognize that it was Jesus.

5 He called out to them, *"Children, do you not have any cooked fish?"*

"No," they answered.

6 He said, *"I command you to throw your net on the right side of the boat and you will find some."*

When they did so, they were unable to drag the net in because of the huge number of fish. 7 Then, the disciple whom Jesus loved said to Peter, "It is the Lord!" As soon as Simon Peter heard him say, "It is the Lord," he wrapped his outer garment around him, for he had taken it off, and threw himself into the water. 8 The other disciples followed after in the boat, towing the net full of fish, for they were not far from shore, about a hundred yards.

9 When they landed, they saw a fire of burning coals there with fish on it and some bread. 10 Jesus said to them, *"I command you to bring some of the fish you have just caught."*

11 So Simon Peter hustled back into the boat and dragged the net ashore. It was full of large fish, 153, but in spite of there being so many, the net was not torn. 12 Jesus said to them, *"I command you to come now and have breakfast."*

None of the disciples dared ask him, "Who are you?" They knew it was the Lord. 13 Jesus came, took the bread, and gave it to them, and he did the same with the fish. 14 This was now the third time [in the gospel of John that] Jesus appeared to his disciples after he was raised from the dead.

#342 Jesus' Seventh Resurrection Appearance, Part II
Jesus Publicly Restores Peter to Ministry
JN 21.15-24

15 When they had finished eating, Jesus said to Simon Peter, *"Simon, son of John, do you continually love me more than these?"*

"Yes, Lord," he said, "you know that I love you."

Jesus said, *"I command you to continue feeding my lambs."*

16 Again Jesus said, *"Simon, son of John, do you constantly love me?"*

He answered, "Yes, Lord, you know that I love you."

Jesus said, *"I command you to continue caring for my sheep."*

17 The third time he said to him, *"Simon, son of John, do you really love me?"*

Peter was hurt because Jesus asked him the third time, "Do you love me?" He said, "Lord, you know all things; you know that I love you."

Jesus said, *"I command you to continue feeding my sheep. 18 Very truly I tell you, when you were younger, you dressed yourself and went where you wanted, but when you are old, you will stretch out your hands and someone else will dress you and lead you where you do not want to go."*

19 Jesus said this to indicate the kind of death by which Peter would glorify God. Then, he said to him, *"I command you to continue following me!"*

20 Peter turned and saw that the disciple whom Jesus loved was following them. [This was the one who had leaned back against Jesus at the supper and had said, "Lord, who is going to betray you?"] 21 When Peter saw him, he asked, "Lord, what about him?"

22 Jesus answered, *"If I want him to remain alive until I return, what is that to you? I command you to continue following me."*

23 Because of this, the rumor spread among the believers that this disciple would not die. But Jesus did not say that he would not die; he only said, *"If I want him to remain alive until I return, what is that to you?"*

24 This is the disciple who testifies to these things and who wrote them down. We know that his testimony is true.

#343 Jesus' Eighth Resurrection Appearance:
"The Great Commission" in Galilee
MT 28.16-20 (Parallel text: I Cor. 15.6)

I Cor. 15.6 After that, Jesus appeared to more than 500 of the brothers at the same time, most of whom are still living, although some have fallen asleep.

^{MT}16 So the eleven disciples went to Galilee, to the mountain where Jesus had directed them to go. 17 When they saw him, they worshiped him, but some doubted.

18 Then, Jesus came to them and said, *"All authority in heaven and on earth has been given to me. 19 Therefore, I command you to make disciples of all nations. Do this by continuing to go to them, by continuing to immerse them in the name of the Father and of the Son and of the Holy Spirit, 20 and by continuing to teach them to constantly obey everything I have commanded you. Look! I myself am surely with you always, until the consummation of the age."*

#344 Jesus' Ninth Resurrection Appearance, to His Younger Half-Brother, James
I Cor. 15.7A (Related Text: James 1.1A)

Then he appeared to James... (I Cor. 15.7A)

"I am James, a bond-servant of God and of the Lord Jesus Christ"... (James 1.1A)

#345 Jesus' Tenth Resurrection Appearance: The Holy Spirit Command and Promise
Acts 1.4-8

4 On one occasion, while he was eating with them, he gave them this command: *"Do not leave Jerusalem, but wait for what my Father promised, which you have heard me speak about. 5 For John immersed in water, but in a few days, you will be immersed in the Holy Spirit."*

6 Having gathered together around him, they were asking him questions, saying, "Lord, are you restoring the kingdom to Israel at this time?"

7 He said to them, *"It is not for you to know the dates or seasons the Father has set by his own authority. 8 But you will receive power when the Holy Spirit comes on you, and you will be my witnesses in Jerusalem, and in all Judea and Samaria, and to the ends of the earth."*

#346 Jesus' Eleventh Resurrection Appearance:
His Ascension Back to Heaven
LK 24.50-53 (Parallel Text: Acts 1.9-12)

50 When he had led them out to the vicinity of Bethany, he lifted up his hands and blessed them. 51 While he was blessing them, he left them and was taken up ᴬbefore their very eyes ᴸinto heaven, ᴬand a cloud hid him from their sight. They were looking intently up into the sky as he was going, when suddenly two men dressed in white stood beside them.

"Men of Galilee," they said, "why do you stand here looking into the sky? This same Jesus, who has been taken from you into heaven, will come back in the same way you have seen him go into heaven."

52 ᴸThen, they worshiped him and returned with great joy to Jerusalem ᴬfrom the hill called Mount Olivet, a Sabbath day's walk from the city. 53 ᴸAnd they stayed continually at the temple, praising God.

CHAPTER 51

Resurrection and Eternal Ministry:

Jesus' Words and Works in the Early Church

#347 Jesus Continues His Ministry in Heaven by
Pouring out the Holy Spirit at Pentecost
Acts 1.1-2; 2.1-5, 16-21, 33, 36

1.1 In my first book, Theophilus, I wrote about all that Jesus did constantly and all that he continually taught 2 until the day he was taken up into heaven, after he had given commands through the Holy Spirit to the apostles he had personally selected.

2.1 When the day of Pentecost had fully arrived, the disciples were all spending time together in one place. 2 Suddenly, a sound like the bellowing of a mighty, roaring wind came out of heaven and filled the entire house where they were sitting. 3 They were able to see what seemed to be tongues of fire that divided up and settled down on each of them. 4 All of them were filled with the Holy Spirit and started speaking in other languages as the Spirit gave them the words.

16 Peter stood and said, "This is what was spoken by the prophet Joel:

17 'In the last days, God is saying,
I will pour out my Spirit on all kinds of people.
Your sons and daughters will prophesy,
your young men will see visions,
your old men will dream various dreams.
18 Yes... upon my male servants and female servants
I will pour forth my Spirit in those days,
and they will preach my word.
19 I will give wonders in the heavens above
and signs on the earth below —
blood and fire and mighty billows of smoke.
20 The sun will be turned to darkness
and the moon into blood
before the great and noteworthy day of the Lord comes.
21 And whoever chooses to call
on the name of the Lord in prayer will be saved.' (Joel 2.28-32)

33 "Because he has been exalted to the right hand of God, and because he has received the promised Holy Spirit from the Father, **HE [Jesus] has poured out what you are now seeing and hearing.** 36 Therefore, I command that all Israel be absolutely certain about this: God has made this very Jesus, whom you crucified, both LORD God and Messiah."

#348 Jesus Adds New Believers to His Church Every Day
Acts 2.41-27; 11.19-21

41 Those who fully accepted his message were immersed in water, and about three thousand people were added to their number that day. 42 They were continually devoting themselves to the apostles' teaching and fellowship, to the breaking of bread, and to various kinds of prayer. 43 Everyone was continually being filled with a sense of awe at the many wonders and signs constantly being performed by the apostles. 44 All the believers were fellow-

shipping together and held everything in common. 45 They sold property and possessions to give to anyone who had any need.

46 Every day, they steadfastly continued to meet together in the temple courts. They broke bread in their homes and shared their food together with glad and sincere hearts, 47 constantly praising God and enjoying the favor of all the people. **And every day the Lord kept adding those who were being saved to their number.**

Six years later...

19 Now those who had been scattered about by the persecution against them when Stephen was killed traveled as far as Phoenicia, Cyprus, and Antioch, speaking out the Word exclusively among Jews. 20 However, some of them — men from Cyprus and Cyrene — went to Antioch and began witnessing to Greeks also, boldly sharing the good news about the Lord Jesus.

21 The Lord's hand was with them, and so a great number of people who believed were turning to the Lord.

#349 Jesus Stands as a Witness and Intercessor at the Death of Steven
Acts 7.54-60

54 Because the members of the Sanhedrin heard this, they were in a state of fury in their hearts and gnashing their teeth at him. 55 But Stephen, being full of the Holy Spirit, looked up intently into heaven and saw the glory of God, and Jesus who was standing at the right hand of God.

56 "Look," he said, **"I am seeing the heavens opened up, and the Son of Man standing at the right hand of God."**

57 At this, they covered their ears, and screaming with a mighty voice, they rushed at him together as one mob, 58 threw him out of the city, and then began stoning him. The witnesses laid their coats at the feet of a young man named Saul.

59 While they were stoning him, Stephen was praying, "Lord Jesus, receive my spirit." 60 Then, he fell to his knees and cried with great voice, "Lord, do not hold this sin against them." When he had said this, he fell asleep.

#350 Jesus' Twelfth Resurrection Appearance: to Paul (Saul) on the Road to Damascus
I Cor. 15.8-9; Acts 9.1-9, 26.14-18

1 After months of persecution, Saul was still breathing out non-stop threats and murder against the Lord's disciples. Going to the high priest, 2 he asked him for letters to the synagogues in Damascus, so that if he spied out any believers there who belonged to the Way, whether men or women, he might arrest and keep them bound as prisoners and drag them to Jerusalem.

3 As he was nearing Damascus on his journey, a bright light from heaven suddenly flashed around him. 4 After falling down to the ground, he heard a voice say to him, *"Saul, Saul, why are you persecuting me?"*

5 "Who are you, Lord?" Saul asked.

"I AM Jesus, whom you are persecuting. (Acts 26.16-18) *"I command you to rise and stand on your feet. I have made myself visible to you for this purpose – to appoint you as my servant and as a witness of what you have seen, and will see, of me. 17 I will deliver you from your own people and from the Gentiles. I, myself, am sending you to them 18 to open their eyes and turn them from darkness to light and from the power of Satan to God, so that they may receive full forgiveness of sins and an eternal inheritance among those who have been permanently dedicated to me by their faith in me.*

6 *"Now I command you to go into the city, and you will be told what you must continue doing."*

7 The men traveling with Saul stood unable to speak, for they had been hearing the sound but were not seeing anyone. 8 Saul rose up from the ground, but when he opened his eyes, he could not see anything. So taking him by the hand, they led him into Damascus. 9 For three days, he remained blind and did not eat or drink anything.

Paul's testimony: I Cor. 15.8-9

"Last of all, like a person of abnormal birth, [Jesus] appeared even to me also. For I am the last of the apostles, and I am not worthy to be to be called an apostle because I persecuted the church of God."

#351 Jesus Reaffirms Paul's Apostolic Calling by Sending Ananias
Acts 9.10-19, 22.14-21

10 In Damascus, there was a disciple named Ananias. The Lord called to him in a vision, *"Ananias!"*

"Look Lord, I am here," he answered.

11 The Lord told him, *"I command you to go the house of Judas on Straight Street and ask for a man from Tarsus named Saul, for he is continuing to pray. 12 He has seen a vision of a man named Ananias come and place his hands on him to regain his sight."*

13 "Lord," Ananias answered, "I have heard reports about this man from many people and he has done much harm to your holy people in Jerusalem. 14 And he has come here with authority from the chief priests to seize all who call on your name."

15 But the Lord said to Ananias, *"I command you to go now! This man is my chosen instrument to declare my name to the Gentiles and their kings and to the people of Israel. 16 I will reveal to him how much he must suffer for my name."*

17 Then, Ananias went to the house and entered it. Laying his hands on Saul, he said, "Brother Saul, the Lord has sent me to you in a decisive way, so that you may see again and be filled with the Holy Spirit. It was Jesus who appeared to you on the road as you were coming here. (Acts 22.14-16) The God of our fathers has personally selected you to know his will and to see the Righteous One and to hear words from his mouth. 15 You will be a witness on his behalf to all people of what you have permanently seen and heard. 16 And now what are you waiting for? Rise, receive immersion in water, and wash your sins away by calling on his name."

18 Immediately, something like scales fell from Saul's eyes, and he could see again. He rose and was immersed, 19 and after eating some food, he was strengthened.

Jesus Spoke to Paul again later (Acts 22.17-21)

17 "When I returned to Jerusalem and was praying at the temple, I fell into a trance 18 and saw the Lord speaking to me. *'Quick!'* he said. *'I command you to leave Jerusalem immediately because the people here will not accept your testimony about me.'*

19 "'Lord,' I replied, 'these people know that I went from one synagogue to another to imprison and whip those who believe in you. 20 And when the blood of your martyr Stephen was poured out, I stood there in full agreement and watched over the clothes of those who were killing him.'

21 "Then, the Lord said to me, *'I command you to go now; for I myself will send you far away to the Gentiles.'*"

#352 Jesus Sets Paul and Barnabas Aside for the First Missionary Journey
Acts 13.1-3

1 In the church at Antioch there were prophets and teachers: Barnabas, Simeon called Niger, Lucius of Cyrene, Manaen, who had been brought up with Herod the tetrarch, and Saul.

2 While they were serving the Lord with worship and fasting, the Holy Spirit said, *"I command you all now to set apart for me Barnabas and Saul for the work to which I have permanently called them."*

[For Jesus had promised:] *"The Spirit will not speak on his own; he will speak only what he hears from me, and he will tell you what is yet to come. He will glorify me because he will take from what belongs to me, and he will make it known to you."* JN 16.13-15

3 So after they had fasted and prayed, they placed their hands on them and sent them out.

#353 Jesus Encourages Paul in Corinth on the Second Missionary Journey
Acts 18.9-11

9 The Lord spoke to Paul one night in a vision: *"I command you to stop giving in to fear, but continue speaking out, and do not be silent. 10 For I myself am with you, and no one is going to attack and harm you because many people belong to me in this city."*

11 So Paul stayed in Corinth for a year and a half, teaching the word of God among them.

John Stephen Wright

**#354 Jesus Reveals Himself to Paul in a Time of Great Weakness
II Corinthians 12.7-10**

In order to keep me from becoming puffed up with pride, I was given a thorn in my flesh--a messenger of Satan--to torment me. 8 Three times I earnestly pleaded with the Lord to take it away from me. 9 But he said to me,

*"My grace is constantly sufficient for you,
for my power is always made perfect in weakness."*

Therefore, I will continue boasting all the more about my weaknesses, so that Christ's power may enfold me like a tent. 10 This is why I remain thankful in weaknesses, in insults, in hardships, in persecutions, in the toughest difficulties for Christ' sake. For when I am weak, then I am really strong.

CHAPTER 52

Resurrection and Eternal Ministry:

Jesus' Words and Works Throughout Eternity

#355 Jesus Appears to John on the Island of Patmos
Rev. 1.4-6, 9-20

4 John, to the seven churches in the province of Asia:

Grace and peace to you from the One who is, and who was, and who is to come, and from the seven-fold Spirits who are before his throne, 5 and from Jesus Christ, who is the faithful witness, the firstborn from among the dead, and the absolute ruler of the kings of the earth.

To the One who is always loving us, and has set us free from our sins through his blood, 6 and has made us become a kingdom of priests in personal service to his God and Father — to him be glory and power for ever and ever! Amen.

9 I myself, John, your brother and fellow participant in the agony and kingdom and endurance that we share in Jesus, was on the island of Patmos because of the word of God and my testimony about Jesus.

10 I was worshipping in the Spirit on the Lord's Day, and I heard a booming voice behind me like a trumpet, 11 which said: *"I command you to write*

what you are seeing in a book and send it to the seven churches: to Ephesus, Smyrna, Pergamum, Thyatira, Sardis, Philadelphia, and Laodicea."

12 I turned around to see the source of the voice that was talking to me. When I turned, I saw seven golden lampstands, 13 and at the center of the lampstands was someone like a son of man, dressed permanently in a long robe reaching down to his feet, wrapped in a golden sash bound permanently around his chest.

14 His head and his hair were white like wool, as white as snow, but his eyes looked like blazing fire. 15 His feet were like bronze that was permanently glowing in a furnace, and his voice was like the roar of many rushing waters. 16 In his right hand were seven stars, and a sharp double-edged sword was coming out of his mouth. His face was radiant like the sun shining in all its brilliance. 17 When I saw him, I fell at his feet like a dead man.

Then, he placed his right hand on me and said, *"I command you to stop being afraid. I AM the First and the Last. 18 I am the Living One; I was dead, and now look, I am alive in God's kind of life forever and ever! And I hold the keys of death and Hades. 19 Therefore, I command you to write what you have seen, what is now, and what will take place later. 20 The mystery of the seven stars that you saw in my right hand and of the seven golden lampstands is this: The seven stars are the messengers of the seven churches, and the seven lampstands are the seven churches."*

#356 Jesus Speaks to the Church in Ephesus, and to All Who Will Listen
Rev. 2.1-7

1 *"I command you to write to the messenger of the church in Ephesus:*

"This is what the One who is firmly gripping the seven stars in his right hand and is walking among the seven golden lampstands is saying.

2 *"I know your deeds, your hard work, and your endurance. I know that you cannot tolerate wicked people; I know that you have tested those who claim to be apostles but are not, and you have found them to be liars. 3 You have persevered and have endured hardships for my name, and you have not grown weary to the point of permanent exhaustion.*

4 *"Yet I am holding this against you: You have abandoned the love you had for me at first. 5 I command you to think seriously about how far you have fallen and remain mired! I command you to change your mind and heart and do the things you did at first. If you do not repent, I will come to you and remove your lampstand from*

its place. 6 But you have this in your favor: You continue to hate the practices of the Nicolaitans, which I am also hating.

7 "Whoever has ears, I command to hear what the Spirit is saying to the churches. To the person who is victorious, I will give the right to eat from the tree of eternal life, which is in the paradise of God."

#357 Jesus Speaks to the Church in Smyrna and to All Who Will Listen
Rev. 2.8-11

8 "I command you to write to the messenger of the church in Smyrna:

"This what the One who is the First and the Last, who became dead and then returned to life again is saying.

9 "I know your agony and your poverty, yet you are actually rich! I also know about the blasphemy of those who called themselves Jews and are not, but they are actually a synagogue of Satan.

10 "I command you not to be afraid of what you are about to continue to suffer. Look! The devil is about to throw some of you into prison to test you, and you will suffer persecution for ten days. I command you to be faithful, even to the point of death, and I will give you the victor's crown of eternal life.

11 "Whoever has ears, I command to hear what the Spirit is saying to the churches. The person who is victorious, will never, ever, be hurt by the second death."

#358 Jesus Speaks to the Church in Pergamum and to All Who Will Listen
Rev. 2.12-17

12 "I command you to write to the messenger of the church in Pergamum:

"This is what the One who has the sharp, double-edged sword is saying.

13 "I know where you are living — where Satan makes his throne. Yet you remain true to my name. You did not renounce your faith in me, not even in the days of Antipas, my faithful witness, who was put to death in your city — where Satan is living.

14 "Nevertheless, I have a few things against you. Some among you hold fast to the teaching of Balaam, who taught Balak to toss stumbling blocks before the Israelites, so that they ate food sacrificed to idols and committed sexual immorality. 15 Likewise, you also have those who hold firmly to the teaching of the Nicolaitans. 16 Therefore, I command you to repent! Otherwise, I will soon come to you and will go to battle against them with the sword of my mouth.

17 *"Whoever has ears, I command to hear what the Spirit is saying to the churches. To the one who is victorious, I will give some of the hidden manna. I will also give that person a white stone with a new name permanently engraved on it, known only to the one who receives it."*

#359 Jesus Speaks to the Church in Thyatira and to All Who Will Listen
Rev. 2.18-29

18 *"I command you to write to the messenger of the church in Thyatira:*

"This is what the Son of God is saying, whose eyes are like blazing fire and whose feet are like polished bronze.

19 *"I know your works, love, faith, service and perseverance, and that your last works are greater than your first ones. 20 However, I am holding this against you: You tolerate that woman Jezebel, who calls herself a prophet, and continues teaching and deceiving my own servants into sexual immorality and the eating of food sacrificed to idols. 21 I gave her some time to repent of her immorality, but she remains unwilling to repent of her immorality.*

22 *"Look! I will surely toss her down onto a bed of agony, and I will cause those who are committing adultery with her to suffer intensely if they refuse to repent of their ways. 23 I will strike her children stone dead. Then, all the churches will be convinced that I AM the One who searches hearts and minds, and I will give to each of you as your deeds deserve.*

24 *"Now I say to the rest of you in Thyatira, to those who are not holding to her teaching and have not learned what they are calling 'satan's deep secrets,' I am not placing any other burden on you, 25 except to hold on tenaciously to what you have, until I come.*

26 *"To the person who is victorious and is staying true to my work until the end, I will give authority over the nations; 27 that person will 'rule over them with an iron scepter and will smash them to pieces like pottery' (PS. 2.9) just as I have permanently received authority from my Father. 28 I will also give that person the morning star.*

29 *"Whoever has ears, I command to hear what the Spirit is saying to the churches."*

#360 Jesus Speaks to the Church in Sardis and to All Who Will Listen
Rev. 3.1-6

1 *"I command you to write to the messenger of the church in Sardis:*

"This is what the One who holds the seven-fold Spirits of God and the seven stars is saying.

"I know your works; you have a reputation for being spiritually alive, but you are actually dead. 2 I command you to become alert! I command you to strengthen what remains of your obedience, which is on the verge of dying, for I have found your deeds seriously incomplete in the sight of my God. 3 I command you to continually remember, therefore, what you have permanently received and heard; I command you to faithfully hold true to it and to repent. But if you do not wake up, I will surely come like a thief, and you will most certainly never know at what time I will come to you.

4 *"Yet you have a few people in Sardis who have not defiled their clothes. They will walk with me, dressed in white, for they are worthy. 5 The person who is victorious will be dressed in white, too. I will never, ever, blot out the name of that person from the book of life, but I will proudly confess that name before my Father and all his angels.*

6 *"Whoever has ears, I command to hear what the Spirit is saying to the churches."*

#361 Jesus Speaks to the Church in Philadelphia and to All Who Will Listen
Rev. 3.7-13

7 *"I command you to write to the messenger of the church in Philadelphia:*

"This is what the One who is holy and true, who holds the key of David, who opens doors that no one can then shut, and who closes doors that no one can then open — HE is saying.

8 *"I know your works. Look! I have placed a permanently opened door before you that no one can shut. I know that you have little strength, yet you have remained faithful to my word and have not denied my name. 9 I will make those who are of the synagogue of Satan, who are claiming to be Jews though they are not, but are liars — I will make them come and fall down at your feet and fully understand that I have loved you. 10 Because you have remained faithful to my command to endure patiently, I will also keep you safe from the hour of trial that is going to come on the whole world to test the inhabitants of the earth.*

11 *"I am coming soon. I command you to continue holding on tenaciously on to what you have, so that no one will take your victory crown from you.* 12 *I will make the person who is victorious a pillar in the temple of my God. Never, ever, will they leave it again. I will write the name of my God and the name of the city of my God on them, the new Jerusalem, which is coming down out of heaven from my God, and I will also write on them my own new name.*

13 *"Whoever has ears, I command to hear what the Spirit is saying to the churches."*

#362 Jesus Speaks to the Church in Laodicea and to All Who Will Listen
Rev. 3.14-22

14 *"I command you to write to the messenger of the church in Laodicea:*

"This is what the Amen, the faithful and true witness, the ruler over God's creation is saying.

15 *"I know your works, that you are neither cold nor hot. You ought to be either one or the other!* 16 *So, because you are lukewarm — neither hot nor cold — I am on the verge of spewing you out of my mouth.* 17 *You say, 'I am rich; I have acquired permanent wealth and do not need a thing.' But you do not realize that you are actually wretched, pitiful, poor, blind, and naked.* 18 *I am counseling you to buy gold that has been fully refined in the fire from me, so you can become rich, and have dazzling white clothes to wear, so that the shame created by your nakedness will not continue to be revealed, and have healing salve to smear on your eyes, so you will be able to see.*

19 *"I make a practice of rebuking and disciplining the people I really love. So I command you to be constantly earnest in these things and to repent.* 20 *Look! I have taken my permanent stand at your door, and I am continuing to knock. If anyone hears my voice and opens up the door, I will come inside with that person and share a meal with him, and he will eat my cuisine with me, also.*

21 *"To the one who is victorious, I will give the honor to sit in fellowship with me on my throne, just as I was victorious and sat down in fellowship with my Father on his throne.*

22 *"Whoever has ears, I command to hear what the Spirit is saying to the churches."*

#363 Jesus is Worshipped by All Creation as the "Lamb that was Slain"
Rev. 5.1-14

1 Then, I saw in the right hand of the One who sat on the throne a scroll, which the front and back had been permanently written upon and sealed with seven seals. 2 And a mighty angel proclaimed in a booming voice, "Who is worthy to break its seals and open the scroll?"

3 But no one in heaven or on earth or under the earth was qualified to open the scroll or even look inside it. 4 I kept weeping and sobbing because no one was found who was worthy to open the scroll nor to look in it. 5 Then, one of the elders said to me, "Stop weeping now. Look! the Lion of the tribe of Judah, the Root of David, has triumphed. He is worthy to open the scroll and its seven seals."

6 Then, I saw a Lamb, showing the evidence that it had been slain, who had taken his stand at the center of the throne, encircled by the four living creatures and the elders. The Lamb had seven horns and seven eyes, which are the seven-fold Spirits of God sent out into all the earth. 7 He went and permanently received the scroll from the right hand of him who sat on the throne. 8 And when he had taken it, the four living creatures and the twenty-four elders fell flat in front of the Lamb. Each one had a harp and they were holding golden bowls full of incense, which are the prayers of God's people. 9 And they sang a new song, saying:

"Worthy! You are worthy to take the scroll
and to open its seals,
because you were slain,
and with your blood you purchased for God — in his name —
people from every tribe and language and people and nation.
10 You have made them to be a kingdom and priests to serve our God,
and they will reign on the earth."

11 Then, I looked and heard the voice of many angels who encircled the throne and the living creatures and the elders, numbering thousands times thousands, and ten thousand times ten thousand. 12 With a deafening voice, they were saying:

"Worthy is the Lamb, who was slain,
to receive all the power and wealth and wisdom and strength
and honor and glory and praise!"

13 Then, I heard every creature in heaven and on earth and under the earth and on the sea, and all that is in them, saying:

"To him who sits on the throne and to the Lamb
be all the praise and honor and glory and power,
forever and ever!"

14 The four living creatures were saying, "Amen," and the elders fell flat on their faces and worshiped.

#364 Jesus Directs the Final Events of History
Rev. 6.1, 3, 5, 7, 9, 12; 8.1; 11.15-18; 19.6-9, 11-16; 21.1-4, 22-23

6.1 My eyes were glued to the Lamb as he opened the first of the seven seals. Then, I heard one of the four living creatures say in a voice like rolling thunder, "Come!" [This same process is repeated for each of the seven seals; Jesus opened them all.]

8.1 When he opened the seventh seal, there was complete silence in heaven for about half an hour. 2 And I saw the seven angels who stand before God, and seven trumpets were given to them. [The seven trumpets are sounded in succession, a process Jesus set in motion by opening the seals.]

11.15 The seventh angel sounded his trumpet, and there were loud voices in heaven, which said:

"The kingdom of the world has become
the kingdom of our Lord and of his Messiah,
and he will reign for ever and ever."

16 And the twenty-four elders, who were seated on their thrones before God, fell flat on their faces and worshiped God, 17 saying:

"We constantly give thanks to you, Lord God Almighty,
the One who is and who was,
because you have permanently set your infinite authority in place, and have
begun to reign.
18 The nations were angry, and your wrath has come.

The time has come for the dead to be judged,
and for rewarding your servants the prophets
and your people who revere your name, both great and small—
and for destroying those who keep destroying the earth."

19.5 Then, a voice came from the throne, saying:

"You are commanded to praise our God, all you his servants,
you who fear him, both great and small!"

6 Then, I heard what sounded like a uncountable multitude, like the roar of gushing waters, and like loud, great peals of thunder, shouting:

"Hallelujah!
For our LORD our God—the Almighty-has begun to reign.
7 Let us continually rejoice, continue exulting in him, and constantly give
him glory!
The wedding of the Lamb has come,
and his bride has made herself ready,
for 8 fine linen, gleaming bright and pure,
was given her to wear."

9 Then, the angel said to me, "I command you to write this. *'Blessed are the people who have been permanently invited to the wedding supper of the Lamb!'"*
And he added, *"These are the true words of God."*

11 I saw heaven standing wide open. Look! A white horse, whose rider is called Faithful and True. He is rendering judgment with perfect righteousness and waging war. 12 His eyes are like blazing fire, and on his head are many crowns. He has a name permanently engraved on him that no one knows but he himself. 13 He is dressed in a robe dipped in blood, and he has been given the permanent title of, "The Word of God."

14 The armies of heaven were following him, riding on white horses and dressed in fine linen, gleaming white and clean. 15 A sharp sword is coming out of his mouth to strike down the nations. "He will rule them with an iron scepter." He is treading the winepress of the fury of the wrath of the Almighty God. 16 On his robe and on his thigh this name stands written:

KING OF KINGS AND LORD OF LORDS

21.1 Then, I saw a new heaven and a new earth, for the first heaven and the first earth had passed away, and there was no longer any sea. 2 Then, I saw the Holy City, the new Jerusalem, coming down out of heaven from God, permanently prepared as a bride who is always beautifully dressed for her husband.

3 And I heard a booming voice from the throne saying, *"Look! God's dwelling place is now among the people, and he will make his home with them. They will be his people, and God himself will be with them and be their God. 4 He will wipe every tear from their eyes. There will be no more death, or mourning, or crying, or pain, for the former order of reality has passed away."*

5 The One who was seated on the throne said, *"Look! I am making everything new!"* Then, he said, *"I command you to write this down, for these words are trustworthy and true."*

9 One of the seven angels who had the seven bowls full of the seven last plagues came and said to me, "Come, I will show you the bride, the wife of the Lamb."

10 And he carried me away in the Spirit to a great and towering mountain and showed me the Holy City, Jerusalem, descending out of heaven from God. 22 I did not see a temple in the city because the Lord God Almighty and the Lamb are the temple. 23 The city has no need of the sun or the moon to illuminate it, for the glory of God radiates its light and the Lamb is its lamp. 24 The nations will walk by its light, and the kings of the earth will bring their splendor into it. 25 Its gates and outer courts will never, ever be shut by day, and there will be no night there. 26 All the glory and honor of the nations will be brought into it. 27 Impurity will never, ever enter it, nor will anyone who does what is shameful or deceitful, but only those whose names are permanently written in the Lamb's book of eternal life.

#365 The Bible Closes with Jesus' Final Commands and Promise to Come Again
Rev. 16.15; 22.1-7, 12-13, 16-17, 20

16.15 *"Look, I am coming like a thief! The person who stays vigilantly on guard and keeps his clothing in order so as not to walk about naked — shamefully exposed — is truly blessed."*

22.1 Then, the angel showed me the river of the water of eternal life, bright and clear as crystal, flowing from the throne of God and of the Lamb 2 straight down the middle of the great street of the city. On each side of the river stood the trees of eternal life, blossoming in twelve crops of fruit, bearing their fruit every month. The leaves of the trees are used for the healing of the nations. 3 There will no longer will be any kind of curse. The throne of God and of the Lamb will be in the city, and his servants will serve him in worship. 4 They will gaze upon his face, and his name will be on their foreheads. 5 There will be no more night. They will have no more need of the light of a lamp or the light of the sun, for the Lord God will shine as their light. And they will reign forever and ever.

6 The angel said to me, "These words are trustworthy and true. The Lord, the God who directs the spirits of the prophets, sent his angel to show his servants the things that must surely take place soon."

Jesus said, 7 *"Look, I am coming soon! Blessed is the one who faithfully holds to the words of the prophecy written in this scroll. 12 Look, I am coming soon! My reward is with me, and I will give to each person according to what they have done.*

13 *"I, myself am the Alpha and the Omega, the First and the Last, the Beginning and the Conclusion. 16 I, myself, Jesus, have sent my angel to give you this testimony for the churches. I AM the Root and the Offspring of David, and the bright Morning Star.*

17 *"The Spirit and the bride are saying, 'I command you to come!' And I command the one who is hearing me to say, 'I command you to come!'*

"I command the person who is thirsty to come; I command any person who wants it, to receive the free gift of the water of eternal life."

20 He who testifies to these things says, *"Yes, I am coming soon."*

Amen! Come, Lord Jesus!

JN 20.30 Jesus performed many other signs in the presence of his disciples, signs that are not permanently recorded in this book. But these stand written so that you may believe that Jesus is the Messiah, the Son of God, 31 and that because you believe, you may continue to have eternal life in his name.

APPENDIX A:

Six Features of The JESUS SAGA

Tatian published the first known harmony of the gospels ("The Diatesseron") around 160 AD. Since then, various harmonies have been compiled throughout Church history; each has its own unique characteristics. Readers who are interested in the history and basic principles of gospel harmonies should go to an excellent introductory work on this subject:

The NIV Harmony of the Gospels by Robert L. Thomas and Stanley N. Gundry
Published by Harper Collins, New York, 1988
ISBN: 0-06-063523-1

Thomas and Gundry's discussion of the history, relevant issues, and merits/disadvantages of the harmony approach to the life of Jesus is thorough and helpful. According to Thomas and Gundry, at least 24 composite style harmonies were published in English between 1845 and 1988. Other composite harmonies have been published since then, including The JESUS SAGA, bringing the total number to over 30 different publications. Of these, perhaps the work by Johnson M. Cheney first published in 1969 ("The Life of Christ in Stereo," Multinomah Press) and its various revisions has enjoyed the widest recent circulation.

There are two main types of gospel harmonies. The "multiple column style" displays the four gospels in four separate columns, and arranges the

301

gospel material in a chronological order. Parallel passages can then be compared between the multiple columns. The "composite style harmony" blends the parallel accounts into one seamless narrative, including everything in the parallel passages while eliminating the repetition between them.

Composite style harmonies combine three components to create their content: (1) chronological arrangement of the four gospel content, (2) "blending" of parallel passages into one composite text, and (3) translation of the four gospels from the Greek manuscripts into English. Most composite harmonies use an existing English translation (KJV and the ASV are the most common) of the four gospels to create their "blended" text. Among the composite harmonies mentioned above, just eight were created by blending and then translating the Greek New Testament. These are the works of Fred Fisher in 1949, Freeman Wills Crofts in 1949, Edward F. Cary in 1951, William f. Beck in 1959, Johnston M. Cheney in 1969, Frank Ball in 2008, Robert H. Mounce in 2010, and The JESUS SAGA in 2013 (Also in print under the Title: The SAGA OF JESUS CHRIST.) The work of Mounce is particularly original because he made Jesus the narrator of the entire story, speaking in the first person. ("Jesus, In His Own Words")

Assuming the validity of the composite style harmony approach to the study of Jesus' life then, and the three components which this genre uses to create its text, the SAGA contains six main features that work together to create a distinct reading experience.

1. Detailed Outline Structure with Clear Chronological and Geographical Arrangement

The JESUS SAGA attempts to give a clear and understandable chronological guide through the life of Jesus through the organizational structure of Nine Stages/52 Chapters/365 Sections with Titles. This chronological organization presents the most detailed outline structure for the life of Jesus among the composite harmonies that have been published to date. The relationship between the Nine Stages/52 Chapters/365 Sections in the organizational structure of the SAGA is explained in the Preface.

Once the gospel content has been organized in this manner, the development of Jesus' life and ministry becomes clearer than when each gospel is read separately. Each of the four gospels uses a different approach to organizing its content, and each maintains its own distinct narrative perspective; no single gospel covers the chronology of the life of Jesus in a balanced way.

For example, few readers realize that John Chapters One through Four cover the first six months of Jesus' ministry, and then Chapter Seven jumps to the final six months of his life. Furthermore, in Chapter Twelve John leaps ahead again, to Passion Week. John's coverage of Jesus' life leaves huge blanks. Yet few readers of the gospel of John are aware of this as they read.

Or, how many readers of Mark's gospel realize that by the end of Chapter Three they are already about halfway through Jesus' 40-month ministry? Because there are 16 Chapters in Mark, this is a bit surprising. In contrast, JESUS SAGA readers know where they are in Jesus' life story on every page.

When we put all the information from the four gospels together in one inclusive narrative, the flow of events in Jesus' life and the connections between them become more clear. Once a believer has studied a chronologically arranged harmony, like the SAGA, well enough to learn the development of Jesus' life story, they will know when each event actually occurred in each gospel. This makes the life of Jesus, faithfully recorded in each gospel, come alive with fresh vitality and glory.

Careful, repeated reading of the gospels reveals many subtle hints about the chronology of events in Jesus' life. Still, much remains unclear. The fruit of my own intensive compilation and blending process in preparing the SAGA is substantially the same as the work done by many students of the New Testament.

The arrangement of the events of Jesus' life in The JESUS SAGA is not inspired. The SAGA chronology involves many interpretive decisions that are consistent with all the Scriptural information about Jesus, but it is not the only possible interpretation. Minor differences in the various schemes have been proposed. The SAGA chronology is therefore a plausible, well-reasoned proposal rather than the only valid interpretation.

2. The "Blended Text" Approach of the SAGA

Roughly one-third of the content of Jesus' life is repeated in more than one gospel. We call these repetitions "parallel accounts." Blending these passages into one streamlined text that includes every word in every account, while also eliminating the repetition among them, presents a complex challenge. Here is an explanation of the blending process used in compiling The JESUS SAGA.

The first step involved selecting one of the parallel texts as a "base text." Because over 90% of Mark's gospel is repeated word-for-word in the other three gospels, Mark is often the "base text." The text that contained the most balanced, comprehensive content was chosen. The "base text" retains every word, and the order of the original gospel passage intact.

After determining the "base text," the next step compared every word of the parallel text(s) with the base, adding the unique words and phrases from each parallel passage into the base text at the most appropriate point in the narrative. In this way the extra insights of every parallel passage illuminate the base text. As a result, reading a "blended text" is like reading all the parallel passages simultaneously. Yet, the flow of thought and perspective of the "base text" gospel is also retained as much as possible in the SAGA.

In order to identify the origin of every word in a "blended text" for my readers, The JESUS SAGA uses a "Superscript ID" system. This system is explained in the Preface. Readers may not care about this "Superscript ID" feature, and it can be ignored without any loss of meaning. However, the impact of a particular passage on the reader might be profound on occasion. If it is a blended text, the reader might want to trace it back to the original gospel and read it there as well. The Superscript ID system will be of value in those situations.

In addition, attentive readers of the SAGA will be able to trace the consistent perspectives of each gospel writer in blended texts. For example, the Superscript ID for Luke will usually appear when references are made to prayer because Luke focused on this aspect of Jesus' ministry more than any other gospel writer. Much insight can be gleaned from close observation of the Superscript ID, but it is tough work.

The JESUS SAGA "blended text" approach has the value of retaining the integrity of the "base text" of Scripture. While the chronological arrangement of the text of the SAGA is different from any of the gospels, each paragraph or section of The JESUS SAGA is composed solely of Scripture. The SAGA is not a Bible *per se*, but it does retain all the Scriptural content, just in a different order. This is important for those of us who believe, as I do, in the full inspiration and reliability of the Scripture as the truthful Word of God.

3. Dynamic Translation of the Original Greek New Testament

I have attempted to translate the Greek of the New Testament into lively, dynamic English. Those who have been blessed with the opportunity to study New Testament Greek and can read the New Testament in its original language know how powerful and clear the Greek text is.

Many nuances and aspects of the meaning in Greek are not usually expressed in English translations. This does not imply any error or inadequacy in the many published English New Testaments. They are excellent and they deserve our full confidence. However, no single translation can convey all the nuances of the original language due to the differences in grammar, syntax, and thinking between the two languages and cultures.

A completely "word for word" translation of the Greek New Testament to English does not exist because of the inherent differences in the languages. Greek does not have an indefinite article, for example, while English does. Many other differences in the vocabulary, grammar, and syntax of the two languages mean that every word in the translation cannot correspond directly to every word in the original. Thus, every Bible translation is an interpretation of the meaning of the original text in the language and culture of its readers.

The JESUS SAGA attempts to bring out more of the nuances of the Greek text than the majority of English translations. Words or phrases have been included in the translation to communicate the fuller meaning of the Greek. (Ideas are usually expressed more compactly in Greek than is possible in English.) The JESUS SAGA also favors vivid verbs that give the sense of energy packed by the Greek.

It is hoped that the freshness of the SAGA translation, and the inclusion of additional information from the parallel accounts in blended texts, will give readers a new stimulus in seeing and hearing Jesus in his Word.

4. Translation of the Greek Tenses, Especially the Greek Present and Perfect Tenses

The Greek verbs involve a special aspect of the dynamic approach to translation mentioned already. Like English, verbs are the heart of communicating in Biblical Greek. The Greek present and perfect tenses, in particular, are more comprehensive concepts than are their English equivalents. The SAGA attempts to bring out these differences. Here is what to look for.

The Greek present tense usually describes an action as a continuing process. The SAGA uses the terms *"continuing to,"* or *"constantly"* to describe the ongoing process described in a Greek present tense verb. When the continuation of the action as a process is a key component of the meaning of a present tense verb, the SAGA translation shows this.

The Greek perfect is a magnificent, comprehensive verb. It describes an action that occurred in the past that was completed. Furthermore, the results of the action remain unchanged until the time the speaker or writer describes it. For example, if the Greek perfect is used to say, "I built my house," it means that the speaker engaged in the process of building their house, they completed it, and the house remains standing in essentially the same condition at the time the speaker makes the declaration. If a 60-year-old man speaks of having built his house when he was 20, the Greek perfect tense describes a house that has remained intact for 40 years and is still standing — the results of building it remain unchanged.

The enduring results described by a Greek perfect verb are often hard to translate into English, but this is a crucial part of the thinking of the speaker or writer in Greek. The adverb *"permanently"* has often been used to communicate this aspect of the meaning of Greek perfects in The JESUS SAGA. Most English translations of the Greek New Testament do not attempt to convey this aspect of the Greek perfect tense.

For example, Jesus (or a gospel writer) often used the perfect tense to describe the way he had healed a person. When the Lord said, *"You have been healed,"* in the perfect tense, it assured a person that what they had experienced was not temporary — the results of their healing remained--they were healed permanently and need not fear a relapse. This is the power of the Greek perfect tense describing a healing.

So, The JESUS SAGA translation emphasizes the underlying meaning of the Greek text, and especially its verbs, more than the beautiful expression of English. The Greek New Testament is the most influential collection of documents ever assembled; it communicates with a depth of meaning, clarity and power that the SAGA translation cannot match.

5. The Commands of Jesus

A final, and most important, aspect of the Greek translation in the SAGA concerns the imperatives of Jesus that were mentioned in the Preface. Greek uses a particular grammatical form to indicate imperative verbs. As a result, they are instantly identifiable, and stand out in the text. (The second person plural form of Greek imperatives is an exception to this. However, these can be identified as imperatives by contextual clues.)

In addition, the notion of authority — and Jesus' authority in particular as the King of Kings and Lord of Lords — is a central, crucial view of who Jesus is for the gospel writers. Both the Greco-Roman and Jewish cultures of the 1st century understood the absolute authority of those in power — whether it be YHWH for a Jew or the Emperor for a Roman — in a way few cultures appreciate in the 21st century. For the original authors and readers of the gospels, then, the authority and imperatives of Jesus were of paramount importance for understanding him.

An imperative assumes that the giver of a command possesses the power to enforce obedience, and that the receiver of the command is in a subservient position of being obligated to obey. Commands require this superior/subordinate relationship to be true imperatives. In the case of Jesus, his authority is affirmed in the gospels to be absolute, the very power and authority of God. Therefore, his commands matter. Jesus had much to say about the central role of his commands throughout his teachings.

In order to make Jesus' commands as plain to English readers of The JESUS SAGA as they were to his original disciples, I have chosen to use the word *"command"* in the translation of Jesus' imperatives. Other translations do not do this, making it easier to gloss over the commands of Jesus when we read the gospels in English. Readers will find the *"command"* structure of Jesus' imperatives in the SAGA to be blunt to say the least, and perhaps repetitive, but they will feel some of the force Jesus intended when he chose to use the imperative mode. Jesus said: *"The person who is holding on to my commands and is obeying them is the one who loves me."* (JN 14.21A) It is hoped that readers will give special attention to the commands of Jesus in the SAGA for the purpose of learning and obeying them.

6. Life of Jesus Scriptures Not Contained in the Gospels

The JESUS SAGA is not just a harmony of the gospels. In order to present the complete life of Jesus recorded in the Scriptures, the words and deeds of Jesus in the Bible that are described outside the four gospels have also been included. Passages in the Old Testament containing the words and deeds of the Pre-incarnate Jesus, and portions of the New Testament that record the things Jesus said and did after ascending back to heaven supplement the gospel material. Why is this important?

The gospels end with Jesus' 11th resurrection appearance, his ascension (Luke 24). However, Luke made it clear in the Book of Acts — the second book in his two-volume set of the life of Jesus — that Jesus continued to *"do and teach"* after he returned to heaven (see Acts 1.1-3). Many passages in the book of Acts record these words and the work of Jesus, such as Paul's conversion and its aftermath. Some of Paul's letters also include quotations of the words of Jesus not contained in the gospels, and accounts of his actions as well. These are all included in the SAGA.

Furthermore, the final book in the Bible is the "Revelation of Jesus Christ." This prophetic book describes the works of Jesus that will consummate this age and bring in the Kingdom. The Bible concludes with the words of Jesus. These passages should complete our Scriptural understanding of the life of Jesus.

The book of Hebrews affirms that, *"Jesus Christ is the same — yesterday, today, and forever."* (13.8) The Lord that every Christian believes in is the same Jesus as the days of his flesh in the gospels. However, he is now eternally alive in his spiritual, resurrection body. It is this eternal Jesus whom we have come to know. The portions of the Scripture that record his words and deeds after his ascension are as essential to the good news about him as everything written in the four gospels. They ought to be known with the same familiarity as every other aspect of his glorious life, for they are HIS words and deeds, and he has commanded all believers to love him by learning them, obeying them, and teaching others to do the same.

Conclusion

The JESUS SAGA compiles ALL the words and events in Jesus' life that are contained in the Scriptures. Doing this in one chronological, seamless blended sequence has the effect of reading all the Scriptures about Jesus in the way the first disciples experienced him, allowing readers to see and hear Jesus in a comprehensive, awe-inspiring way.

As a composite harmony of the complete life of Jesus then, The JESUS SAGA is a unique kind of book. It is comprised of Scripture, but it is not a Bible because the content has been rearranged chronologically. Nonetheless, because the SAGA is a compilation of Scripture, the Holy Spirit can use it to reveal the Lord of Glory to hungry, seeking minds and hearts.

The combination of the six features discussed above make the SAGA a powerful new discipleship tool for in-depth study of the life of Jesus. The author of the SAGA desires that readers will see Jesus in all of his glory in a way that will cause them to know him, love him, and become more like him. Thus, they will be equipped to make him known in making disciples of all the peoples in the world ... until he returns.

Dear reader, may this be your experience in reading this Scriptural witness to the Lord Jesus Christ.

=.=.=.=.=.=.=.=.=.=.=.=.=.=.=.=.=.=.=.=

REMEMBER--free, indepth study material by John Stephen Wright on every section of The JESUS SAGA is available at the ATJ Ministries website, or by daily e-mail delivery. Visit www.atjministries.org today.

APPENDIX B:

Index of Scriptures in The JESUS SAGA

(The 3 digit number to the right of the = sign indicates The JESUS SAGA section number corresponding to the Scripture passage on the left side of the = sign. Books are listed in Biblical order)

The Book of Genesis

Ch. 1.1-2.3=002

The Book of Psalms

Ch. 110.1-2, 4=004

The Book of Isaiah

Ch. 6.1-10=003

The Book of Daniel

Ch. 7.13-14=004.

The Gospel of Matthew

Ch. 1.1-17=028, 1.18-25=014
2.1-12=020, 2.13-18=021, 2.19-23=022
3.1-3=024, 3.4-10=025, 3.11-12=026, 3.13-16=029
4.1-11=030, 4.12=049, 4.13-16=052, 4.18-22=053, 4.23-35=055
5.1-12=068, 5.13-20=069, 5.21-26=070, 5.27-37=071, 5.38-48=072
6.1-4=073, 6.5-15=074, 6.16-18=073, 6.19-24=075, 6.25-34=076
7.1-6=077, 7.7-12=078, 7.13-23=079, 7.24-29=080
8.1=081, 8.2-4=056, 8.5-13=081, 8.14-16=054, 8.23-27=096, 8.28-34=097
9.1-8=057, 9.9-13=058, 9.14-17=059, 9.18-19=098, 9.20-22=099, 9.23-26=098, 9.27-34=100, 9.35-38=102
10.1-8=103, 10.9-15=104, 10.16-23=105, 10.24-31=106, 10.32-42=107
11.1=108, 11.2-6=083, 11.7-19=084, 11.20-30=085
12.1-8=064, 12.9-14=065, 12.15-16=065, 12.17-21=066, 12.22-37=088, 12.38-45=089, 12.46-50=090
13.1-9=091, 13.10-17=092, 13.18-23=091, 13.24-30=093, 13.31-33=094, 13.34-35=095, 13.36-43=093, 13.44-50=094, 13.51-53=095, 13.54-58=101
14.1-12=109, 14.13-14=110, 14.15-21=111, 14.22-33=112, 14.34-35=113
15.1-9=119, 15.10-20=120, 15.21-28=121, 15.29-31=122, 15.32-39=123
16.1-4=124, 16.5-12=125, 16.13-16=127, 16.17-20=128, 16.21-28=129
17.1-8=130, 17.9-13=131, 17.14-18=132, 17.19-20=133, 17.22-23=134, 17.24-27=135
18.1-6=136, 18.6-8=214, 18.7-9=137, 18.10-14=138, 18.15-20=139, 18.21-3=140
19.1A=141, 19.1B-2=202, 19.3-9=229, 19.10-12=230, 19.13-15=231, 19.16-22=232, 19.23-30=233
20.1-16=234, 20.17-19=235, 20.20-28=236, 20.29-34=237
21.1-7=242, 21.8-9=243, 21.10-11=245, 21.12-13=247, 21.14-17=245, 21.18-19=246, 21.20-22=252, 21.23-27=252, 21.28-32=253, 21.33-46=254
22.1-14=255, 22.15-22=256, 22.23-33=257, 22.34-40=258, 22.41-46=259
23.1-12=260, 23.13-24=261, 23.25-36=262, 23.37-39=198 + 266
24.1-5=267, 24.6-14=269, 24.15-22=268, 24.23-31=225 + 270, 24.32-44=226 + 271, 24.45-51=272
25.1-13=273, 25.14-30=274, 25.31-46=275
26.1-5=276, 26.6-13=241, 26.14-16=277, 26.17-19=278, 26.20=279, 26.21-25=282, 26.26-29=286, 26.30=290, 26.31-35=284, 26.36-39=300, 26.40-46=301, 26.47=302,

26.48-54=303, 26.55-56=304, 26.57=306, 26.58=308, 26.59-61=306, 26.62-68=307, 26.69-75=309

27.1=310, 27.2=311, 27.3-10=312, 27.11-14=313, 27.15-21=315, 27.22-23=316, 27.24-26=318, 27.27-30=319, 27.31-34=320, 27.35-38=321, 27.39-44=322, 27.45-49=324, 27.50=325, 27.51-56=326, 27.57-58=328, 27.59-60=329, 27.61-66=330

28.1-4=331, 28.5-8=332, 28.9-10=335, 28.11-15=336, 28.16-20=343

The Gospel of Mark

Ch. 1.1=001, 1.2-4=024, 1.5-6=025, 1.7-8=026, 1.9-11=029, 1.12-13=030, 1.14-15=049, 1.16-20=053, 1.21-34=054, 1.35-39=055, 1.40-45=056

2.1-12=057, 2.13-17=058, 2.23-28=064

3.1-6=065, 3.5-6=025, 3.7-12=066, 3.13-19=067, 3.2-21=090, 3.22-30=088, 3.31-35=090

4.1-9=091, 4.10-12=092, 4.13-20=091, 4.21-29=095, 4.33-34=095, 4.35-41=096

5.1-20=097, 5.21-24=098, 5.25-34=099, 5.35-43=098

6.1-6A=101, 6.6B=102, 6.7=103, 6.8-11=104, 6.12-13=108, 6.14-29=109, 6.30-34=110, 6.35-44=111, 6.45-52=112, 6.53-56=113

7.1-13=119, 7.14-23=120, 7.24-30=121, 7.31-37=122

8.1-10=123, 8.11-13=124, 8.14-21=125, 8.22-26=126, 8.27-29=127, 8.30=128, 8.31-38=129

9.1=129, 9.2-8=130, 9.9-13=131, 9.14-27=132, 9.28-29=133, 9.30-32=134, 9.33-37=136, 9.38-41=138, 9.43-50=137

10.1A=141, 10. B-2=202, 10.3-12=229, 10.13-16=231, 10.17-22=232, 10.23-31=233, 10.32-34=235, 10.35-45=236/279, 10.46-52=237

11.1-7=242, 11.8-10=243, 11.10-11=245, 11.12-14=246, 11.15-18=247, 11.19=250, 11.20-26=251, 11.27-33=252

12.1-12=254, 12.13-17=256, 12.18-27=257, 12.28-34A=258, 12.34B-37=259, 12.38-40=260, 12.41-44=263

13.1-6=267, 13.7-13=269, 13.14-20=268, 13.21-27=270, 13.28-32=271, 13.33-37=272

14.1-2=276, 14.3-9=241, 14.10-11=277, 14.12-16=278, 14.17=279, 14.18-21=282, 14.22-25=286, 14.26=290, 14.27-31=284, 14.32-36=300, 14.37-42=301, 14.43=302, 14.44-47=303, 14.48-52=304, 14.53=306, 14.54=308, 14.55-59=306, 14.60-65=004/307, 14.66-72=309

15.1A=310, 15.1B=311, 15.2-5=313, 15.6-11=315, 15.12-14=316, 15.15=318, 15.16-19=319, 15.20-23=320, 15.24-28=321, 15.29-32=322, 15.33-36=324, 15.37=325, 15.38-41=326, 15.42-45=328, 15.46=329, 15.47=330
16.1=330, 16.2-4=331, 16.5-8=332, 16.9-11=334

(note: MK 11.26 and 15.28 have been omitted from the text of the SAGA because they do not appear in many of the most reliable, early manuscripts of Mark. They were probably not part of the original edition of Mark.)

The Gospel of Luke

Ch. 1.1-4=005, 1.5-10=006, 1.11-17=007, 1.18-25=008, 1.26-38=009, 1.39-45=010, 1.46-56=011, 1.57-66=012, 1.67-80=013
2.1-7=015, 2.8-14=016, 2.15-20=017, 2.21-35=018, 2.36-38=019, 2.39-40=022, 2.41-52=023
3.1-6=024, 3.7-10=025, 3.11-18=026, 3.19-20=049, 3.21-22=029, 3.23A=027, 3.23B-38=028
4.1-13=030, 4.14-15=049, 4.16-30=051, 4.31-42=054, 4.42-44=055
5.1-11=053, 5.12-16=056, 5.17-26=057, 5.27-32=058, 5.33-39=059
6.1-5=064, 6.6-11=065, 6.12-16=067, 6.17-26=068, 6.27-30=070/072, 6.31=078, 6.32-36=070/072, 6.37-42=077, 6.43-46=079, 6.47-49=080
7.1-10=081, 7.11-17=082, 7.18-23=083, 7.24-35=084, 7.36-50=086
8.1-3=087, 8.4-8=091, 8.9-10=092, 8.11-15=091, 8.19-21=090, 8.22-25=096, 8.26-40=097, 8.40-42=098, 8.43-48=099, 8.49-56=098
9.1=108, 9.1-2=103, 9.3-5=104, 9.6=108, 9.7-9=109, 9.10-11=110, 9.12-17=111, 9.18-20=127, 9.21=128, 9.22-27=129, 9.28-36A=130, 9.36B=131, 9.37-43=132, 9.43B-45=134, 9.36-48=136, 9.51-56=149, 9.57-62=143
10.1-3=170, 10.4-9=171, 10.10-16=172, 10.17-20=173, 10.21-24=174, 10.25-28=175, 10.29-37=176, 10.38-42=177
11.1-4=178, 11.5-13=179, 11.14-26=180, 11.27-28=181, 11.29-36=182, 11.37-41=183, 11.42-54=184
12.1-7=185, 12.8-12=186, 12.13-21=187, 12.22-34=188, 12.31-34=189, 12.41-48=191, 12.49-53=192, 12.54-59=193
13.1-9=194, 13.10-17=195, 13.18-21=196, 13.22-30=197, 13.31-35=198, 266, 13.35-40=190
14.1-6=203, 14.7-14=204, 14.15-24=205, 14.25-35=206
15.1-7=207, 15.8-10=208, 15.11-24=209, 15.25-32=210

16.1-13=211, 16.14-18=212, 16.19-31=213

17.1-4=214, 17.5-10=215, 17.11-19=223, 17.20-21=224, 17.22-25=225, 17.26-37=226

18.1-8=227, 18.9-14=228, 18.15-17=231, 18.18-23=232, 18.24-30=233, 18.31-34=235, 18.35-43=237

19.1-10=238, 19.11-28=239/274, 19.29-35=242, 19.36-40=243, 19.41-44=244, 19.45-48=247

20.1-8=252, 20.9-19=254, 20.20-26=256, 20.27-39=257, 20.40-44=259, 20.45-47=260

21.1-4=263, 21.5-8=267, 21.9-19=269, 21.20-24=268, 21.25-27=270, 21.28-33=271, 21.34-36=272

22.1-2=276, 22.3-6=277, 22.7-13=278, 22.14-16=279, 22.17-20=286, 22.21-23=282, 22.24-30=279, 22.31-34=284, 22.35-38=285, 22.39=290, 22.40-44=300, 22.45-46=301, 22.47=302, 22.48-51=303, 22.52-53=304, 22.54A=306, 22.54B-55=308, 22.56-62=309, 22.63-65=307, 22.66-71=310

23.1=311, 23.2-5=313, 23.6-12=314, 23.13-19=315, 23.20-22=316, 23.23-25=318, 23.26-32=320, 23.33-34=321, 23.35-37=322, 23.38=321, 23.39-43=322, 23.44-45A=324, 23.45B=326, 3.46=325, 23.47-49=326, 23.50-52=328, 23.53-54=329, 23.55-56=330

24.1-=331, 24.4-8=332, 24.9-11=333, 24.13-32=337, 24.33-34=338, 24.35-49=339, 24.50-53=346

(note: LK 23.17 and 24.12 have been omitted from the text of the SAGA because they do not appear in many of the most reliable, early manuscripts of Luke. They were probably not part of the original edition of Luke.)

The Gospel of John

Ch. 1.1-2=001, 1.3-5=002, 1.6-9=024, 1.10-14=027, 1.15=025, 1.16-18=027, 1.19-28=031, 1.29-31=032, 1.32-34=029, 1.35-42, 033, 1.43-51=034

2.1-11=035, 2.12-22=036, 2.23-25=037

3.1-10=038, 3.11-15=039, 3.16-21=040, 3.22-24=041, 3.25-36=042

4.1-2=041, 4.3-6=043, 4.7-14=044, 4.15-19=045, 4.20-26=046, 4.27-38=047, 4.39-42=048, 4.43,45=049, 4.44=051, 4.46-54=050

5.1-14=060, 5.15-20=061, 5.21-30=062, 5.31-46=063

6.1-3/=110, 6.3-15=111, 6.16-21=112, 6.22-29=114, 6.30-40=115, 6.41-51=116, 6.52-59=117, 6.60-71=118

7.1=119, 7.2-10/=141, 7.11-19=144, 7.20-27=145, 7.28-36=146, 7.37-39=147, 7.40-52=148

8.1-8=149, 8.9-11=150, 8.12-20=151, 8.21-24=152, 8.25-30=153, 8.31-36=154, 8.37-40=155, 8.41-47=156, 8.48-53=157, 8.54-58=158

9.1-7=159, 9.8-12=160, 9.13-17=161, 9.18-23=162, 9.24-34=163, 9.35-41=16

10.1-6=165, 10.7-10=166, 10.11-13=167, 10.14-18=168, 10.19-21=169, 10.22-26=199, 10.27-30=200, 10.31-39=201, 10.40-42=202

11.1-6=216, 11.7-16=217, 11.17-27=218, 11.28-37=219, 11.38-44=220, 11.45-53=221, 11.54=222, 11.55-57=240

12.1=240, 12.2-8=241, 12.9-11=240, 12.12=242, 12.13-19=243, 12.2-26=248, 12.27-33=249, 12.34-36=250, 12.37-43=003/264, 12.44-50=265

13.1-11=280, 13.12-20=281, 13.21-30=282, 13.31-32=283, 13.33=284, 13.34-35=283, 13.36-38=284

14.1-11=287, 14.12-14=288, 14.15-26=289, 14.27-31=290

15.1-8=291, 15.9-17=292, 15.18-27=293

16.1-6=293, 16.7-15=294/352, 16.16-22=95, 16.23-32=296, 16.33=290

17.1-5=297, 17.6-19=298, 17.20-26=299

18.1=300, 18.2-9=302, 18.10-11=303, 18.12-14=305, 18.15-18=308, 18.19-23=305, 18.24=306, 18.25-27=309, 18.28-32=311, 18.33-38=313, 18.39-40=315

19.1-6=316, 19.7-12=317, 19.13-16=318=19.17=320, 19.18-24=321, 19.25-27=323, 19.28-30=325, 19.31-37=327, 19.38=328, 19.39-42=329

20.1=331, 20.2-9=333, 20.10-18=334, 20.19-23=339, 20.24-31=340

21.1-14=341, 21.15-24=342

The Book of Acts

1.1-2=347, 1.3=331, 1.4-8=345, 1.9-12=346, 1.18-19=312

2.1-5, 16-21, 33, 36=347, 2.41-47=348

7.54-60=349

9.1-9=350, 9.10-19=351

11.19-21=348

13.1-3=352

18.9-11=353

20.35=189

22.14-21=351

26.14-18=350

Paul's First Letter to the Corinthians

11.23-26=286
15.3-5=338, 15.6=343, 15.7A=344, 15.8-9=350

Paul's Second Letter to the Corinthians

12.1-10=354

The Book of James

1.1A=344

The Book of Revelation

1.4-6, 9-20=355
2.1-7=356, 2.8-11=357, 2.12-17=358, 2.18-29=359
3.1-6=360, 3.7-13=361, 3.14-22=362
5.1-14=363
6.1, 3, 5, 7, 9, 12=364
8.1=364
11.15-18=364
16.15=365
19.6-9, 11-16=364
21.1-4, 22-23=364
22.1-7, 12-13, 16-17, 20=365

ABOUT THE AUTHOR

Missionary church-planter (in Japan), pastor, and seminary teacher John Stephen Wright earned his B.A. with honors at Baylor University in Texas, USA; double minoring in Greek/Christianity, and majoring in Oral Communication. He went on to earn a M.Div. in Theology from Southwestern Baptist Theological Seminary in Texas.

John has more than 35 years of experience as a Bible teacher and preacher in the USA and Japan, has planted two Japanese language churches, and pastored two other international churches in Japan, as well as taught New Testament Greek and other New Testament courses at Tokyo Baptist Theological Seminary from 1991 to 2012. He makes his home and continues his writing ministry in the mountains of Nagano, Japan, and travels regularly to the Tokyo area for ministry.

John is married to Rhonda, another MK (missionary kid) from Japan. They have been blessed with two children and one grand-daughter so far. Rhonda serves with John in ATJ Ministries.

The Lord Jesus brought John to faith in him at the age of 6. In his Jr. year in college, John discovered the Greek New Testament, and began his life-long love of reading and studying the Bible in Greek.

John began "According to Jesus" (ATJ) Ministries in 2007 to equip churches and believers to fulfill the Great Commission by *"teaching them to carefully observe everything I have commanded you."* (MT 28.19) A lifetime of immersion in the Greek New Testament and has equipped John to prepare the comprehensive studies of the life and teachings of the Lord Jesus Christ that are the core of John's writing ministry, and ATJ Ministries. John developed these materials over the 35 plus years of preaching, teaching, and disciple-making ministry in American and Japan.

"Having known and ministered alongside John Wright for more than a decade, it is with great pleasure and without reservation that I endorse ATJ Ministries.

I had the privilege of working with John on a church plant west of Tokyo. Weekly I sat in a rather jealous awe as I heard him teach in fluent Japanese using the Greek New Testament and an English outline. John is a scholar. But more than his scholarship, he is a passionate disciple of Christ.

God has placed a clarion call on John's life – to obey Christ's command to make disciples of all people groups. I can think of no one better qualified to provide doctrinally sound and culturally unbiased discipleship materials. I heartily recommend John and the resources he has developed."

–Mark Edlund, Executive Director, Colorado Baptist Convention

It is John's passionate desire for Jesus Christ to be glorified by the power of the Holy Spirit through his life and ministry. You can contact him at:

john@atjministries.com

Visit www.atjministries.org to learn more about books concerning the life and teachings of Jesus by John Stephen Wright. Books are available in either print e-book, and PDF formats.

The "SAGA" Series

THE JESUS SAGA (Also available as "The SAGA OF JESUS CHRIST")
THE SAGA STUDY GUIDE
THE SAGA STUDY LEADER'S GUIDE
ALL THE SAYINGS OF JESUS CHRIST

The "Life of Jesus" Series

A CHRONOLOGICAL GUIDE TO THE LIFE OF JESUS
THE LIFE OF JESUS: IN THE BEGINNING
THE LIFE OF JESUS: HIS GREAT GALILEAN MINISTRY
THE LIFE OF JESUS: HIS FINAL YEAR
THE LIFE OF JESUS: HIS PASSION
THE LIFE OF JESUS: HIS RESURRECTION AND ETERNAL MINISTRY

The "Everything You Need to Know — According to Jesus" Series

ALL THE COMMANDS OF CHRIST
ALL THE PROMISES OF JESUS CHRIST
ACCORDING TO JESUS: The Joy of Christ-centered Living (A free e-book)
EVERYTHING YOU NEED TO KNOW ABOUT ME— ACCORDING TO JESUS
EVERYTHING YOU NEED TO KNOW ABOUT MY FATHER — ACCORDING TO JESUS
EVERYTHING YOU NEED TO KNOW ABOUT THE HOLY SPIRIT-- ACCORDING TO JESUS
EVERYTHING YOU NEED TO KNOW ABOUT LOVE--ACCORDING TO JESUS
EVERYTHING YOU NEED TO KNOW ABOUT GOD'S POWER-- ACCORDING TO JESUS
EVERYTHING YOU NEED TO KNOW ABOUT PRAYER--ACCORDING TO JESUS

EVERYTHING YOU NEED TO KNOW ABOUT THE PRESENCE OF GOD--ACCORDING TO JESUS

EVERYTHING YOU NEED TO KNOW ABOUT YOUR MINISTRY--ACCORDING TO JESUS

EVERYTHING YOU NEED TO KNOW ABOUT GOD'S WORD--ACCORDING TO JESUS

EVERYTHING YOU NEED TO KNOW ABOUT FAITH--ACCORDING TO JESUS

EVERYTHING YOU NEED TO KNOW ABOUT DISCIPLESHIP--ACCORDING TO JESUS

The "Discipleship Boot Camp" Series

ONE THING: The Goal of Discipleship — According to Jesus
THE JOURNEY: The Process of Discipleship as Jesus Practiced, Taught, and Commanded It
JESUS ALONE: The Preeminence of Jesus in Discipleship
A CALL FOR SERIOUS FOLLOWERS OF JESUS
THE OFFERINGS AND MINISTRY OF A SPIRITUAL PRIEST

Each of these publications surveys every word and deed of Jesus' life and ministry concerning the topic. Nothing is left out. If you want to know everything the Scriptures record about what Jesus said and did regarding these topics, these books deliver it. Available as e-books, in print, and as PDFs.

CPSIA information can be obtained
at www.ICGtesting.com
Printed in the USA
LVHW112153290819
629476LV00001B/51/P